RUDOLF MEYER (1896 Christian Community work helped shape spir in the twentieth centur he studied theology and philosophy in Kiel, Göttingen—briefly under Edmund Husserl—Freiburg and Heidelberg. As a member of the founding circle of The Christian Community, he served as a pastor in North Germany, Saxony, Prague, Düsseldorf and Zürich, later teaching at the Stuttgart seminary from 1932. Deeply inspired by Rudolf Steiner, Meyer attended the influential Agricultural Course at Koberwitz in 1924 and supported Karl König in the development of education for special needs. He authored more than thirty books including biographies of Christian Morgenstern, Novalis, Rudolf Steiner and Albert Steffen, and on themes including mythology, relgion and the spiritual meaning of fairy tales. Rudolf Meyer died in Göppingen in July 1985.

Knights of the Round Table with a vision of the Holy Grail,
Évrard d'Espinques, circa 1475

STORY OF THE GRAIL

Where Time Becomes Space

An Esoteric Study

RUDOLF MEYER

Translated from the German by Maren and Alan Stott

Edited by Neil Franklin

TEMPLE LODGE

Temple Lodge Publishing Ltd.
Hillside House, The Square
Forest Row, RH18 5ES

www.templelodge.com

First published in English by Temple Lodge in 2026

Originally published in German as *Der Gral und seine Hüter* by Urachhaus, Stuttgart, in 1956. This translation is based on the second edition entitled *Zum Raum wird hier die Zeit, Die Graalsgeschichte* (Urachhaus, Stuttgart, 1980 / Fischer Taschenbuch Verlag GmbH, Frankfurt am Main, 1983)

The publishers authorised representative for product safety in the EEA can be found at www.templelodge.com

A CIP catalogue record for this book is available from the British Library

ISBN 978 1 915776 45 7

Cover by Morgan Creative featuring painting by Ninetta Sombart
Typeset by Symbiosys Technologies, Visakhapatnam, India
Printed and bound by 4Edge Ltd., Essex Rudolf Meyer

Contents

Additional Notes

Preface

This book appeared in 1956 and 1958 with the title, *Der Graal und seine Hüter* ('The Grail and its Guardians'). It aimed to pursue the origin of the Grail legend, and to look at its uniquely powerful influence up to today. What this symbol expresses is in no way limited to the literary realm and thus concludes its development. It proves to be something that grows and still today moves the world on, from within.

Meanwhile, many publications have appeared with the Grail as their theme. This book is published in a third edition. The text remains unchanged; only the title is different. Why? Because this saying—used by Richard Wagner in his music drama, *Parsifal*, giving the initial instruction to the Grail seeker—is a *keyword* with a central meaning for all the chapters of this book. It depends everywhere on overcoming the limits of space and time, of mastering a soul-space in which the Grail-event can be experienced as something contemporary. This characterizes the book.

Certainly, one can approach these motifs as a historian. It may even be found sufficient to remain simply registering them. One may astutely analyse what the different poetic authors of the Grail story have managed to achieve in giving their insufficient contributions to this material. One should also become aware how the sacred content repeatedly escapes this onslaught. For the Grail is a cosmos in itself. It can deny itself and it can graciously open itself—there are many ways of access. Heights of worlds and depths of Earth are part of it; the Mysteries of the stars and the glittering of gemstones. The widths of the world—the East with its ancient wisdom, and the European races with their youthful forces. Angels and demons are at work throughout this universe. Legendary beings of all kinds populate it. Yet the central part is formed by the human being—courageous adventurers and ardent prayerful souls, devoted women and radiantly beautiful maidens, in addition to knights who ride for their ideal loves. Suffering and erring people are given space in this world, also those who have died with their mysterious longings. And all this seems to be held together through an all-encompassing power from which it receives meaning and glory.

It has been attempted to bring out the variety of viewpoints in this account. Yet in order not to make the flow of presentation too arduous, certain asides are relegated to endnotes. As additions and explanations, they may appear essential for some readers, yet not essential to an initial reading of the book. The author is conscious how many things could only be addressed through indications that really require further explanation. The seedlike character, opening new points of view, may correspond most closely to the style of a study on the Grail. An inexhaustible nature of this Mystery comes to the fore—the invitation of researching further, the call to search for the Grail.

Rudolf Meyer
January 1980

1. Experiencing the Grail

The initial appearance of the Grail saga

The Grail legend belongs to those spiritual treasures of humanity that repeatedly engage the human mind, which touch the deepest layers of the soul able to guide seekers to the Mysteries of Christ. This is without any dogmatic conclusions, not moving in the paths of Church traditions. In it, the sacred element proceeding from Golgotha grows in artistic pictures clothed within a super-earthly magic. In a mysterious manner these legendary motifs are suddenly present. Their appearance and growth within poetic works over several centuries present many problems for the literary researcher. In the high flowering time of the Middle Ages around 1180 the world receives the first announcement of the Grail and of Perceval, the Grail seeker, through the recognized master of knightly epic, Chrétien de Troyes. The poet introduces his *Conte du Graal*, the 'Story of the Grail', which he regards as 'the best story' ever to be told in a king's court.[1]

He little reaps who little sows,
And he who'd have good harvest knows
To sow his seeds in such a field
That they a hundredfold will yield;
For good seed in a barren place
Will shrivel there and fail apace.
Now Chrétien sows here the seed
From which a story will proceed,
And sows it in so good a place
Great profit shall his efforts grace,
For what he does is for the best
With whom the Roman Empire's blessed.
He is Phillip, Count of Flanders,
Of greater worth than Alexander,
Of whom they give such good account.

[1] Translation of Perceval (or the Story of the Grail, c. 1180) by A.S. Kline. https://www.poetryintranslation.com/PITBR/French/DeTroyesPerceval-PartI.php/French original, https://fr.wikisource.org/wiki/Perceval_ou_le_conte_du_Graal/

We read:

> It is the story of the Grail;
> The book he has from the Count;
> Judge how he renders his account.

The description goes far beyond any normal praise for a generous patron of the arts. This Count did not act out of a conceited search for fame; it was the love of God that lived in him. He acted from this alone.

> And know this then, of a verity,
> Those gifts are gifts of charity
> That good Count Phillip doth give,
> For naught counsels him so to live
> But his own heart, frank, debonair,
> Which teaches him to act the fair.

It seems that the poet clearly points towards a quite special decision that led to the publication of this legend. It is a gift of the love of God itself that wants to impart itself to the age with the proclamation of the Holy Grail. We know the picture of the sower from Christ's parable.[2] Here, too, it is used to show the spreading of the gospel. And indeed, these seeds quickly germinated; they increased in an astonishing way. For one Grail epic after another suddenly germinates, enthralling listeners and readers of the epic arts as seldom before.

Shortly after this, possibly around 1190, a second epic in French appears—*Joseph d' Arimathie* by Robert de Boron, thought to form a part of a vast Grail epic. The first part was to announce the origins of the Grail vessel; in the second part, weaving into it, the Merlin and Arthur legend, and the third part was to describe the suffering of the Grail as well as the saving deed of a prophesied redeemer, probably through Parsifal. The work remains fragmentary.

In the beginning of the thirteenth century, poetic works in German took up the content. Wolfram von Eschenbach, linking to Chrétien's epic, fashioned with his *Parzival*[3] the most profound

---

[2] Matt. 13; Mk. 4; Lk. 8.

[3] Online prose translation: https://ia600908.us.archive.org/24/items/Parzival/Parzival.pdf. Also Eng. tr. by Jesse Weston: file:///Users/macuser/Desktop/pg47297-h/pg47297-images.html. Eng. tr. by A.S. Kline: https://www.poetryintranslation.com/PITBR/German/Parzivalhome.php

poetic work of the German Middle Ages, a work that was completely reborn out of the primordial power of his Christian and philosophically attuned personality. He is the first able truly to round off the event. The previous poetic works remained incomplete; they found various further developments of other French poets, but none could deal with the greatness and sanctity of the content. Through what Wolfram himself indicates at the end of his poetic work, *Parzival* is continued by other German poets in a description of the mission of Lohengrin. Around 1280 a poetic work on Titurel appears, which today is attributed to Albrecht von Scharfenberg. It encompasses the destinies of the Grail and the Grail dynasty in a detailed manner, for our taste not always artistically fashioned. Today it is hardly read, yet it is acknowledged for its most significant motifs. Here for the first time, the Grail Castle is described. The Grail Temple with its splendour and mystical secrets is presented here for the first time; it enthused the medieval world and ever again enchanted the Romantic sensibilities. Step by step over a hundred years, we consequently see the Grail's Mysteries are revealed to the astounded world, unfolding like a seed, completing the holy events with additions.

What, especially in prose stories, later appeared in an unformed heaping up of content during the following centuries, essentially added no motifs to the legend—they simply responded to the popular hunger for reading, the greed to lay hold of increasing details about the Grail and its heroes. Towards the end of the fifteenth century, this interest subsides. In 1477 the German poetic work on the Grail is printed in Strasburg. But the Age of the Reformation and of humanism, in its most inner turning away from the Gothic period, did not always give the right resonance for this world of legend and what spiritually shines and sounds behind it, and even less during the centuries of the Enlightenment. Only the nineteenth century asks again for the Grail, seeking for its Mysteries. This happens with those touched by the Romantic spiritual movement, slowly opening perception of the world of fairy tales and legends, for whom the Christian Middle Ages were not simply the 'Dark Ages'. Novalis ceremonially greeted this new Spirit of the Age in a poetic fairy tale,[4] with the words *'die Wärme naht, die Ewigkeit beginnt'*—

[4] Novalis, *Heinrich von Ofterdingen*, Berlin, 1802. https://www.deutschestextarchiv.de/book/view/novalis_ofterdingen_1802/?hl=nach&p=282/

'the warmth approaches, eternity begins'. As if a layer of ice, or the intellect, began to melt away, the pictures now began again to receive inner life. They regained their radiance. They began to sound, to make music. As the last great Romantic, Richard Wagner (1813–1883) renewed the proclamation of the Grail through his music dramas, *Lohengrin* from his earlier period (1848), and *Parsifal* (1882), his last testament. As a poet and composer, he was able to breathe new life into the figures and symbols of the world of the Grail, so that from the stage they began to enter numerous hearts. The search for the Grail, interest in its riddles, came to life again, not only in the sense of historic research or a romantic, aesthetic longing, but as a *call of the age*.

'Do you hear the call?' asks the Grail-teacher Gurnemanz, who shakes awake the sleeping guardians in the borderland of the Grail. 'Now give thanks to God that you are called to hear it.'

Since the Romantic era, literary criticism has taken extraordinary strides to fathom the connections of the various poetic works on the Grail. Unresolvable contradictions seem to arise. What was it about the book from Count Phillip that no later Grail poets seem to know about? Did other sources exist at all, from which the various poets could draw? One of the philologically most thorough researchers of the previous epoch, Wolfgang Golther, thoroughly denies this. He states that it was the intention of the later poets, through such cited sources, to surpass Chrétien.

Perhaps one could ascribe such motifs to the authors of the later prose novels on the Grail. But if one could gain an impression of the sublime moral seriousness that penetrates the work of a Wolfram, one should be careful with such claims regarding him. Wolfram, as little as he is a scholarly writer and thus misses the exactitude of academic standards regarding names and historical facts, nevertheless exhibits a most deep moral relationship to the poetic motifs he employs. Towards his pictorial figures he acts responsibly in a manner seldom to be found in modern literature. Here is no playing, no arbitrary dealing with the imaginative content. Consequently, in literary and historical research one can, for example, come across the opinion today that none of the Grail poets has a clear idea of what the Grail actually is and what it serves. But particularly this unresolved, mysterious question repeatedly stimulates the drive towards creating fables, calling up new inventions. If we take only the first three epics, we can regard them as the pillars for the construction of all further poetic work on the Grail.

- Chrétien describes the Grail as the vessel for the Host, as it is used by the Church for Communion of the Sick.
- Robert de Boron presents it as that chalice from which Christ gave His disciples to drink during the Last Supper and in which Joseph of Arimathea collected the blood of the Redeemer.
- Wolfram, on the other hand, simply calls it a 'stone'; this stone, whose heavenly origin he describes to us, is renewed each Good Friday in its miraculous power, in that a dove descending from heaven places on it a Host.

'Who is the Grail?'

We see how each time a connection is made to the symbolism of the sacrament at the altar. But each poet feels the right freely to fashion the pictures. For each in their own way approaches a higher Mystery that is so comprehensive that one feels the necessary to point towards it always with new Imaginations. Wagner approached the content of the legend with such an intuitive, sensitive gift that gave him the power to construct the whole story once more. By smelting the various events from here and there into his composition, something miraculous arose. He possessed to a high degree what Goethe meant by 'exact Imagination'.

'Wer ist der Gral?' 'Who is the Grail?' he makes the young Parsifal ask, who for the first time hears this name from the lips of Gurnemanz. The latter answers:

'Das sagt sich nicht;
doch, bist du selbst zu ihm erkoren,
bleibt dir die Kunde unverloren.
Und sieh'!
Mich dünkt, dass ich dich recht erkannt:
kein Weg führt zu ihm durch das Land,
und niemand könnte ihn beschreiten,
den er nicht selber möcht' geleiten.'

'That cannot be said;
but if you yourself are called to its service
that knowledge will not remain withheld.
And see!

I think I know you aright;
no earthly path leads to it,
and none could tread it
whom the Grail itself had not guided.'

Wagner made a staging indication that while the two appear to walk, the stage should change in an unnoticeable manner. The forest disappears. In the walls of rock a gate appears, receiving the walkers, until in ascending passages they are allowed to enter the Grail Castle. Parsifal says:

'Ich schreite kaum,	'I scarcely tread,
doch wähn' ich mich schon weit'.	yet seem already to have come far'.

The Grail teacher answers him:

'Du siehst, mein Sohn,	'You see, my son,
zum Raum wird hier die Zeit'.	here time becomes space'.

In the dramatic events themselves an initial answer to the Grail-question is given. The human being does not achieve the Grail by walking towards it. The Grail must come towards him. It is *grace* to be allowed to experience it, but of course the human being has to begin to walk, has to become active, if the Grail is to come towards him. This walking is an overcoming of sensory existence with its laws of space and time. A soul-space is reached, as it were, a sphere in which what otherwise occurs one after another and side by side, appear simultaneously. An explanation coined by Wagner here opens a way to an understanding. It seems to be drawn from the depths of mystical experience. What in the language of spiritual science is called 'entering the astral plane', is here exactly described with this formula that here 'time becomes space'. It concerns a realm where what has long passed continues to have its effect, as well as what has not yet occurred having an effect from its nascent forces. Where time has become space, the event of Golgotha can reveal itself as a sacrificial event continuing to be effective in earthly existence. One no longer needs to experience it out of reports and Church traditions. As an event, it is not finished in Palestine but is revealed as a continuous dying of Christ's Being into the life of humanity and its ever-fresh resurrecting out of the grave of the soul. For such an experience, Christianity has become a 'mystical time', although at the beginning of our reckoning of time it also occurred as an historical fact.

Rudolf Steiner at the beginning of the twentieth century wrote his book *Christianity as Mystical Fact* (1902). With it a foundation stone was laid towards a knowledge of Christ, which meant a complete overcoming of that historical-critical method through which the Gospels and other documents of Christianity have been reduced to an intellectual study. The events of Palestine are revealed to the spiritually awake gaze in direct vision without any historical mediation. They can be read in that 'scripture', which with eternal signs are imprinted into the 'book of life' of humanity. But with this we approach the riddle of those mysterious books to which the poetic works on the Grail relate and from which they claim to be written.

Consequently, the key to the riddles and contradictions the various Grail narratives present to us seem only to lie in the activity with what we seek to penetrate to the Grail experiences themselves as they are presented to us each time in their legendary pictures. Initially, the groundbreaking poetic work of Chrétien de Troyes will be explored in this way.

Chrétien's Perceval *and the Imagination of the Grail Castle*

Chrétien describes how Perceval rides during the day, in the evening of which he finds the Grail Castle. He had left Blanchefleur, the beloved, to find his mother, for whom he is concerned in his heart since he saw her fainting at his departure. He does not yet know that she has died—for the whole day he remained on his path, that is, he did not meet anything earthly, no male or female Christian who could show him the way, and he prayed unceasingly to God, the highest Father, that he may find his mother again in health.

From this unceasingly prayer he awakens towards evening, when he sees he has arrived at a river where the surging floods deny his crossing. He follows the river until he reaches a rock protruding into the water, thus barring his way. He sees a boat drifting downstream. Two men sit in it, the one rowing the other fishing. He greets them, asking how he could cross. The fisherman answers that there is no bridge or ferry far and wide, but that he himself is prepared to host him for the night. He points out an opening that leads into the rock and then towards a path leading upwards. Perceval rises on this path to the summit and from a gorge the peak of a tower appears. Towards this he guides his horse. He becomes aware of a strong castle, clearly described to the reader. He rides to the gate; the drawbridge is already let down. How he is received and led into the hall, all this points to the fact that he is already expected. After discarding his armour, he is robed in a crimson mantle. Thus, he is led before the lord of the castle who sits on a couch beside a mighty fireplace, excusing himself for not rising to meet his guest. Later we hear that he is called 'the rich Fisher-King'. A squire brings in a sword with precious adornments, giving it to the lord of the castle as a present from his niece, a beautiful maiden. The lord immediately puts it on the youth, making it clear to him that it was meant for his possession. But then, out of a chamber another squire enters with a naked lance that he holds in the middle of the shaft. He passes between the fire in the hearth and the one sitting on his bed. They all see the lance and from its iron tip a drop of blood oozing that flows down to the hand of the squire. Here the youth wanted to ask, but he recalls the teaching of that noble man who not long ago made him a knight, warning him against idle talk. Perceval forbears to ask concerning the bleeding lance.

After this, however, the beautiful maiden appears, accompanied by squires with magnificent lights. She bore, we read, 'a grail in her two hands' [Part 3, 3205]. With it such a great light enters the room, the candlelight pales against it, as the stars do when the Sun or the Moon rises. But the Grail, made of pure gold was studded with the purest gemstones of the Earth—it is emphasized that without doubt they surpassed any others. The Grail was followed by another maiden with a silver platter. These objects, too, like the lance are carried from one room to another. Again, Perceval does not dare to ask a question, whom one served with the Grail.

Only five years later, from the holy hermit to whom he confesses his sins, he hears that the rich fisherman is the son of the noble king who is being served by the Grail [Part 4, 6207ff.]:

> A single host, assuredly,
> That in the grail one brings to him,
> Sustains and warms the life in him.
> So holy a thing is the grail,
> And he, so spiritual, without fail
> The host within the grail, no more,
> Maintains his life, so it endure.

Then we read that this old king for twelve years has not left his chamber into which the Grail entered to feed him.

Perceval was around fifteen years old when he ventured out and was allowed to see the grail for the first time; five years have passed since then. The old king has been held for the same time in the mysterious chamber, in which he is nourished by the strength of the Host, for the same duration as Perceval has lived in his earthly body. Is it perhaps possible from this aspect that the veil could be lifted that lies over the miracle of the feeding miracle? For the grail is a miracle of nourishment.

It is now described in detail how the hosting of the guest is carried out. The meal is served on a table with an ivory surface resting on wooden legs of ebony. It is claimed that this wood can neither rot nor break, and of the tablecloth on it we read that neither legate nor cardinal, nor a pope had eaten from a whiter cloth. With this non-decaying wood and shimmering white cloth we are directed beyond the sphere of transitory things, but at the same time beyond the ecclesiastical hierarchy. For the grail that bears the Host is not carried by a priest. A maiden guards it.

It may appear strange, how down to earth the meal is described with its rich courses. The first course is a whole haunch of venison joint, roasted and with peppers, with which a squire serves the host and his guest. Clear, fine wines are not missing from the meal. Yet unceasingly the Grail openly passes by as the food is brought, one course after the other. The noble man excuses himself and is carried by the squire on a blanket into the adjoining room. But Perceval finds his bed in the same room where the meal took place. There he sleeps far into the morning. When he awakens, he finds nobody to serve or greet him. He has to arise and dress himself alone, takes up his weapons—but the doors of the rooms are locked. It appears he is imprisoned in the hall. He calls and knocks loudly. No one opens; it is completely silent. Finally, he finds one door open; he climbs down to the courtyard, sees his horse, saddled. Making towards the gate, he rides over the drawbridge that clearly has been let down, so that nothing holds him back. He intends to ride after the squires who certainly left early to hunt. Then he will ask them those questions strongly lying on his heart that he could not utter. Before he can make it over the bridge, he suddenly feels the feet of his horse are being lifted. With a great jump he just makes it to reach the ground; the drawbridge meantime has been pulled up. He turns and calls—but receives no answer. He has to ride away without having found an explanation for all the mysteries of the night …

The way someone waking in the morning initially feels caught in the castle, hopelessly seeking exits, how he is thrown out roughly and abruptly—all these are clearly experiences that take place on the threshold of waking up, when the soul emerging as from another world can only with difficulty connect to sensory consciousness. It must wrestle to be able consciously to dive again into the body.

Shortly afterwards, Perceval hears from the maiden who holds a slain knight in her lap that there is no hostelry in that region for five miles around. The one where he was a guest of the Fisher-King cannot be found again despite all his searching. Consequently, it cannot be a castle to be perceived with earthly senses in which Perceval had been. This castle is entered in falling asleep and one is thrown out of it when one awakens. But the meal takes place in the same room in which shortly afterwards one falls asleep. It can only be the human body itself in which such mysteries take place. Yet seldom do people, and only chosen ones, seem to be able to participate consciously. A certain strength of soul is necessary to stay awake in falling asleep, whilst the sensory expressions are fading away and the soul begins to remove itself from the body. It is consequently a letting go and at the same time a looking back onto the body that sinks into slumber—an inner awaking. Wonderful mysteries take place every night in that castle of the body; they can only be presented to the spiritually awakened person in imagination while remaining protected from the day-consciousness. For that would be difficult to bear, or attempts would be made to interfere destructively.

Such a strengthening of the soul that made it possible to remain conscious while entering the world of sleep, the youth could achieve during that day when, in great anguish for the mother he had abandoned, he rode in unceasing prayer. The concentration on an essential thought, or the devotion towards a strong feeling, concentrates the soul-forces. Through this, in the declining of sensory impressions, these soul-forces are still able to remain awake in themselves. The soul and spirit learn to be loosened from the body; in looking back on it before the inner eye, the streaming life-forces first appear, while the sensory world recedes. Perceval notices he cannot proceed in the same direction in which his horse carried him during the day. And so, a check in consciousness arises, a racing stream over which no passage is evident before the soul's gaze. Two men appear in a boat. A hidden dreamer that lives in us emerges. He appears twofold—in so far that the human being of wishes plumbs into the depths (the one fishing) and the bearer of wisdom who mysteriously guides him (the one who rows), working in the instinctive life of the soul. Seen in its duality, this dreamer is truly 'the rich Fisherman'. For to him belongs the depths of human consciousness that contain immeasurable treasures, of which the day-person is hardly conscious, or only divines it.

In the world of fairy tales and legends we often meet the picture of the fisherman. It appears where the soul begins to go on paths that lead it towards the border of firm earthly things, where it becomes aware how all sensory existence is surrounded by hidden life-forces. Thus, the soul can be felt to be placed on the shore of the ocean of the ether and begins to bring out of it the revealing pictures which are the true soul-nourishment. It becomes a fisherman. Life in Imaginations has taken its start.

This wants to announce itself to the young Perceval. Now, whilst his 'I' is lifted from his body it nevertheless looks back on it. Its gaze is directed towards the protruding rock—the fisherman in the boat points the direction to him, leading like a cleft into the interior of the rock; he penetrates into it until before him the majestic castle arises from the depths.

Like a mighty rock-bone there appears to the spirit and soul of the human being the shape of the skull, out of whose organs he had just been released. The etheric forces that have been fashioning in this and continue to retain it, expand before its gaze. These grow towards the sublime imagination of the Grail Castle. The one who has become clairvoyant in falling asleep enters these forces. He beholds processes arising from the depths of the bodily nature which slowly reconstruct the head-nature of the human being. Mysteries of construction, mysteries of nourishment of the hidden human being, bliss-awakening and yet woven through with painful processes that at first remain for him a riddle, painfully weighing on him, pass by the beholder until he finally loses the power of the waking experience; he falls into a deep sleep in the same place.

In his spiritual-scientific lectures, Rudolf Steiner undertook to shed light on the Grail Imagination from various angles. He also precisely describes the physiological mysteries that are reflected in these pictures.[5] He describes how our human nature here on Earth is initially enchanted into a castle, how it must live enclosed by rock walls. What from outside appears to us as the top of the skull is a mighty castle if we regard the etheric forces lying as its basis. Towards this castle during our sleep, forces stream up out of the whole organism which sustain the human being. At first that force is made of everything that burns through the human being, making him strong through the nerves. This force appears like the mighty sword which the human

[5] *The Effect of Occult Development* (GA 145), The Hague, 20–29 March 1913.

being himself has forged on Earth. With this sword of thinking, as far as it is well smithied, a unique power is given to him. Perceval is made aware of this when he receives the grail-sword. But then the forces of the blood surge up, those which cause hurt to the brain-person lying in the magic castle of the skull. For in the blood selfishness streams, it poisons all the noble strivings and intentions. A bleeding lance appears, with which all misfortune is connected; Perceval should have asked about the ailment of the Fisher-King because it concerns his innermost being. The Grail is mentioned, which with its noblest nourishment feeds alone that which with any other nourishment would be killed. Rudolf Steiner calls it 'the human *Heros*' [Gk. for 'widower'], the father of the Fisher-King, in Wolfram called Titurel. This hidden member of the human being can only be contained throughout an entire human lifetime through the wonder of etheric nourishment, although we are sentenced to death from the moment we are born. It is the Spirit-Man in us, which at birth must dive down into the bodily nature as if confined within a prison cell. Now it is understandable why the hermit could say to Perceval that this holy man who is only able to strengthen his life from the Grail for twenty years—that is, as long as Perceval has lived on Earth—could not leave that room into which the Grail repeatedly enters.

Digestive processes flood the human head when we sink into sleep. All earthly nourishment taken during the day now streams upwards, transformed by the blood, towards the upper human being—animal, plant and mineral substance. But they would dull the noblest part of the brain, which is the seat of Spirit-Man, unless a finest extract is separated and carried to Spirit-Man. This is why the Grail during the feeding goes round repeatedly taking what the father of the Fisher-King is allowed to enjoy without being killed by it. Here Rudolf Steiner explains that it concerns the mineral aspect from our nourishment, which can unite with specific impressions from the sense organs.

> The noblest element of light, the noblest element of sound, the noblest element of warmth, here touch the noblest products of the mineral realm, for the noblest part of the brain is nourished by the connection with the noblest sense-impressions, with the noblest mineral products. From this noblest part of the human brain, the ether-body extracts everything coming from the plant and animal realm.

Initially, this concrete description may appear sobering, in contrast to all the poetic words with which the Grail wants to escape towards a symbol for the highest religious and moral ideals. This is only as long as one has learnt not to view together the spiritual and moral element with the material and physical element.

For what is united there, carrying from below the purest substances, penetrating from above the noblest raying from the cosmos, is a Sun-filled illumination—transfiguration forces making their effect through human nature. With the most precious stones that adorn the Grail the mineral substances are indicated; with the golden glow of the vessel and its Sun-like raying of light, the cosmic influence is indicated that is perceived with our sense impressions. What we usually call our sense-perception is only a small part of what penetrates us through seeing, hearing, tasting, and so on. In perception, we only take up a part of what cosmically radiates in; this we reflect as the content of our consciousness. But the highest effects which enter us through sense-impressions, are continuously received by our hidden soul-life. These are the effects of the Sun, which cannot be grasped by day-consciousness and thus remain completely pure. They are received by that deeper consciousness that remains virginal, because the nature of the urges does not reach it. Its seat is the vegetative nervous system, with a certain centre in the solar plexus. From it proceed all the healing and building-up processes in the human organism. A maiden appears before Perceval. She carries the Grail up to the enchanted Castle when the day-consciousness is extinguished; she governs the forces of transfiguration in human nature.

But why does the nourishment of the Grail appear in the form of a Host, by which 'the holy one' is nourished? This can only be understood when the cosmic Mystery of Christ's Being is once again recognized. On the beams of sunlight, this sublime Being from the cosmos entered historical, earthly existence, lived a human destiny and within the ether-forces of the Sun became internalized into pure Love. When the three most pure disciples on Mount Tabor beheld their Master in the transfiguration of the body, the Grail appeared for the first time on the Earth. There to the disciples' view the Grail shone like a Sun from the head of Christ. But through suffering death, the Grail is given to the life of the Earth. To find it in earthly existence, as it were to breathe it in with each sense-perception and unite with it in everyday nourishment, has become possible since the sacrifice of Golgotha. In the sacrament of the holy meal, this receiving of the holiest life-forces becomes visible. What happens during the night in the depths of our organism as the power of transfiguration, becomes raised through the action of the priest, when it appears in the right way, into devotional experience.

Perceval, who for a moment becomes inwardly clairvoyant, experiences the 'holy nocturnal meal', which for us otherwise takes place unconsciously all the time. What Chrétien intends to describe is neither a sacrament of the Church, nor a concession to some Church tradition, for then he would not have a maiden carry the vessel with the Host. It is rather the archetypal picture for that which in the sacramental service can approach us from without. The sacrament at the altar imitates externally for our beholding what takes place in us in a hidden manner. It would give to the believers the strength to learn to connect ever more closely with these healing processes, to lay hold of them as fully conscious human beings.

An ancient Nordic legend of Perceval exists[6] that arose in the thirteenth century and mainly follows Chrétien. It expressly says of the Grail, 'And this is a holy thing which that rich man had carried before him, for comfort and support of his soul and his life; this holy thing is something spiritual, nothing physical.' Later, we shall discuss this early Nordic account, which clearly strives to penetrate the inner content of the Imaginations.

[6] In Riddarasögur (legends of the knights).

2. The Origin of the Grail

The missed question

Perceval finds the Grail without a search. He did search for his mother, but he does not fulfil what is expected of him. He does not pose the question that would have brought about the healing of the sick Fisher-King. The holy hermit to whom, five years later, he confesses this guilt out of a deep plight in his soul, explains to him why he was unable to ask: 'Sin bound your tongue when you saw before you the point of the lance that never ceases to bleed, and you did not ask what it means.' He was caught in the same situation regarding the question, whom does the Grail serve? The sin with which he unconsciously burdened himself was the great pain he inflicted on his mother, which broke her heart. Nevertheless, it was the prayers of this mother which on destiny's path protected him from death and imprisonment. His life was actually finished. Only through the protection of her who died was he able to live.

We see Chrétien's work exudes the spirit of a deep piety. He possesses a chaste relationship to the Imaginations; except for dressing the events in the forms of knighthood, he leaves the pictures untouched. Consequently, in his work they possess the greatest transparency. On the other hand, his work misses the crowning. For five years Perceval searches for the Grail, but how he finds it is not described. It is obvious that with this completion for the search for the Grail, we, [and] Perceval himself, would have experienced what the Grail is. With the instructions through the hermit, already a part of this Mystery is revealed, but only after Perceval has gone through many trials and borne many pains for the Grail. A certain maturity of life is necessary to be able to ask questions of the Grail. Being held in a heavy, although unconscious guilt, does not allow the soul to awaken in the world of spirit, as would be necessary to do the right thing at the right moment. For in this case *asking* would be acting in the spirit. An engagement of the full human being was asked of him.

Perceval possesses the purity and impressionable capacity of the soul to receive the Grail Imaginations. Yet he remains stuck in the beholding the pictures. A strengthening of the 'I' in the spirit was necessary, an act of innermost freedom, to place and question and thus receive answers. This marks the cognitive step that leads from the

Imaginative experience to that of Inspired recognition. At this level the pictures are superseded; the 'word' wants to be born in the soul. The spirit only reveals its Mysteries when the right questions, those of the heart, are brought towards it. To be able to ask shows the grade of maturity. *'Gradweise'*—*'gradatim'* of medieval latin—the Mystery only reveals itself *gradually*, which on the first level approaches the soul in pictures woven like dreams. Consequently, it is called the Grail (= '*gradale*'): that which only by degrees can be revealed. This word had to bear many attempts at interpretation. People attempted to trace it back to the early French word *'graal'* (Old Provençal, *'grazal'*), which describes a key. This is not necessarily wrong. In the Middle Ages word games were much favoured. From an everyday word, traces of mysterious names were sought, or even to indicate with an innocent term a deeper meaning for those in the know. This has always been the custom in the language of the Mysteries.

Perhaps without human intention, there nevertheless lies in the way succeeding poetic works on the Grail 'gradually' illuminate the Mystery, something like a guidance of the medieval souls through the various 'grades' of an enlightenment given them within the time of approximately 1180–1280.

Robert de Boron's Joseph of Arimathea

Robert de Boron is the next Grail-author. With his poetic work *Joseph d'Arimathie*,[7] the first part of a planned comprehensive Grail narration, he takes on the task of describing the origin of that vessel. The tension with which Chrétien's epic leaves the reader demands this. Nevertheless, it is naïve to imagine that only out of this tension, that is, out of a novelistic need for sensation, such an artistic legend breathed through by a sublime mood could have been contrived, as is given us in this story of the foundation of serving the Grail and its destiny. (1)[8]

Robert is the first to present the connection of the Grail to the events of Palestine. He brings the early Christian world to arise in our imagination. According to his interpretation, the Grail is that vessel out of which the Saviour during the Last Supper gives His disciples to drink, in which later the holy blood of the Redeemer is collected.

---

[7] *Merlin and the Grail: Joseph of Arimathea, Merlin, Perceval.* D.S. Brewer 2008.

[8] Numbers in brackets refer to the Additional Notes. For an initial reading of the text, it is not necessary to look these up immediately.

We read that during the Lord's arrest, a Jew found this vessel and brought it to Pilate. Joseph of Arimathea, a member of the Sanhedrin, who according to the Gospel narrative took the body of Christ from the cross and interred it in his own grave near the hill of Golgotha, is described as a knight, who with his men had faithfully served the Governor for many years and now as a favour asked for the body. Pilate granted this request and gave him the vessel in addition. But when Joseph with Nicodemus took the body from the cross and washed it, once again blood flowed from the wounds. He gathered it in the vessel and sought to keep it in his house. But after the Resurrection of the Lord, the Jews accused him of disposing the corpse secretly. In their rage they put him in a tower, both high and deep, securely locked. But the Risen One Himself came to his prison, filling it with radiant glory. He brought him the vessel with the precious blood and comforted him by assuring him of His love.

> You have taken me from the cross and laid me in the grave. No offering in the Mass will occur without remembrance of your deed. The cloth with which you wrapped me will be called the 'Corporal'.[9] The vessel which received my blood will be called the 'Chalice', and the 'Paten' laid on it, shall signify the stone with which you closed my grave. Everyone who in future beholds this vessel will experience eternal joy and blissfulness of the heart.

The Risen One now entrusted to him secret words that are to be spoken to consecrate the Grail and comforts him regarding the future.

The release of Joseph, nevertheless, only takes place with the destruction of Jerusalem by the Romans. Vespasian has himself lowered into the prison on a rope and finds the ancient man, who without food and drink was kept alive through all the years in a super-earthly light. (2)

Such descriptions tend to point in pictures towards the conditions of mystical contemplation, as was practised by individual hermits in

---

[9] The corporal is an altar linen used in Christianity for the celebration of the Eucharist. Originally called *corporax*, from Latin *corpus* ('body'), it is a small square of white linen cloth; modern corporals are usually somewhat smaller than the width of the altar on which they are used, so that they can be placed flat on top of it when unfolded. During the Liturgy of the Eucharist, various altar vessels are placed on the corporal, including the chalice, the paten, and the ciborium containing the smaller hosts for the Communion of the laity—*Wikipedia*.

strict asceticism. The mystic who can remove himself at times from the sensory world to merge completely with an inner beholding truly experiences himself held in a windowless tower. The head is the prison of the soul. But when illumination occurs from the heart, this prison is illumined by a light extinguishing all darkness. With Joseph of Arimathea a founder of Christian mysticism is presented to us who, in the inner connection of the Mystery of the cross, was allowed to experience in himself the transformation of the nature of blood. A deep entering into the experience of the Mystery of the Passion leads the blood through purification through annihilating all lower urges. Through this, it begins to release an etheric light out of itself, which is the beginning of a new clairvoyance.

Novalis, although in his writings nowhere connecting with Grail symbolism, knew it out of the deepest Christian discipleship. In his novel *Heinrich von Ofterdingen*, he has the old hermit speak words that could also have been spoken by Joseph of Arimathea.

'In the vale I gladly linger,
Smiling in the dusky night,
For to me with rosy finger
Proffers Love his cup of light.

With its dew my spirit sunken
Wafted is toward the skies,
And I stand in this life drunken
At the gate of Paradise ...'[10]

Historical research has found a medieval theological work, an introduction to the Mysteries of the Sacrifice of the Mass, *Gemma animae* of Honorius von Autun,[11] that uses almost the same pictures as Robert de Boron to honour the significance of the first Guardian of the Grail. We read how the Deacon, who after the words *per omnia saecula saeculorum*

[10] Novalis, *Henry von Ofterdingen: A Romance*, Dover 2015, 54. Unabridged republication of the work originally published by Cambridge Press, Cambridge, Massachusetts, 1842.

[11] Honorius Augustodunensis's Gemma animae, or Jewel of the Soul (Gerhard Eger 2023), stands out among the treatises of the pre-Scholastic blossoming of commentary on the Franco-Roman liturgical rite—*Wikipedia*.
https://sicutincensum.wordpress.com/2023/05/01/translation-of-honorius-augustodunensiss-gemma-animae-now-available-for-purchase/

raises the chalice, places it on the altar and covers it with a cloth, introduces in the Offertory Joseph of Arimathea, how he took down Christ's body and covering His face with a sweat cloth, laid Him in the grave and closed it with a stone.

We see how within Christian devotion of those days a stream was present—*Gemma animae* derives from the same twelfth century—seeking inwardly to connect the celebration of the altar service with Joseph of Arimathea. But with this the Sacrifice of the Mass derives from the Easter experiences of early Christianity. In them it finds its origin. Focus on the Risen One, which Joseph as a mystic was allowed to experience, becomes a source of inspiration for the stream which through the centuries has poured into celebrating the altar sacrifice. Robert de Boron appears to have been part of such an esoteric, spiritual stream. (3)

People want to see the Grail legend fashioned by Robert as a glorification of the honouring of relics—the Chalice with the most holy Blood as the most precious relic of Christendom. It should not be denied that devotion to relics ever since the earliest days is linked to an ardent piety. The longing to bridge the abyss separating us from the early Christian times and the work of the Apostles, increased in certain groups during the Middle Ages to such surges of emotions that many hearts could experience a deep satisfaction in being allowed to see or to touch a relic, an heirloom, from those days. For them it carried into the present day, as it were, a breath of the holy event, of Christ's divine-earthly existence. But piety towards the Grail demands something completely different. It leads attention towards a source of experience, from whence that most holy event can be ever renewed. Each chalice of the Mass, it says, can be the grave into which the Redeemer can be lowered; each corporal, with which one covers the chalice becomes the cloth into which Joseph of Arimathea once wrapped the body of the Crucified and from which He rose to new life on Easter morning. In the mystic's experience, the gap of time is overcome. For him the holy event becomes the continuous present, because it can be experienced in one's own blood as the influence of the Grail.

The Grail on its way from East to West

Up to this point the Grail legend of Robert de Boron seems to place itself naturally into Christianity of the Church and the stream of sacramental life. It only wants to show the esoteric foundations from which this can be repeatedly renewed.

But now the legend moves to describe to the reader the company of the Grail table and of a Grail community. It presents a picture of early Christian life, standing outside the development of the recognized Church and outside the traditional Apostolic activity, quietly unfolding and finally finding its path into the world. It describes how Joseph, freed from prison, is joyfully welcomed by his sister and brother-in-law Bron (an abbreviation of Hebron). They gather a community; together they move to a foreign land after the destruction of Jerusalem. There they farmed and finally became wealthy. But when opulence appeared amongst them, the blessing withdraws from their community. Pursued by misfortune and hunger, a great helplessness overcomes them. It consequently has to do with an early form of Christian community, which in a special sense might have fostered the ideal of holy poverty.

Joseph kneels in ardent prayer before the holy vessel, imploring help. A voice in his spirit commands him to separate the impure from the pure. 'You will test the sinners amongst your people, by placing before them my blood and myself.' He is to replicate the table of the Lord's last supper. There, the betrayer sat at table receiving the sop, and through it excluded himself; the same thing should happen here. According to the divine instructions, Joseph sets up the Grail table. In the middle the chalice with the previous blood is placed. Opposite it a fish is laid, which, at Joseph's command, had to be caught by his brother-in-law Hebron. This fish is to present Christ in his pure form.

What is the deeper reason for this fish-symbol, which we also meet in the representations in the Catacombs? The fish within cosmic development embodies that level of life that has not yet begun to form warm blood; it is the bearer of the yet guiltless life. It was imagined that Christ in His cosmic existence was akin to this level of the fish. He wants to lift us, too, towards this guiltless form of existence in the ether-realm. To arrive at this, however, He Himself had to go through human incarnation—He had to take on warm-blooded life. In this way He connected Himself out of love with humanity's guilt that in the red blood streams through the generations. But He purified this blood of all selfish urges and tendencies. The disciple of the Grail's Mystery is to look at both forms of existence of Christ and be able to contemplate them, in that the fish and the chalice with the sacred blood are present on the table.

Quite a different viewpoint may be added. At the Grail table the Redeemer does not appear as the Lamb, corresponding to the symbolism of the Passover feast. As long as the Sun passed through the spring point of the Ram (Aries) in the zodiac, the Ram, or the Lamb, had been the great cultural symbol of the religions. But the vernal, or spring point passed on to the zodiac sign of the Fishes (Pisces), where it is still to be found today. The rising of the Fish-symbol is to be seen as a mirroring of this fact of the cosmos. Early Christianity saw itself as preparing the way for future spiritual forces that began through grace to be given to humanity, as the Sun moved into a new zodiac sign. The wisdom of the Grail also knows the picture of the 'rich fisherman', in which the Grail king appears. This wisdom in a special sense prepared Christianity of the 'age of the Fishes', whereas the traditional Church with its strong roots in the Old Testament and the cultures of antiquity, was still caught in the declining 'age of the Ram', as it were, forming a transitional link before the Christian impulse was able to struggle through to its own form. Through this, the rigidifying of Christian traditions and the search for completely new starting points for Christianity in the present age becomes understandable.

Robert de Boron describes the service of the Grail. The people are invited to sit at the table. Between Joseph and Hebron an empty place remains, signifying the seat of Judas. Whoever sits at that place, the Earth will open and swallow him up. After a deceitful disciple had to experience this, a warning voice advises to leave the place unoccupied until a grandson of Hebron is born. It is reserved for him. It is described how the pure ones in beholding the Grail are allowed to experience sweetness and bliss of the heart—but the impure ones remain with empty hearts and shamefully withdraw. This is the test causing at the same time a division of spirits. Around the third hour of the morning, the community gathers daily for the Grail service.

We see how here, in a calm manner away from Church tradition, a community life is founded in the centre of which a ritual stands from which everything radiates that can bless souls and is penetrated by the light of Christ. Perhaps some things have come from the traditions of the Essene brotherhood into this community of the Holy Spirit. The holy service here is not presented in the form of a eucharistic meal, which in the form of bread and wine wants to distribute the Body and Blood of the Redeemer. It is a trial of beholding. In a symbolic manner events and exercises are depicted, which by itself is to ignite the light of Christ in the participants. Only when the light of the Grail is ignited in the soul is the trial passed; with this the purpose of the celebration is fulfilled.

At the end of the presentation, it is confirmed that Robert de Boron brought this account to the light of day with the permission of the Church and following the request of the Count of Montbéliard. But one may consider that in the south of France in those days the first war against the Albigenses was fought (1181/82). The Church of the Cathars in Provence, which had to be an annoyance, a thorn in the side for Rome, began their battle to the death. The Roman Church was only able to extinguish it in 1229 in what is called the 'peace of Toulouse' after the terrible devastation of the Heretic Crusades to extinguish 'the pestilence' of the Cathars. Towns and proud castles, in which free spirits and courageous hearts had unfolded a rich culture full of brilliance and inner devotion, were reduced to ash and rubble. Into this stream free from Rome many things from the first millennium could be saved of primordial Christian wisdom and the inner striving to receive the Holy Spirit. Especially in those decades when the destiny of the Cathar community entered its decline, in the view of those in the know the urge arose to save these spiritual treasures in a different manner through the storm of the time.

In the same way, to get through the winter, plants draw back in the form of the seed, the spiritual striving has to be clothed in pictures of sagas and legends. It was known—if these pictures are potent, they will also be strong enough at a given time to bring forth a new spiritual life. The publication of the Grail legend is a precautionary measure issuing from a group in the know. In this subdued way, the rays of the Grail light can enter the divining soul under the veil of legendary events.

The destiny of the Grail stream—as was laid out for it on the path from East to West, is indicated to us in the legend. Hebron with his wife, the sister of Joseph, had twelve sons who were all prepared to serve God. Eleven married; only the twelfth remained single. His name was Alain ('Alan' in the Celtic-Breton stream), chosen in a special sense to be the carrier of the elevated testimony that Joseph of Arimathea before his parting could still impart to him on his way. Joseph himself is able repeatedly to receive divine advice in contemplation before the Grail. He lives on the comfort of the Holy Spirit, acting on Its advice. Thus, he receives the instruction to introduce this youngest of his nephews into the Mysteries of the Grail and to entrust to him his own Christ-experiences from the time of his imprisonment. For Alain is to become a messenger of Christ. But from him a destined descendant will one day guard the Grail in the right way.

Thus, with his brothers Alain moves to the far West to proclaim the name of Christ, whereas Hebron is to receive from the departing Joseph the vessel of the Grail and those mysterious words that belong to its rightful guardianship. Of him it is said that he is called the 'rich fisherman', since he had caught the fish for the Grail table. This name appears again, which we know from Chrétien's epic. If we recall the Orphic Mysteries of the Greek culture, the mystagogue carries the name 'fisherman'. Here we see especially clearly the connection to that early Christian cultic community with the Mysteries of the antiquity. Joseph of Arimathea and his esoteric group might have been closely connected to the Order of Essenes. He could draw on a rich ritual symbolism coming from the Eastern Mysteries into this Order. The fishermen from the Lake of Gennesaret, who later became the Apostles of Christ, were in this sense fisher-priests.

Hebron, too, moves towards the West, for the Valleys of Avalon (in Wales) are mentioned. A bridge is made towards Celtic Christianity, to that stream free from Rome, which from early on went its own ways and which has gained the highest honour of missionizing Western Europe. The spiritual leadership of humanity pursues hidden paths. References to them could be revealed in such legendary pictures. Our gaze is directed towards the West; all our expectation goes towards this unnamed descendant who will guard the Grail. Until then people looked for the light in the East. The Crusaders also set forth, because the motto *'Ex Oriente Lux'* kept them directed to the East. But this highest light that once radiated from the chalice with the most previous Blood, has been extinguished in the East. The Grail has been carried to the West, the legend wants to say—Seek the light, which arises in the West!

Wolfram's Parzival and Master Kyot

Wolfram von Eschenbach expresses himself much more courageously [than de Boron] and he leaves the path of Church tradition, also in the clothing of the Grail Mystery. Whilst the seedbeds of all heresy in Provence were under the observation of the Inquisition and disaster already beginning to brew over them, Wolfram at the end of his great epic confesses:

> 'The true tale was sent complete
> From Provence, to us, to greet
> Its audience in German lands.
> And found itself in my fair hands'.

For this he draws on his master, to whom he is indebted for the true knowledge of the Grail—Master Kyot, whom he calls a person from Provence. Indeed, in a protest against the first great bard of the Grail, he ends his poetic work with:

> If Chrétien of Troyes the story
> Has marred, good cause to be angry
> He has given Kyot, who sent
> The true tale here, with clear intent.
> [Book XVI]

We have to ask wherein lies Wolfram's judgement (whereby he appeals to Master Kyot) of the insufficiency of Chrétien's story? Initially, it seems that Wolfram owes a lot to this French example, indeed, that he followed him quite far in presenting Parsifal's destiny.

Let us test how he describes the Grail experiences themselves. Seen artistically, all the events seem to have become much more down to earth. The Imaginations have distanced themselves one step further from their spiritual origin. The fashioning of knightly adventures and the adjustment to the courtly life of the high Middle Ages, that is, the Hohenstaufen dynasty [1138-1254], are throughout composed with a sovereign poetic freedom. The figures arising before the Imaginative gaze and initially wanting to point to Mysteries of the inner life, gain here their own life and destiny. The fisherman of the Lake Brumbane who invites the youth as a guest is named Anfortas. The old man, who spends his life in the secluded chamber, living only from the strength of the Grail, is here called Titurel—we meet him as the ancestor of the noble family of the Grail. Chrétien describes the hall of the mysterious castle that could house four hundred knights. Consequently, Wolfram has four hundred Grail knights in a specific order sitting around the hall, to participate in the festive meal. Although in the garb of knightly attire, it concerns a community of the Grail as described by Robert de Boron, yet it cannot be found in any place on Earth. Parsifal only finds access to its realm, by travelling so far that day as hardly a bird can fly. With this, Wolfram clearly leads our attention beyond the sensory realm.

The Grail, however, is brought in, carried in procession. Twenty-four maidens, artistically arranged according to their different tasks, enter the hall one after the other, before the bearer of the Grail herself appears. It is Repanse de Schoye, the same who had sent her cloak in advance to the guest. Only because he had taken off his armour containing the forces of earthly prestige and was allowed to clothe himself in the cloak of pure feelings of a virginal soul is he able to perceive the holy events.

> She bore, on green silk Achmardi,
> The perfection, here, of paradise,
> Root and blossom, before their eyes;
> A thing it was they called the Grail,
> Beside which Earth's perfections fail.
> [Book V]

What is it that has been preserved in Paradise and is praised as the aim of humanity's longing? The 'Tree of Life', the fruits of which gives human beings eternal life, if today they could eat of it. That a tree is meant, we can see from line 3 of the quotation. Not only its golden fruit, of which legends and fairy tales tell us, but the tree itself with its roots and twigs becomes visible here. Whilst Parsifal exchanges his earthly awake consciousness against that virginal, faultless consciousness, there appears before his vision the Mystery of the restorative processes of life.

In discussing the Grail Imaginations in Chrétien's poetry, we pointed out how these Imaginations have their seat in the vegetative-nerve system, particularly the solar plexus. The strongest effects of the Sun, which with sensory impressions always penetrate us but cannot be held by the day-consciousness, can be reflected, but which on the other hand are graciously received by this deeply hidden consciousness. This organization appears in the Imagination of a tree with many branches and twigs, which is present in all innocent life-processes, whereas the central nervous system, which from the head branches down through the body, corresponds to the other tree that continuously sends death-bringing forces into the body. In the Bible this is the 'Tree of Knowledge'. Wolfram, when speaking of the Mystery of the Grail, adds '*erden wunches überwal*', 'high over all earthly wishes'.

> Root and blossom of Paradise Garden, that thing which men call 'The Grail',
> The crown of all earthly wishes, fair fulness that ne'er shall fail!
> [Book V, tr. Jesse Weston]

The Grail, however, is not that Tree of Life itself but what can be experienced and received through it. It is that which goes beyond all choosing of earthly wishes. But this means it conveys experience that cannot be grasped by earthly nature of wishing, cannot even be imagined.

Consequently, it is so difficult to lay hold of the Grail in a clear Imagination. At best one can describe the effect and results of its activities. Wolfram describes an elaborate miracle of feeding. A hundred pages appear who full of reverence receive from the Grail bread in white napkins, which they then distribute throughout the hall. Who would not recall the miraculous feeding of bread told in the Gospels?—At this meal the Grail offers food of all kinds, whatever is wished. Drinks in golden vessels, also spices according to taste in small golden vessels, are presented.

But the picture of the golden chalice with the Host, which we know from Chrétien's narration, does not appear. Wolfram consciously avoids that Imagination, taken from the realm of sacramental life. But what is carried in on the green silk cloth? We only hear about it in Book XI, when after long wanderings Parzival re-enters the realm of the Grail and is to receive the teachings of Trevrizent. The Mystery of the Tree of Life is not the only thing mentioned. The spiritual vision of this honourable teacher penetrates further than the youth in his knightly experience was able. Trevrizent has, as it were, penetrated to a deeper level in Grail knowledge. It is a *stone* that long ago had been carried down from heaven. But now when Parzival hears through the ancient hermit this 'secret knowledge of the Grail', the poet expressly says that earlier on one was not allowed to ask.

> ... For Kyot asked
> Me to hide them, thus I was tasked,
> Because his source had forbidden
> Kyot too, from making mention
> Of them till the story attained
> The point where they must be explained.
> [Book IX]

Stages of wisdom exist, towards which the soul has first to aspire. If imparted too early, such seeds would not find the right soil in which to unfold. Gradually, by stages, the Mystery of the Grail's life will give itself only to the one who is striving. According to the poet, only the one who with Parzival could follow the painful tests and trials will also gain the maturity to receive what is now to be imparted.

Wolfram now introduces his master, already mentioned in Book VIII as a bardic singer (*Kyôt la schantiure hiez*), whose art it is said made people happy. He, a man from Provence, had seen the *âventure* of

Parzival written in a 'heathen' manner; what he said about it in French he wanted now to attempt to tell Wolfram in German. The Master Kyot found the source of this legend in the dust of Toledo, 'in a rough heathen script', probably meaning in Arabic letters. This script he must have diligently studied, not needing 'necromancy' (the art to communicate with those who have died):

> That he was a baptised Christian
> Helped him, for otherwise no man
> Had learned the tale; no magic art,
> No hidden wisdom, on the part
> Of the infidels could e'er avail
> In learning the nature of the Grail,
> And how its secrets might be known.

Only through the Christian light in the soul, do we see the full splendour of the Grail revealed, although knowledge of it goes back to pre-Christian times. For a heathen—he is called Flegetanîs—discovered the first trace of the Grail, before baptism existed, an illumination in the Christian sense. This Flegetanîs, we read, wise in the knowledge of nature, explored in detail the circling stars and how the destiny of human beings is connected to them. But this knowledge of the stars led him to discover one 'thing called the Grail'. To this he gently refers in his research.

Concerning this wise master, we read he was born in the line of Solomon, which here probably means his contemporary. His father was a heathen who still worshipped a calf, whereas his mother came from Israelite stock. Now, we know from the Old Testament of such a contemporary of Solomon. He is the master builder Hiram, the 'son of a widow'. Of him it is reported, his father hailed from Tyrus (who there would have served the cult of the Bull), and his mother was an Israelite of the tribe of Naphtali [1 Kings 7:13–14]. This master, famous for his art, built as is known the two brazen column pillars in Solomon's Temple, which he called Jachin and Boaz; he cast the brazen sea and all the other wonderful work for which the temple in Jerusalem became famous and for centuries became a centre of powerful influences. The great master builder was always named with veneration by the wisdom streams of the Middle Ages. He is everywhere known in brotherhoods, where the symbolism of the temple was fostered. The esoteric Temple Legend sees in Hiram the master who goes through all ages, who once built Solomon's Temple, and after it was destroyed becomes the teacher of all those who intend to work on the 'invisible temple' of humanity. In a hidden yet nevertheless recognizable manner for those who know, Wolfram points to this exalted individuality, who was well known in the symbolism of the guilds and later in the traditions of Freemasonry. (4) The Grail knights themselves are called by Wolfram '*Templeisen*', for they are the guardians of the new Temple Mystery.

The Grail as a 'Stone'

Of the Grail, the name of which the wise master was able to read in the starry script, the following is now narrated.

> ... A host of angels this marvel to earth once bore,
> But too pure for earth's sin and sorrow the heaven they sought once more,
> And the sons of baptized men hold It, and guard It with humble heart,
> And the best of mankind shall those knights be who have in such service part.
> [Tr. J. Weston]

> ... A heavenly band
> Left it here, upon earth did stand
> And then they rose above the sky,
> If innocence drew them on high.
> Then a pure Christian progeny,
> Bred to a pure life, had the duty
> Of its guard. Worthy, says the tale,
> Are all those summoned to the Grail.
> [Tr. A. Kline]

Angels carried the Grail to the Earth; human beings have to receive and care for it. It consequently has to do with something holy, which was sacrificed from heaven to the Earth. Only 'baptized men' are called to care for it. These are the *Templeisen*, who are nourished by the Grail itself.

Only here is revealed that the Grail is a 'stone'. Its name is '*Lapsit exillis*'. Certainly, with this name (Wolfram uses names very freely, loves thereby to indicate some deep meaning), the imagination is to awaken to something that falls from heaven—*Lapis ex caelis*, or also *Lapsit ex caelis* (= it fell from heaven). Everything suggests it concerns an alchemical concept. The name could originally have been *Lapis exilii*, deriving from *exilium*, meaning 'pushing out, or destroying'. Then the substance would be meant that derives from a process of decay, of a destruction. For this stone reveals its true strength:

> It is named there 'Lapsit exillis'.
> It is by virtue of this stone
> That the Phoenix dies, alone,
> Burns to ashes, and is reborn
> Moults and rises with the dawn;
> For then it shines as bright as ever,
> Fair as before, in every feather.

The legend of the magical bird, the Phoenix, which at certain intervals repeatedly plunges into the fire to burn to ashes, then to rise from it rejuvenated, belongs to those Mystery teachings that seek to clothe the law of dying and rebirth into a picture. Initially, it should enter the feelings of humanity before it could be uncovered as knowledge. The Phoenician Mystery centres from where the great master-builder Hiram had come, knew the Phoenix Mysteries.

What does the eternal human personality do when it incarnates in a body? It dives into the fire of the blood. The 'I' is only able to incarnate into the warmth processes of the blood. It needs this eternal burning process to be able to unfold. In death it wrests itself, rejuvenated from this fire-process; it rises out of the formation of ash. In going through deaths and births, out of each death it draws new rising strength towards eternal life. But to do this, not to remain in death but to wrest from each dying a spiritual birth, requires a unique strength. This strength has to be carried from heaven to Earth, if human selves are not to succumb to death. The strength to overcome death that wants to become effective in the earthly body can only be received from Christ's sacrifice—from His becoming human and His dying, which from the grave wrested the form of a new body. His 'I am', if we take it up in ourselves, proves to be temple-building. It has become a foundation stone of a new temple—a foundation stone able out of itself to grow can also be related to the Tree of Life. This foundation stone is to be laid into each human soul. In becoming aware of this, the Phoenix in us can accomplish the sublime art of 'die and become'.

Only now we begin to understand Flegetanis, the wise natural philosopher, for what he could read in the starry script. He beheld what through long stretches of time moved from the heavens towards the Earth as a new impulse for the development of humanity. But then came that Holy Night in which, carried by angels with that Child, that impulse entered the earthly stream of humanity, which then could be called the 'new Adam'. In Him, 'the wish of Paradise' was fulfilled. The forces of the Tree of Life, access to which had to be denied to guilty humanity, began to give themselves afresh. Through this, the Virgin who gave birth to this Child became at the same time the prototype of the Grail-bearer. We may only receive this Grail into the virginal forces of our being. The Grail awakens the Tree of Life in our depths, from which all life-renewing effects proceed for sick human nature that has succumbed to death.

This can be *perceived.* It is the Mystery of the Phoenix that awakens the higher human being in passing through the experiences of death towards a body-free beholding. Trevrizent explains to Parzival this experience, connected to a painful wrestling with conditions of death and yet it leads one to find life in dying.

> 'Further, all mortals, however ill,
> On seeing the stone, live on still
> For a week, and from that day
> Lose not their colour in any way;
>
> And tho' faint be the man and feeble, yet the day that his failing sight
> Beholdeth the stone, he dies not, nor can, till eight days be gone.'
> [Tr. Jesse Weston]

He means to say that such experiences of resurrection, which arise before the spirit-vision, last for a week. The rhythm of the seven days lies deep in human nature; it is fundamentally significant for Christian experience. Each Sunday marks the day on which the inner Easter experience for the salvation of human mortal nature is to be renewed in us. It says that youthful forces are imparted through it, retaining the body's vitality even when the hair becomes grey. Trevrizent assures the student of the Grail:

> 'Such power the stone confers, I say,
> On mortals, that their flesh and bone
> Renews, for young they have grown.
> This stone they also call "The Grail"'.

The teaching of Grail wisdom, as Master Kyot taught, concerns the effect of the Resurrection, right into 'flesh and bone', that is, right into the skeleton. Consequently, Wolfram emphasizes the fact that it is a 'stone', which is beheld and shines from within.

The pre-Christian Mystery-centres, too, knew an initiation through death—the awakening of the supersensory human being, who leaves behind the physical body; when raised in the etheric body, he awakens to behold. In this way they experienced the Phoenix Mystery, but they knew the nature of the physical body, formed in the firm mineral substance, has to be left behind untransformed. It is mortal. Only one day when the One comes Who is stronger than death, can the physical human being also be laid hold of by the forces of transformation, right into the mineral structure of the skeleton. This is the victory over death of Golgotha. That this unique power will approach humanity in future was seen in the stars by this wise man who here is called Flegetanis.

In his description of the Grail, Chrétien de Troyes remains with Imaginations that possess a very tender, almost dreamlike character. A mystery of the nourishment of the higher human being is experienced, presenting itself in the picture of the sunlike, radiant vessel for the Host. Transformative powers in the blood are engaged. On the other hand, Wolfram, following Master Kyot, is of the opinion that with this, 'the story is unjustly treated'. For he is a human being with a strong self, penetrated with the forces of personality. His Christ-experience penetrates 'flesh and bone'; it shines right into death's depths where it enkindles the new life leading to the resurrection of the human form.

This highest force that wants to become active 'in the Stone', which means, in the mineral part of the human bodily nature, proceeds alone from the Mystery of Good Friday. It is not simply there; it has to be produced ever anew. Trevrizent teaches Parzival about this on a Good Friday.

> 'On this Good Friday, a dove doth sail
> Downwards from heaven, and doth bear
> That which governs the Grail there;
> A small white wafer it doth bring,
> And leaves it there, and then takes wing,
> All dazzling bright, and doth return
> To Heaven; of it the stone doth earn
> Its highest virtue, for the dove I say
> Brings a wafer each Good Friday.'

The Mystery of the Dove has to connect with the Mystery of Good Friday. Christian tradition in the Creed does speak of the Holy Spirit, but it limits itself to the outpouring of the Spirit at Whitsun whose effect to a certain degree was still active in Apostolic times. It does not foster the thought that this Spirit, through Whom in people's hearts Christ's renewed sacrifices are drawn continuously towards the Earth, wants unceasingly to pour Itself into human beings. Wolfram conjures up the picture of the Host before the inner gaze; through this the effect of the Grail relates to that which full of grace wants to give itself in the sacrament to human beings. But this Host, the seed-force of the new body, is received directly from the world's heights as a spiritual effect. Trevrizent, the holy hermit, describes this. There are experiences of contemplation to which he has penetrated. He was allowed to experience cosmic communion, not only in nocturnal Imaginations, of a dreamlike quality, but in full spiritual awareness he received this experience.

*

Literary criticism almost everywhere today denies the existence of Kyot as a person, because on the one hand, despite diligent research, a similar work in French has never been found that could have been written by a Guiot (as the name would originally have been spelt). On the other hand, because the German Parzival epic bears so much the form of Wolfram's personality it would hardly be conceivable to think the whole epic was a copy of a French original. The latter point of view is fully justified. The original achievement of Wolfram cannot be doubted. In no way does it concern an epic form according to which he would have written. His creative imagination was itself able to produce the poetic figures and situations which establish the moral and artistic value of this poetic work. Another aspect is the spiritual background whence Wolfram feels called upon to speak. The events of the Grail concern spiritual contexts that can only be represented with the highest responsibility. Here the desire to fantasize reaches its limits, for Imaginations, as far as they want to express spiritual experiences able to awaken spiritual forces in those able to receive them, demand to be dealt with in a certain way into which no personal, arbitrary whims or aesthetic moods should enter.

Wolfram names his master to whom he feels indebted. In his day, those who knew would have understood what was involved. It is quite conceivable that his descriptive manner, perhaps even in the naming, may seek to wipe out the traces for those whom one does not like to see pursuing them. For the beginning of the thirteenth century is the time when the Cathars living in Provence stood in utmost danger, to be extinguished by the will of the Roman Inquisition. Kyot is that master who was able to take the ancient wisdom of the stars that in Arabic or Kabbalist traditions via Spain could be saved into the modern age, to penetrate it with the Christian spirit-light, and thereby able to renew it in a contemporary manner. He must have known the great streams of humanity in which Eastern and Western traditions flowed together.

Wolfram wrote his poetic work out of a comprehensive world-orientation that uses a well-fashioned language of symbolism. This work can only be really understood as born out of an esoteric Order.

3. The Grail Dynasty and the Grail Temple

The genealogical tree in Wolfram

Master Kyot, of whom Wolfram speaks with deep respect, pursues a second path to penetrate the Mysteries of the Grail. He looks for the dynasty worthy of caring for the Grail, 'Who were true and pure in their dealings and a lowly heart might bear' (Tr. A. Kline).

For this reason, he researched the chronicles of France, Brittany and Ireland. But neither in these countries nor others could such a dynasty be found—'until he found it in the land of Anjou'.

Here one initially meets the royal House of Anjou. But it is expressly said, neither in France nor Brittany could this dynasty be found, yet the Anjevins originate in France, and they reigned at that time on the throne of England. Parzival's ancestors Gamuret and Gandin do not bear on their coat of arms the Lily of the House of Anjou but the Panther. Most diligent genealogical research has been undertaken to discover this genealogical tree. The most enlightening trail points towards Steiermark [Styria, a province in Austria]. For Trevrizent, reporting to Parzifal of his travels through the world, through Europe as well as Africa and Asia, told him that he came once from Seville to Gandin [a town in the Slovenian region of Drauebene close to Pettau]. From this town the grandfather of Parzival received his name, Gandin. According to this, the dynasty originates from Styria. But Styria did have a panther in its coat of arms. Trevrizent adds that anyone who, like him, wanted to practise humanitarian deeds would be driven far and wide. This report gives the impression as if Wolfram wishes to indicate his own journeys. The idea of a cosmopolitan-oriented knighthood seems to shine through, of a life woven in a network of relationships. We know that between the Cathar communities from the south of France and the Bogomils, who from the Balkans carried up the Danube a mystical [neo-Gnostic] spiritual teaching to Europe, an exchange of spiritual knowledge existed through the centuries. Is it not possible that behind these pilgrimages, as mentioned here, such spiritual messages were hidden deriving from Seville, the seat of Spanish-Arabic wisdom tradition, leading to Styria, and then to the Far East?

In Lower Austria, too, a dynasty of 'Anschau' existed, related to the Burgrave of Styria. But to us it seems, if one looks at Wolfram's very free way of coining names, that here a play with words could be present. The dynasty called to the Grail has to bear in itself the utmost prerequisites, the power of spiritual vision. Kyot looks for souls able to lift themselves from mere belief to *behold* (*Anschauung*) the highest. They are true managers of the land of 'Anschauwe'. This was the inheritance that was to come to the young Parzival after his father's death; he was called upon to be the King of 'Anschauwe'.

Who, however, is the founding forefather of this noble dynasty? Wolfram names Mazadan. This name is interpreted as 'Mac Adam', which points to 'son of Adam'. This dynasty is a carrier of impulses for humanity, not of narrow clan and family aims. Mazadan was taken by the fairy Terdelaschoye to Feimurgan. It seems that Wolfram changes the name of the fairy for that of her country. The enchantress Morgane is meant, who according to the ancient Celtic legend lived in Avalun [Avalon], this much-praised 'country of joy' (= Terdelaschoye). From her Mazadan received two sons, who became the forefathers of the dynasty of Anschau and of Arthur. It is consequently fairy-blood, a heritage of ancient atavistic abilities, which streams in the veins of this double genealogical tree. Through this the Grail and the Arthur streams are marked with sublime spiritual forces through which impulses of super-earthly life are to be imparted to humanity.

Through his mother Herzeloyde, who was married to Gamuret of the House of Anschau, Parzival belonged to that ancient, honourable dynasty that till then had to guard the Grail—the dynasty of Titurel. This dynasty is in decline. It consequently awaits the one who is able to lead the Grail dynasty into a new lineage, to rejuvenate it.

But when does all this happen? Wolfram gives a clear indication in the moving passage where he describes how Herzeloyde at the farewell of her son, struck by pain drops down dead.

> Thus from true virtue's root we see
> Rose that stem of humility
> To seek the path that brings souls gain,
> Ah, that her scions no more remain
> To the eleventh generation;
> For lack of them, woe to our nation!

The writer means, his time would be a better one if the Grail dynasty were still alive and active. Then eleven members would have continued the inheritance from Herzeloyde. Each generation of thirty years would mean 330 years separating his time from hers. Thus, counting back from around 1200 we arrive at the second half of the ninth century.

At that time Herzeloyde lived with her son, Parzival. This is the time of Carolingian rule that once extended from Spain over France and Germany as far as Austria [751–919 CE].

According to Wolfram's genealogical tree—it deviates somewhat from that of Chrétien—Herzeloyde is a sister of the sick Grail King, Anfortas and at the same time of the holy hermit Trevrizent. They are the children of King Frimutel who had died early, the son of Titurel. Another two sisters belong to the family: Repanse de Schoye, whom we have already met as the maiden carrying the Grail, and Schoysiane, who was married to the Duke of Katalangen. She died at the birth of her first child Sigune. Sigune is deeply woven into the destiny of Parzival. As an orphan she is educated by Herzeloyde, the sister of her mother. There she meets the tender youth Schionatulander, the squire of Gamuret, who is Parzival's father. This squire woos her. Wolfram dedicated a whole poetic work to these lovers and their tragic destiny. It is known as the *Titurel Fragment*[12]—called thus because it begins with a speech of the old Titurel. He narrates the whole history of his dynasty before passing on to describe that intimate and noblest love, which surpasses everything in tenderness coming to us from the time of the Minnesingers. Right into the melodically changing forms the poet uses here for the first time, we are convinced it is the pinnacle of Wolfram's poetic works.

In contemporary literary criticism, Wolfram's genealogical trees are usually dismissed as invented fables, simply because the origin of the names cannot be traced. It is viewed as a tribute of the poet to the world of the court, where the imagination often delighted in noble genealogical trees. But if one is open for these clearly defined figures and their meaning for the course of the whole plot, then one becomes convinced—here a network of destiny is uncovered, mysteriously woven between the branching relatives. Although clothed in myths, individuals come to the fore in all significance at an historical turning point. They appear to carry the destiny of a spiritual Christianity, but at the same time also the destiny of the progression of the highest concerns of humanity.

The figure of Titurel in Albrecht von Scharfenberg

From another poet, who at first seeks to speak behind the mask of Wolfram, we are given a comprehensive poetic work on the Grail, which

---

[12] https://www.loc.gov/resource/gdcwdl.wdl_14681/?sp=2&st=gallery/

wove into its fabric Wolfram's fragments of the love of Sigune and Schionatulander. This poetic work is called *Der jüngere Titurel,* 'The Younger Titurel',[13] written c. 1270–1280, attributed today to Albrecht von Scharfenberg after it was for a long time mistaken to be by Wolfram. 'The Younger Titurel' takes up all the indicated connections in Wolfram's *Parzival,* supplementing them in all sorts of ways; there arises a painting of the complete destiny of the Grail. This genealogical tree points to the East and back to the first Christian century. King Senabor of Cappadocia, it is told, had three sons who excelled under Emperor Vespasian at the conquest of Jerusalem. One of the sons, named Barille (also called Berillus), receives the emperor's daughter Argusille as his wife, together with the throne of France. The other brothers, too, receive kingdoms in the West. These three brothers who had received baptism, convert those Western countries to Christianity.

Again, we see the destruction of Jerusalem becomes the starting point for those spiritual streams that have taken on the task to preserve the Christian wisdom and carry it from the East into the West. It is the stream that answers to the decisive fact of the destruction of the temple with the impulse, which is a deeply inward one, to build up 'the invisible temple'.

It needs no explanation that all these kings of whom the Grail legend speaks cannot be found in the documents of historians. They are 'spiritual kings', like the Three Wise Men from the Orient, highly venerated in the Middle Ages. They rule legendary realms. Their crowns would have been invisible to earthly view. They shine in the spirit. Cappadocia, the homeland of the three brothers, points us to that region on the Black Sea, which since ancient times contained important Mystery-centres. The son of Barille was called Titurison. His marriage with Elysabel, the daughter of the King of Arraguon, remained childless for many years. Consequently, they undertook a pilgrimage to the holy grave. Their prayer was heard; a son was given them, whom they called Titurel. At his birth an angel prophesies that in his innocent youth he will become a warrior for the faith; one day himself will become a companion of the angels. With super strength he will defend Christianity against the heathens; as a reward he will be able to clothe himself with the Sun. This Grail tradition leads us to Spain. Wolfram

[13] Albrecht von Scharfenberg, *Der jüngere Titurel,* Legare Street Press 2022. Digitalised copies: https://www.loc.gov/item/2021668074/ and https://www.bavarikon.de/object/bav:BSB-CMS-0000000000004612?lang=en/

had already mentioned Catalonia as the Dukedom into which Sigune is born. Aragonia appears now as the homeland of Elysabel.

> 'Whoever has been to Galicia
> Most likely will know St Salvator and Salvaterre',

says Albrecht, meaning that Galicia in the north of Spain, where the realm of the Grail (Salvaterre) and Mont Salvat, the revered mountain, are to be found. In Wolfram, however, nothing points to the Grail Castle as situated in Spain. The battles Titurel with his father is to fight against the heathens mirror the historical battles of the Goths, which had to defend Christian culture in Spain against the thronging of the heathen population. Later in the eighth century, defence against Islam threatening the whole of Europe could only be checked with the help of the Carolingian sword.

The Grail Temple

Ludwig Uhland in his retelling *Titurels Gralstempel*, reduces (to our taste) the over-abundant richness of the Titurel epic to a few simple lines. Here is a section:

> In the same way as for the watchman after a long cold night the rising Morning Star appears, as to all living things, the blissful May, as after a cold frost the Sun, as in the heat of midday a well and the airy linden tree casts its shadow, as to the troubled person a gentle friend, as to the robber person who demands justice, the attention of the king, as to the blind man if he could regain his eyesight, as to the thirsty one the sweet clear wine, to the tired guest the hostel, as for the lover his beloved, beyond all this making the heart rejoice, is the sight of the beautiful youth Titurel. Perhaps the women offer their sweet greeting to him, a hermit would have been stirred by it. But Titurel is mindful of the angel's proclamation at his birth. In the battle for Christianity, he will earn from God to be kissed one day by ruby lips. With his father he goes to battle against the Saracens of Auvergne and Navarra. Like two falcons, the two swerve about in swift flight until in all Western lands the heathens have been subdued.
>
> So he works in unfaded youthfulness until his fiftieth year, then an angel brings the message that Titurel, because of his virtue, has been chosen by the Grail. He takes leave of his parents, who in tears praise God. Led by the song of angels, he comes to a pathless forest that on all sides stretches for sixty miles. Cypresses, cedars and ebony trees, trees of all kinds are entwined. Strange birds sing in their branches. In the

midst of the wood a mountain arises, which nobody can find, except one led by angels, the preserved, protected mountain, Mount Salvat. On this mountain, in many tents lies Titurel's future army. Above it there hovers the Grail richly enclosed, held by invisible angels, since it will be a long time before the one who may touch it is born. What they need the Grail gives to them, whatever vessel one holds under it is filled with the best nourishment. The land, Salvaterra, is rich with gold and precious stones, known to those who travel in Galicia. Here Titurel reigns, glorious before all kings. He builds a broad castle on Mont Salvat. From here he serves God with spear and sword against the heathens who want to settle in the wilderness. Still the Grail remains hovering, so Titurel decides to dedicate a temple to it, the splendour of which nobody can surpass, made of precious stones and pure gold, where the seats are made of aloe. Whatever is needed for one's work is provided by the Grail.

The rock of the mountains is onyx, one part of it, more than 100 fathoms in circumference, Titurel cleared it of grass and herbs; he had it polished so that it gleamed like the Moon. One morning on it he finds an engraved plan of the temple. The building rises circular with 72 choirs, each octagonal in shape. The inside and the outside shine in red gold, and each precious stone according to its colour. High bell towers rise each time between two quires; all around it stand octagonal towers, with many windows, forming a wreath. In the midst one arises twice as high as the others. The pinnacles are burning rubies on which there are crosses made of mountain crystal, on each cross an eagle of gold glitters. From a distance it appears to hover in flight; the cross on which he rests disappears from vision. The pinnacle of the middle tower is made of carbuncle, which shines through the night for the knights of the Grail when they are delayed in the forest. Two bells with golden clappers summon to the temple and to monastery, to meals and to battle. On the outer walls of the temple are engraved and moulded in reliefs how its servants daily fight in arms to protect the Grail. There are three portals of midday, evening and midnight, each ornamented with rich anterooms. Most of the quires are directed towards the morning, towards midday the cloisters lead to the dwellings of the brotherhood. Inside the temple the ceiling is a blue sky of sapphires, with carbuncles as stars, which even shine in the dark night. In between move the golden Sun and the silver Moon, indicating the seven times of the day for singing. The screed floor a crystal ocean, where one sees as under thin ice fishes and wonders of the deep in combat. The walls

> are made of emerald, on it golden trees full of birds ... Nothing in the temple was unadorned. The windows, instead of glass were made of beryl; on them, so that the glare does not harm the eye, pictures made of coloured stones through which the rays of the Sun became coloured. Although the brightness of the windows is lacking, the precious stone give an abundance of light, the sheen of which is ignited by the pure gold ... Whatever voice sounded in the temple through the precious stones, the width and height of the space, the resonance is extended in a bright musical sound, as if the organ were sounding in the forest. One of the greater quires is dedicated to the Holy Spirit, Who is Patron of the whole temple. The neighbouring quire is dedicated to the pure Mother of God, and the third quire to John, the ones remaining to the twelve envoys, or apostles. But in the middle of the temple stands an exceedingly rich work, presenting the temple in small, yet only with one altar—here the Grail is to be kept, when it will descend. The building took thirty years to build. A bishop consecrates temple and altars, then the angel leads the Grail into the precious abode prepared for it.

This account points towards an elevated personality, who may not be judged only according to physical appearance. The earthly body is subject to the law of ageing and dying, the etheric form can ray over it with youthful forces. Consequently, it is understandable when in his fiftieth year Titurel appears in the strength of unwilted youth. Concerning him, it is even said that he chose a spouse and founded an earthly dynasty. John the Baptist, only after a long time of waiting, prophesied to his parents; it is similar with Titurel. Through a pilgrimage to the Holy Sepulchre, his devoted parents through their prayers were able to receive this son. Here we may point to the deep connection of this individual with the events of Golgotha—the calling to the Grail, the accompaniment of the angel into the loneliness of the mountains, helps us to divine that here a person frees itself from life in the world, choosing the life of a hermit.

Again, the Grail appears, the chalice carried by the hands of angels as a Mystery of nourishment. With his company of knights, Titurel for thirty years builds the temple which is to incorporate this holy thing. Once the purest Temple was built on Earth during the same period of time, before the highest Spirit could dwell in it—the body of Jesus of Nazareth, who for thirty years was surrounded by the glory of Christ until, in the Baptism in the Jordan, this sublime Sun-spirit could enter Him.

It is said of Titurel,

> With strength he weighed up,
> Asleep or awake, the work on the temple.

All the building material required for completing the temple comes from the Grail itself. Consequently, the Grail provides not only food and drink; in a mysterious way it also provides gold and precious stones for building the sanctuary. For the Grail is the source of all forming of substance. In it at the same time, the Mystery is contained of the Earth of light, created out of the Spirit, of the New Jerusalem.

Clearly, this is a picture of the processes of meditation to be described with the building of this temple. Whoever seeks to form the hidden spirit-body within has to do some work that finds its continuation during the night. For, especially during the time of sleep, the higher human being fashions the organs of the supersensory body. Invisible powers lay hold of the fruit of soul-exercises and build up the temple of Spirit-Man according to higher laws.

It concerns what may be experienced in contemplation by those who have begun the path towards spiritual life. The contemplatives are the true temple builders; they construct a temple of reverence. They build it out of the forces of community. This temple is an image of the whole cosmos. The human body too, according to its hidden forces and laws is a microcosm. When in death it is freed out of its narrow earthly form, it grows with its formative forces that were compressed in matter, into something elevated—its cupula opens into a dome made out of heavenly blue sapphires, when in the human head the wisdom of the cosmos was thought; an inner starry heaven can shine in earthly man, an inner Sun out of the forces of the heart, and inner Moon can become active out of the mirroring of the forces of thought and work through the soul-life in sacred rhythms.

This temple building was attempted to be rebuilt architecturally, but it seemed to be impossible.[14] The Gothic spirit, which wants to wrest earthly gravity from all matter and wants to dissolve the walls, so that light can flood all the halls finds its intensified expression in this Grail temple. It is the overcoming of the Romanesque style that inspired the early Middle Age buildings. The darkness of the vault is

[14] E. Droysen, *Der Tempel des heiligen Gral nach Albrecht von Scharffenberg*. Bromberg 1872.

illumined, the crypt disappears. The grave is burst open. Life that has gone through death wants to grow into the heights and widths.

The uniqueness of this poetic work of the temple forming the magnificent prelude of the younger Titurel was well respected. Sulpiz Boisserée, whose enthusiastic involvement for the completion of Cologne Cathedral during the first decades of the nineteenth century is known, dedicated a special essay on this theme, because he felt in that poetic work the impulses alive to which as a Romantic, he too was prepared to give all his energies.[15] He says:

> The description of the temple of the Holy Grail, is the only truly significant passage on the art of building that has hitherto been found in the German poetic works of the Middle Ages, but it is also of great importance for the history of our art of building and even for our art of poetry.

He represents the opinion that the author must already have experienced the flowering of our Gothic art of building and consequently only in the fourteenth century was able to write these verses. Yet it has been found, what was then not known, that Albrecht had already finished his work about 1280. We see from this that the Gothic building concept must have been fervently fostered with visionary power in the souls of certain people before they found the possibility to embody this in stone. The poet does not always need to describe only what he already finds in sensory perception. True poetry possesses groundbreaking power, as Goethe maintains in his *Vermächtnis* [1829].

> *Denn edlen Seelen vorzufühlen*
> *Ist wünchenswertester Beruf.*
> To lead where the elect shall follow—this
> And this alone is worth a hero's choice.[16]

Today, we would say that the description of the temple in Albrecht's *Titurel* has an innovating effect on several buildings. Even Boisserée in his writing mentions that the fairytale-like glory of the Grail temple, not long after the completion of the poetic work, was somewhat realized on a small scale with the sacred Chapel of the Cross in Castle Karlstein near Prague. Emperor Charles IV had it built in his castle to keep the treasure of the Empire. Still today one can admire this chapel.

[15] S. Boisserée, *Über die Beschreibung des Tempels des Heiligen Grales in den Helgengedicht Titurel*. München 1834.

[16] Tr. Anon. https://lyricstranslate.com/en/vermachtnis-legacy.html/

The walls are covered with polished agate, amethysts, chrysoprases, and other colourful precious stones. Even the windows were made of many beryls and amethysts held in gilded lead. The vaults present the firmament; the ribs and keystones were adorned with precious stones and pearls. Boissertée mentions that the magnificence of the adornment, reaching the fantastic realm, of the Grail temple must have been inspired through the apocalyptic description of the heavenly Jerusalem, for is not this at the consecration of any church held as an ideal? In *Titurel* we also find a passage in which the New Jerusalem is praised as the ideal of the Grail temple.

Who are these *Tempeleisen*, the Grail Keepers, or Guardians, who under the leadership of Titurel build the archetypal picture of the cathedrals in the etheric realm? They are *those who have died*. This is indeed a key to understand many Mysteries of the Grail, as Rudolf Steiner has given it. He describes,[17] how the young Nordic peoples took up Christianity in a different way than initially the southern, Latin peoples did. They still brought with them traditions of early clairvoyant faculties when they entered into the Christian cultural world from the fourth–fifth century until the twelfth–thirteenth century. They still possessed an immediate, although shadow-like, perception of the continuing life and continuing activities of those who had died. With their soul-vision they followed beyond his death the hero who fought and fell in battle. They beheld how he was received into the company of the *Einherjer* [in Norse mythology, those who died in battle enter Valhalla] and—if he had already worked for Christianity—they saw how with his fellows he was allowed to gather around Christ, to continue the battle for the high goals for which he had dedicated his life on Earth. For these people no abyss existed between the physical and the spiritual world.

'The dead remained with the living,' says Rudolf Steiner,

> and especially distinguished, honoured people. In the initial period after death, that is, after being born into the spiritual world, they go through as it were, the novitiate period to become the saintly ones … A number of these people who were alive after their [earthly] death, when specially chosen, were made Guardians of the Holy Grail … One will never completely understand the Grail legend if one does not know those who actually were the Guardians of the Grail. Simply to say the Grail Guardians were not real people would have appeared to people of the time as most comical. They would have said, 'You shadowy figures who wander

[17] In the lecture *The Mystery of the Trinity*, Dornach 28 July 1922, GA 214.

> on the Earth, do you believe that you would be more eligible than those who have died and now gather around the Grail?'

That sublime individuality called Titurel in the legend penetrates into the realm of the dead when he sees the mountain, 'which nobody can find, except the one led by the angels'. On this 'Mount of Salvation' are encamped that host of knights, nourished in a miraculous way by the Grail. It is not the intention of the poetic work to characterize the Knights Templar Order, as has often been thought. This Order carried the Cross as a symbol, but the Temple Guardians in the poetic word carried the Dove, for they are a community of the Holy Spirit. On the Earth the Church tradition allowed the Spirit to die away, not allowing it to remain as a living principle, as the onward striving principle in Christian development, whereas the stream of true Christianity continues in another world. It goes over to the realm of those who have died. A supersensory communal Order is indicated that dedicates its forces to the Holy Spirit. Through exercises of the soul the Grail temple is built up in the ethereal spheres, not through an individual but by that which is achieved in the combined spiritual work of a community. It condenses here before the spiritual gaze into a building, which is built in thirty years. This temple is the result of the community's contemplation.

The Grail legend wants to point out that in the spiritual world a powerful centre has been formed from which proceeds the direction of Christian matters on the Earth. It is not in Rome that the guardians of Christian impulses are to be found; the authority of the Roman Church is never mentioned. It is also not to be found in the earthly Jerusalem, which the Crusaders see as the spiritual centre of Christianity. The Christian development stands in the protection of the great ones who have died, but who are the truly living ones. To become part of this continuing inspiration, Christian development must seek the connection to those spheres. It was the concern of those who as sowers spread these great legendary pictures into the life of the times, to awaken souls to search for the Grail.

And indeed, at that time the Roman Church had reached the climax of its power. Wolfram created his *Parzival* precisely in the years when Innocent III developed the strongest principles of power. He too was the first Pope who around that time (1208) listened to the complaints against the Templar Order, who had risen to their highest glory, and threatened them with the removal of privileges. Nevertheless, we know how this Order was still allowed to unfold its work of blessing in

Europe for another century, until the diabolical trial took place which turned all their strivings and work into a caricature and finally led to a confession forced under torture. In 1314 the great Master, Jacques de Molay with his followers, confessing his innocence, went to die at the stake. Of this Order one can well say that in its courageous and Christian activity, it presented to a certain degree an earthly reflection of the true Grail Guardians, who in the spiritual world assemble around the Grail. The battle against the Templars and their ruthless destruction has to be understood as an attack of annihilation, which certain powers want to direct against the Grail.

If the poetic work *Titurel* leads us to the country of Salvaterra to the north of Spain, with this it only points to the fact that in those regions a community—perhaps a monastic settlement, or a secret brotherhood on one of the mountains—could be found, able to foster conscious connections to the world of those who have died, and at the same time, in their earthly strivings could already participate in the Mysteries of the Grail. Of this place in the north of Spain, Rudolf Steiner describes how here up to the beginning of the age of the Crusades true initiation Mysteries were guarded. What was fostered there, he called the late Gothic Mysteries.[18] In the realms north and south of the Pyrenees, for centuries the culture of the Cathars blossomed, in which in a hidden manner the wisdom and attitudes of Manicheism could influence Western countries. (5)

Goethe in old age still retained a view of such contemplative communities and was able to divine their Mysteries. His poetic work *Faust* ends in presenting such a place, which he puts into the rocky landscape of Mont Serrat, difficult to access. From Alexander von Humboldt, he received a description of those hermitages in the mountainous region of northern Spain. There the holy Padres live, as we meet them in the final scene of *Faust*, secluded from the world, and through their soul-exercises they raise themselves to such a condition in which they can converse with the world of the dead. One in particular, Pater Seraphicus, even becomes a guardian of the children who had prematurely died. He instructs them to find the transition into the higher spheres, where they can enter the service of the angels. Goethe helps us to divine a supersensory, living connection. It is a place of learning

[18] Steiner's principal communication on this subject is to be found in the lecture appearing in English as 'The Secret of the Grail in the Works of Richard Wagner', Landin, 29 July 1906, in GA 97.

leading by degrees upwards to the realm of the spirits, which is prepared to receive the individuality of Faust. He seems to be one of those who have been long awaited. Faust is received in the world of the heights as a teacher, although he went through the depths of the Earth and had burdened himself with heavy guilt. He assumed a daring attitude by taking on the Manichaic life, not shying away from meeting the dark forces.

The poetic work *Titurel* describes how the Grail Castle within a circumference of sixty miles in surrounded by unsurpassable forest. Only one called to the Grail finds access to it. Whoever penetrates into the realm of Salvaterre uninvited is thrown back by the Guardians of the Grail. The company of knights is given the task to protect the holy realm. For the supersensory world does not without punishment allow unauthorized entrance into their realm. But the Guardians also carry responsibility for the world. They have to be active for Christianity in the sign of the Dove, which means, for the approaching age of the Holy Spirit. For this they often have to take on the 'adventure' of earthly life. In the teaching of the Grail, which Parzifal receives in Wolfram through the hermit Trevrizent, we read:

> 'Tis known to me, and 'tis no tale,
> That many bold warriors reside
> At Munsalvaesche, and forth do ride,
> In search of adventure, and whether
> They reap glory, or something other,
> For their sins, they must bear it well.'
> [Bk IX. Tr. A. Kline]

For the one sent by the Grail takes up the trials of life in a deep affirmation of his destiny. If he works for the Grail on the Earth, he has to accept suffering and calumny. He does not complain by accusing others; he regards what meets him as a balancing for his own life's unatoned guilt.

Christ speaks to His disciples of the joy they should feel that 'their names are written in heaven'. Of those who are chosen for the Grail, it is said that around the Grail there appears each time an epitaph announcing the name and the lineage of the one who is chosen for the path of salvation. Those belonging to the Grail are blessed individualities who already from earlier lives bring that maturity through which their essential being in the spiritual world is consciously illumined when they enter once again on their earthly path.

> And then the name itself doth pale,
> Such that no need for erasure
> Appertains to it for, whether
> It told of man or maid, outright,
> The writing vanishes from sight.

What is meant with this? When such a soul descends to Earth, its name appears at the rim of the Grail. It extinguishes as soon at it enters incarnation. It is a law that individualities of such calibre already in early childhood find connections to that other world. In certain experiences this world flashes up in them. Through this, the work and guidance of the Grail remains, initially unconsciously, or only divined, in the deeper grounds of the soul. It possesses a destiny-forming power. It wields as a calling within the course of destiny.

> Those there who are full-grown came
> As children, summoned by their name.
> Happy the mother of any child
> Destined to serve there; if their child
> Is chosen, both rich and poor, of grace
> Bidden to send them to that place,
> Rejoice; from many a land they come,
> From many a place in Christendom ...

Souls belonging to the Grail can incarnate in the most varying countries and peoples. They form a race that has no significance for national differences. Herzeloyde was such a soul, who from early on knew she belonged to such a spiritual stream. She took her son away from all traditional connections. In his youth, Parzival neither met the culture of knighthood nor Church tradition, but heart forces manifested early in him a deep compassion for all creatures. In the depths of his soul a calling led him in early life towards a spiritual awakening.

In the description of the Grail temple a carbuncle is mentioned that forms the knob on the central tower of the building and which even during the night points the way for the Grail knights who might have gone astray in the wilderness. With this is shown how those souls belonging to the Grail possess a permanent orientation that never deserts them within the darkness of Earth and the confusion of life. In ancient wisdom, precious stones were always seen as mediators of exalted forces in the world. The Eternal City, Jerusalem of the heights, too, rests with its walls on twelve foundation stones, which are adorned with certain precious stones. Thus sapphire, beryl and ruby and other stones are used to adorn the Grail Castle, each one fulfilling its special task. The carbuncle is a stone which addresses the deepest heart forces. It awakens etheric light in the blood, through which Christ's continuous presence can be experienced. The legend, by mentioning it lit the path for the knights of the Grail even during the night, points towards those forces of the Imagination that gives to the human heart the spirit-presence to make the right decisions in any situation of life. It is the Mystery of the blood that gives the 'I' the inner conviction regarding its path. Consequently, it gives a feeling of protection even where the guidance of destiny sometimes remains hidden from being recognized. In *Heinrich von Ofterdingen,* Novalis in poetic words describes the Mystery of the carbuncle.[19]

> A mystic token deeply graved is beaming
> Within the glowing crimson of the stone,
> Like to a heart, that, lost in pleasant dreaming,
> Keepeth the image of the fair unknown. (6)

*

Who are the Guardians of the Grail?

The figure of Titurel cannot be grasped through any standards of an earthly biography. If it is said of him that he was 400 years old when he received permission to marry the king's daughter Richoude, with whom he produced the Grail line, this can only mean that from this point onwards the Grail stream is expressed in earthly personalities. In the spirit-realm one could find Titurel throughout the centuries. He continuously stood behind the development of Christianity in the West. When it is said that he served the Grail with spear and sword against the heathen who want to settle in that wilderness, this indicates the times in which the Christian impulse first had to fight for European territory to become a cultural factor in which the spirit of Christ could live. This occurred from the time of the migrations. Faced with the declining Roman Empire, the young tribes established new kingdoms, which then could become bearers of Western Christianity. So it was that the hidden spiritual guidance emerged through mighty battles and the founding of kingdoms. Particularly in the eigth century when the Moslem conquerors from North Africa sent their armies

[19] Novalis, *Henry von Ofterdingen,* Dover, Thrift Edition 2015, p. 24. Online: https://www.gutenberg.org/cache/epub/31873/pg31873-images.html/

to Spain, overran the West Gothic kingdom and shortly crossed the passes of the Pyrenees, this spiritual leadership had to intervene. Karl Martell beat back the Arabic armies in bloody battles. The Carolingian sword attempted to help the Christian peoples of Northern Spain who were oppressed.

The deeds of Charlemagne, as described, for example, in the legends of Roland, express the shielding of the cultural space of the Christian West against Arabism. These battles and the connected Carolingian politics carried by an ordering, planning will, arose out of the responsibility for the Grail. The other epic, too, which has survived through Wolfram's *Willehalm*, according to its content, is taken from that time when the Carolingian culture had to deal with the surging threat of Islam. With his thinking and feelings, we see Wolfram von Eschenbach focusing on a specific time, allowing it to arise in his poetic works, because his own time, admittedly on another level, is concerned with similar questions. The concern for the continuation of Western culture and its Christian mission at that time penetrated the soul of those who were aware and to whom Wolfram belonged. For the Carolingians, to establish a national kingdom was not the point, but rather a cosmopolitan imperium. A generous cultural exchange with the court of Harum al Rachid was attempted, despite the necessity on European ground to push back the Arabs. Moreover, despite the willingness of the Christian Church to protect with the sword, the Carolingians were not willing simply to obey the Roman throne. Accordingly, Rudolf Steiner could say that the epoch of the Carolingian founding occurred at the time, in which those high spiritual leaders, who, hiding behind the mythical figure of Titurel, sought directly to impact historical development. It was Charles the Great himself whom they had chosen as the instrument of their cosmopolitical activities.

To be able to honour such spiritual facts, a view is required that penetrates other layers of the historical context than the aims of outer historical research. We know the ruthless politics of Charles. Who would not recall the relentless way he forced Christianity onto the Saxons? Many other things, too, which are reported of him do not suggest a favourable picture of him from a moral standpoint. The agreement with the Roman throne, from when he took his Emperor's crown, seems to have reduced him to a tool of the Pope's power. All these observations show a less favourable side, that of the power politician, yet a hidden layer in his being inherited from his maternal side allowed him also to be open to other influences. It formed the legendary side of his being. The wreath of legends that has become so rich around the figure of Charles the Great, points towards this side of his activities. Whenever he was not the son of the ambitious politician Pippin, but the son of Bertrada, the legendary lady Berchta, there his connection with the deeper forces of the folk became evident, rendering him the vehicle for spiritual leadership. With a glance at his spiritual advisors, one clearly finds at his court two mutually wrestling streams. One cannot say that the spiritual one, striving for an inner intensification of Christianity, always gained the upper hand. Clearly, for the security of outer rulership, it was more successful to connect with the powerful Roman Church. During this European age, the sublime spiritual leadership must have felt it was often condemned to a powerless role. For especially from that time onwards, we have entered an epoch in which the most conscientious persons frequently gave rein to what is all-too-personal and self-willed.

The tragic situation is expressed in a legendary picture. The Guardian of the Grail, Anfortas, of the stock of Titurel, suffers from the wound of the Spear. Although he is chosen as the main Guardian, he cannot bring the Grail to its full potential. That which in his blood reigns as selfishness darkens for him his spiritual nature. If one regards his depths of soul, which contain great treasures of ancient wisdom, one may call him the 'rich Fisher-King'. Yet if one looks at his earthly personality with its limitations, he is the guilty one, the Guardian of the Grail lamed in his activity, because of which the world of the Grail has to endure great plight. Wolfram describes how from time-to-time Saturn emerges with its full effect, increasing the suffering of Anfortas. These are the hardening forces, the burden of the untransformed past threatening to separate human nature from the spirit.

For the access of spiritual leadership, intending to make Europe the carrier of the highest Christian impulse, this impenetrable nature increased with those who inherited the Carolingian crown during the ninth century. Beyond the Carolingians, the cosmopolitan nature of the concept of empire in the progress of the Middle Ages becomes increasingly distorted by local politics and nationalistic interests. But the Grail temple includes 72 choirs with their altars. This number always points towards a differentiation of humanity according to languages and nations. According to an ancient Hebrew tradition, 70 angels gathered around the Lord when He descended to the Earth, to lead those people who wanted to build the Tower of Babel into the separation of languages [Gen. 11]. The Holy Spirit has been poured out to lead to the day that separation of languages shall be overcome. It is the patron of the Grail temple. One of the main choirs is dedicated to it. A Christianity, where all peoples and cultures find each other, and each one in its own language stepping to the altar worships in their way, is presented as the ideal picture of universal religion. (7)

This form of religious life was not yet to be found on the Earth, moreover a tolerant thinking was only able slowly to emerge. But it lived in the longing of the noblest spirits of the Middle Ages. What on Earth is longing, in the life after death becomes a creative force in the life after death. The ideals we are able to carry beyond the threshold of death—particularly those for which we have made sacrifices—are temple-building powers. In this human temple, the angels together with human souls build the temple of humanity. With them we fashion our ideals. They grow continually; like everything living, they transform with time according to the experiences the souls gather from earthly life to earthly life and bear them into the spiritual sphere. The way the souls of people who have passed through death co-operate with the heavenly hierarchies to build the temple of the Grail in the etheric realm determines the power with which they are able to enter their coming earthly life to realize their ideals. The office of the temple guardian is to prepare in the spiritual realm the future of humanity.

4. The Celtic Stream in the Service of the Grail

The chronicle of Helinandus and the hermit in Brittany

Some peoples are particularly called upon to direct their forces to serve the progressive Christian impulse. Consequently, they undergo an educational destiny which purifies them for the high task, smelting them, or even leading them through the outer annihilation of their existence. Mysteriously they take part in the great Passion of Him they are to serve, but Who from suffering and doom wrested higher life. The mission of the Celtic folk-spirit is intimately connected with this Mystery.

If we turn to a quite different source, which with great determination presents the sunrise of the Grail experience into the history of the eighth century, in the chronicle of the *Helinandus*,[20] which year by year registers the world-events that appear important. It is reported of the year 717: around that time a hermit in Brittany received a wonderful vision in which he was instructed by an angel concerning Joseph of Arimathea who has taken the body of the Lord from the cross, and about the bowl out of which the Lord with His disciples had eaten. The hermit is said to have given a report concerning this, 'The History of the Grail'. In this Latin text, the Grail is called *'gradalis'* or *'gradale'*, which expression refers to a wide, deep bowl, called like this because on it the food was arranged stepwise (*gradatim*).

Literary studies connect this expression with that 'History of the Grail', which presents the first ancient French prose story on this theme as *'Li livre dou St Graal'*. This is called 'The great Holy Grail' to distinguish it from Robert de Boron's poetic work. In this book we are simply told of the hermit who in a wild region of 'bloie Bretaigne' is said to have a vision of Christ. This took place in 717 after the Passion of Jesus Christ, from the night of Maundy Thursday to Good Friday. It is assumed Helinandus took his indications from that story of the Grail. But then he would have committed an error regarding dates, for the counting 'after the Passion of Christ' would have to be the correct one. And so, he would come 750 after the birth of Christ, that is, to the same epoch into which we could place Titurel's activities.

---

[20] The Latin Chronicon of Helinand of Froidmont, written c. 1211–1223. The passage on the Grail is translated at catholicbookwriter.com/goldenarrow/holy-grail/translation-of-helinandus-gradale-text/

Nevertheless, one problem remains unsolved for historical research. Helinandus ends his chronicle with the year 1204, yet the Grail story from which he is supposed to take his facts, for various reasons would have been written somewhat later. But if one takes the communications of the hermit's vision of Christ not necessarily as an invention of the Grail story, but reckons with a true account, then the difficulties are solved. The poets and writers of romances draw from sources, which for centuries were sacred traditions that began around 1200 to come in a poetic garb into public light.

One may hear in which way this 'Book of the Gail' is supposed to have come about. The hermit, who is beset with doubts about the Holy Trinity, went to sleep in his hut when he was awoken by a voice calling him three times by his name. He awakens and sees the Redeemer standing before him in radiant glory. After addressing him in admonishing words regarding his doubts, He passes on a little book no bigger than the palm of His hand. This book is said to have been written by Himself; it will resolve all his doubts. Yet only those who have fasted and confessed may approach this book. Then the Redeemer disappears. The hermit, however, in the morning (Good Friday) finds the book and reads the opening words, 'This is the beginning of your genealogical tree ...'. It concerns the genealogical tree of the Grail that reaches back to Joseph of Arimathea. The hermit is to know that he is part of this; with this a spiritual succession is indicated, into which he is included.

Heavenly appearances interrupt his devotional reading. Finally, his spirit is being taken up by an angel and ennobled, in order that with his own eyes he sees the Holy Trinity. Thus, the hermit is released from his doubts. It concerns a 'book', which does not convey theological content, but is able to pass on key strengths, that is, symbolic figures as are known from occult traditions. For example, Goethe has Faust appear with such a book 'by Nostradamus' own hand' and describes how through meditative contemplation of the signs he is strengthened to attain spiritual vision.

The report, moreover, becomes still more mysterious. When the hermit returns to his earthly consciousness, he begins to celebrate the Mass. For this reason, he carefully closes the book. But when on Easter Sunday he intends to take it up again, it has disappeared. Following heavenly instructions explaining to him that he can only regain it through trials and suffering, he sets out on a wonderous journey. After two weeks he finds it again in a chapel on the altar. On Saturday evening he returns with it to his hut. In a dream-vision, Christ Himself tells him to take down the contents of the book. The copy is to be finished by Ascension Day. And thus it transpires. Afterwards it is confirmed that after His resurrection our Lord wrote nothing except this single, noble writing of the Holy Grail.

This little book, which disappears and can only be regained on a pilgrimage after heavy trials is clearly no tangible book. One may imagine it written in Imaginative signs—as an etheric chronicle, which can only be deciphered by someone who travels on paths of the soul.

Certain impressions approached the soul of the hermit, initially in pictures, delivered in a dreamlike state of consciousness. Yet they only carried an indicative meaning. Through this, a *searching* of the soul is set into motion, which is to lead to a higher level of illumination (always called a 'reading of the occult script'). When this pilgrimage is now placed into the Easter week and leads the seeker towards an altar, where the mysterious writing, after it had disappeared, can be received anew, then it becomes clear that we shall be led over with the wisdom of the Grail into the sphere of the Risen One. Those blessed conditions into which the disciples were lifted, when they were walking with their Master during the forty days between Easter and Ascension, in a new way want to become part of the souls of those who now enter the Grail's teachings. From now on, the light of Easter can flow directly into the human soul that gives itself to Christ. With this a new epoch of Christianity begins. It is significant, however, that this experience occurs in Britain, pointing towards the realm of Celtic Christianity. (8)

The Arthur saga and the mission of Merlin

Such a mysterious book was already known to Robert de Boron, the first poet to bring the message of the Grail's origin. When he presented the wonderful appearance of the Risen One before Joseph of Arimathea, who was imprisoned in a tower, and the teaching of the Holy Vessel, he confesses, 'I would not dare to tell and present this, had I not the great book in which these stories are written. In it, the great Mysteries are written down, which is called the Grail.' At the end of this first part of this extensively planned poetic work, where he points towards the future paths of the Grail's messengers who had travelled to the West (we have already heard of the valleys of Avalon), he points out that it is difficult to bring together these different paths of destiny in the presentation:

> During the time I was able calmly to deal with the great story of the Grail at the court of my lord Gauthier de Montbéliard, it had never been attempted by a mortal man. But I want all who would like this book to know, that if God grants me health and life, I intend to gather these parts if I can find them within a book.

Nevertheless, amongst those who know there is no one who believes that these parts have been lost and is ignorant concerning their fate. That is why he withholds himself before writing about it and commences to present the story of Merlin.

Only a few verses of this second part have been saved. Perhaps the poet was unable to complete the epic of Merlin. With the existing prose narrative, it is not completely clear how much is really by Robert de Boron, also the third part, connecting Parzival, the expected Grail hero, with the Round Table of King Arthur. But through this description the stream of the Grail is most intimately connected with the destiny with the decline of Celtic culture and its last shining figure.

King Artus, or Arthur, for the dying British tribes throughout the Middle Ages, was the last legendary hero who defended Britain against the invading Saxons and conquered them in twelve glorious battles, until he himself—in the battle against his traitorous nephew Mordred, who seduced his wife, Queen Ginevra [Guinevere]—mortally wounded, is brought for healing to the Isle of Avalon. From there his return is awaited. Artus symbolized all hope for the maimed Celtic race towards a glorious rebirth.

Through Geoffrey of Monmouth's *History of the Kings of Britain*, which appeared at the beginning of the twelfth century, these national hopes were rekindled. But through this *History* particularly the figure of Arthur with the heroes of the Round Table has become in the folklore of Western Europe a shining centre of all the epic poetic works.

He was said to be the son of Uther Pendragon (that is, 'dragon head'), of the King of Britain and the beautiful Ygerne, whom he had forcefully taken from her husband the Duke of Tintagel. When Arthur was fifteen years old, during the time of the wars with the Saxons, which finally led to the enslaving of the Celtic tribes and to the conquering of England, he begins his rulership. He is said to have died in 357. What is related of him in legends may point towards a much earlier epoch. Out of the grey mist of earlier times, a sublime leader, who was educated and advised by a teacher of ancient Druidic wisdom, shines out of the traditions. This wise teacher is called Merlin. 'Merddin, the bard', he is called in old hymns and prophecies ascribed to him. It is said of Merlin that he was the son of a pure maiden, who was tricked by the ruse of the devil. Merlin's birth was planned by the counterattack of Hell against the appearance of Christ, whose victory over death had provoked great fear among the hellish spirits. In the same way as the Virgin Mary had received her Child from the Holy Spirit, a son of Lucifer was to be produced, to annul the deed of salvation. But the arch enemy was unable to stain the purity of that maiden when he overcame her in her slumber; through the leadership of a pious priest, it was possible that this child was seized from the adversary. From his progenitor, Lucifer, he inherited the knowledge of past things, but from God he received from his mother's innocence, the wisdom of future things. In Merlin's soul the archetypal wisdom of ancient magic was paired with prophetic knowledge from Christian grace. He helps Uther Pendragon, advising him to establish 'the Round Table', at which at all times the best knights are to gather.

According to other traditions, Merlin was the teacher of the young Arthur, the son of Uther Pendragon, and who prepared him to establish the Round Table. This was to imitate that Table which at one time Joseph of Arimathea had founded for the Grail. The wise Merlin said that there are three mysterious Tables:

- the first formed by our Lord before His death, when He gathered around Him the twelve disciples for the holy meal;
- the second prepared by Joseph of Arimathea as the Table of the Grail;
- the third was to be inaugurated in honour of the knighthood gathering around Arthur.

This third one, too, was to have left one empty seat, as at the Table of the Saviour a place for Judas, and at the Table of the Grail; it was the 'seat perilous'. Whoever takes this seat uninvited is swallowed by the Earth, which is rent open with a groan. Only one knight is able to do it without such consequences. This is the chosen one for the Grail. In the early traditions it is Perceval; in later Grail narration Galahad steps in as one sent from heaven.

What is this Table of King Arthur, from which the noblest heroes are sent to enter adventures with fabulous creatures and to enter the highest trials of courage? Gawain, Lancelot, Eric, Iwein, and other favourite figures around whom garlands of legends had begun to weave, for the world of the Middle Ages were the archetypal pictures of all true knighthood.

The Hibernian civilization and the decline of the Celts

The greatness of the Celtic race that once from the British Isles spread their culture over Galicia of Northern Spain, Gaul, and the whole of Middle Europe, indeed down the River Danube into the East, possessed the quality of a spiritual heritage from Atlantis, which had passed away. The Druids, that Order of wise priestly people, was for a long time responsible for the spiritual education and leadership of the Celtic peoples; for some time, their culture also spread over the Germanic peoples. A liturgical service of the Sun, in which the wisdom of the early Atlantean oracle centres echoed on, was faithfully preserved by them. As witnesses of the ancient culture penetrated by cosmic forces, there stand today in southern England and the northwest coast of France, those mighty stone circles, the dolmens and alignments. They served those mysterious ceremonies of the wise Druids who knew how to question the cosmos, allowing the insights they gained at such places to stream into all social life. It is what remains of the Hyperborean culture, through which a sacred inheritance of the Sun could be preserved for the rigidifying earthly existence. This gave the Celtic culture its unique glory, which today we can only feel in a divining manner.

Where the ancient Greeks once spoke of that strange people, the Hyperboreans, of the eternal land of the Sun, whence at one time Apollo, led by swans, began his journey to Hellas to appear at the Castalian Spring in Delphi, in order as the giver of songs, the teacher of the muses, to bless the peoples—here is indicated those Mystery-centres which still knew how to guard the Mystery of the innocent origin of the human race, the connection to the springs of eternal youth. And so, it is reported of Perseus, the Greek hero, that he initially dwelt with the Hyperboreans and participated in their holy meal, before he could gain victory in the battle with Medusa. Heracles had to seek to find the Mysteries when he sought to gain the golden apples of the Hesperides. The poets celebrated the Hyperboreans in song, to whom one could not find one's way 'neither by land nor sea'.[21] The inaccessibility of their way of life can be compared to the realm of

---

[21] The recent appearance of *Celtic Wonder-Tales* from the Gaelic, retold by Ella Young (Dover Publications 1996; Floris Books 2002), describes the descent of the elevated Sun-beings in Ireland, the green island, in which Brigit, the soul of the world, spread her heavenly mantle. This descent is presented as a sacrifice of the Sun-beings to the world of darkness; one feels reminded of a Manichaen view.

the Grail, which no striving could reach that remained in a sensory existence. When its eternal youthfulness is praised, which knows neither sickness nor age that loses its strength, we recall Titurel, who also remained for many centuries in unbroken heroic strength. For it is a rebirth of the Hyperborean Mysteries out of the forces of Christianity, shining in the world of the Grail; this world, too, is protected in deepest seclusion by a strict hierarchical Order who everywhere send their messengers to the people, that the world does not lack beauty and wisdom through which the holy element can enter souls.

The last people fostering the Hyperborean Mysteries worked in Hibernia, that 'Island of the Saints', in which no snake can live, as is said concerning Ireland. Consequently, it is not surprising that at these centres, as is repeatedly said in the legendary tradition, the Christian messengers were immediately recognized and accepted when they carried to the West the message of the events in Palestine. We know that wherever the holy, cultural centres of Druidic worship were, the missionary Christian centres, free from Rome, could blossom; even on the Continent, for example, the region of the Carnutes, or Carnuti, from which the later Chartres took its name, had been a central sanctuary for the Gauls. Or let us think of Odilienberg (Alsace), which through its mighty stone circle, of which only fragments remain, points to such a Druidic sanctuary. Later it hosted a centre where spiritual Christianity was fostered, inspired by the spirit of St Odilia, and was able for a long time to fulfil an exalted task. The [monastic and eremitical] Culdee Church of Irish monks flourished out of the decline of Druidism.

From the time when Caesar conquered Gaul, and with it introduced the destruction of the ancient Celtic culture through the Roman Empire, it was sought everywhere to strike the living nerve with the destruction of their Mysteries and cultural centres. But out of the sacrifice of a great culture and its sanctuaries that had become overripe—although outwardly initially sentenced to powerlessness, invisibly and politically—strong impulses were born for the promotion and spread of a spiritual Christianity.

The state-building power of the Celtic race was extinguished; the missionary responsibility that had been taken over from the pupils of St Columba and many Irish messengers of the faith, formed a community of cultural carriers, consecrated by the spirit, who planted oases of a Christian way of life onto the European mainland, particularly in France, the Alpine countries and deeply into the German realms, initially in monastic communities—we may name Luxeuil in France, St Gallen and the island Reichenau in the Lake of Constance. But then, proceeding from such places expressed in a broad stream of activity full of blessing, which within the Church ever more usurped by Rome, took care that artistic impulses could be fostered, and traditions of wisdom could not completely fade away.

One of the most radiant figures of esoteric Christianity, as planted from the Celtic centres on the Continent, John (or Johannes) Scotus Erigena (800–877) may be named. Although he also felt the resistance of the Roman representatives, he managed in the middle of the ninth century (that is, to the same time we may ascribe the lives of Herzeleide and Parzival) to develop a deep Christian philosophy at the court of Charles the Bald. It is his achievement to have made known the writings of Dionysius the Areopagite from the Greek, especially his teaching on the angelic hierarchies, which always presented the heart of spiritual Christianity.

In his lectures on *The Mission of the Individual Folk-Souls*, Oslo 1910 (GA 121), Steiner spoke on the activities of the archangels, how they reign protectively over the development of peoples. After the completion of such a mission, they always raised themselves to higher tasks. In this context, he always emphasized the uniqueness of the Celtic folk-spirit, which at the time of the inception of Christianity made a great sacrifice. It is said that this spirit took on a special mission by becoming 'the inspiring spirit of esoteric Christianity'. The outer side of this occurrence is the disappearing of the Celtic peoples, the decline of their state-building power and their national cultural context, but the inner side is the glorious task of a spiritual mission. 'In the west of Europe, the mysterious place was to be found for those who were initiated into these Mysteries.' Under the effect of these archangelic beings, a centre of inspiration was formed from which everything radiated that was to be further developed from the Mysteries of the Holy Grail and through Rosicrucianism.

We notice the Druids retreat under the Roman leadership in Gaul and Britain, and their best representatives soon afterwards dedicated themselves to Christian activities. Yet another strength greatly significant within Celtic culture is able to contain and protect them longer: the national tradition. These are the Bards who were organized in Orders and through guilds of singers. We hear that 'Chairs' existed in several locations. They formed several ranks with regalia and robes. They preferred to gather in stone circles that remained from Druidic times. Without weapons one entered the circle—only a sword, which as a sign for peace was held at the point, was carried into the gathering. This sword was not there to inflict wounds, it was *the sword of the word*. It lives in poetry, wanting to be celebrated through song.

A 'system of the Round Table' existed. This, it is said, was established under the protection of King Arthur, that is, in the sixth century. The bardic conventions of the eleventh century under the protection of the Church, usually culminated in the celebration of Pentecost (Whitsun). In the legend, the glorious Pentecost celebrations in the court of King Arthur are repeatedly described. In Wolfram we still read, 'Artus, the man blessed by the spring.' Later, this custom becomes secularized in the courtly feasts of the knights, which was celebrated in France at Pentecost under the name of the Round Table. At Pentecost 1184, Emperor Barbarossa hosted such a glorious feast at Mainz for the knights; singers assembled from many lands.

With the decline of national hopes, the bardic community took up their cosmopolitan task. A Pentecostal mood was fostered in those circles who guarded the 'rule of the Round Table'. In their poetry lives the educational ideals that were to enthuse the Christian knight. Moral-forming power emanated, wanting to plant into souls the character of knighthood with responsibility towards Christian culture beyond nations. There are three virtues that stand as ideals before such a knighthood:

- the dignity of human personality (shown in an exaggerated feeling of honour),
- the courage to give one's life for this personality (continuously sought for and proven in 'adventure'),
- the ennobling of the forces of love (purified to the tenderest feelings in the service of the Minnesingers).

These ideals lead to knighthood of the Grail, where the male honour is raised to the highest spiritual responsibility, where the courage penetrates to daring in the supersensory realm, where the ability to love matures to transfigure the blood towards the complete devotion to Christ. Amongst those aspiring to be Arthur's knights, only a few find the way towards these ideals. But they are those who set out in search of the Grail.

In the legend, King Artus still holds his splendid court at Kaerlleon (Carduel) in Wales. Later, however, also in Wolfram's work, he reigns in Brittany, in the capital town Nantes. Remains of the British population, hard pressed on the island by the Saxons, fled to the Continent. The north-western region of France, then still called Armorica, becomes their new homeland. Later it becomes 'Brittany'. This landscape, with its alignments and Druid stones still today retains the mood of primordial worlds. It is as if the souls, who wandered here through the lonely stretches of land were still touched by a cosmic piety, which during the pre-Christian millennia was fostered in this area. Consequently, it is understandable that the legends of Arthur and the Grail like to choose Brittany to stage the events. These Arthurian Round Table events are structured guilds, which later in the Western world continued in the Lodges, although in a very vague form. One can imagine them as secret brotherhoods, concerned with law and order; their members vow to be prepared to protect with their shields what is helpless and with their sword to fight the unruly. Thus, throughout the centuries there always was a King Arthur; his activities are hidden from public view. One must seek for him, if one wants to enter his circle. If accepted, one can enjoy a special education; tasks will be received when one is dedicated to his service.

Perceval achieves entrance to the Arthurian circle, yet for him it is one step. A law of his inner development drives him beyond this.

German Minnesingers and French Troubadours

Here, however, we have to look at a phenomenon that gives the world of the Middle Ages that quite different *fluidum*, a fluidity giving life a poetic magic. It is the blossoming of the Minnesingers. In its homeland, Provence, the art of the Troubadours was the basis of a whole culture, closely related to the mystical-religious teachings of the Cathar communities. It became the '*gai savoir*', to that which Nietzsche imagined at a certain point in his inner development, as 'the joyous science' (*gaya scienza*). In them, he admired the 'free spirits'. In Provence there were what is called the *Minne* courts at the castles and noble seats. From there 'strict *Minne* laws' were issued, which the members of the courts had to follow. We read that these laws were given to the first Troubadours from a falcon sitting on a branch of a golden oak tree. The oak is the sacred tree of the Druids. In the picture of the golden oak the first enlightened Druid himself appears. He is penetrated by the wisdom of the Sun—a spiritual messenger—the falcon—whispers to him. As an inspiration of Druidic origin the '*Minne* laws' consequently enter into the cultural life of the West. They are an educational impulse deriving from the Celtic spirit, which seeks to stands facing the ascetic ideal coming from the Orient in the customs of the monks. The Toulousian Troubadour says, 'Lovers should be of pure heart and only think of Minne. For Minne is no sin but virtue that makes the bad good and the good better. Minne makes one chaste.' The Minne service, when taken seriously, excluded any bodily connection between lovers. It established a soul-connection that was to inspire the hearts continuously for the highest deeds. Whoever fostered thoughts and feeling in faithfulness and was able to experience it as forces overcoming space and time, experienced the living power of Minne. Through this such a person entered the reality of the world of soul and spirit.

The path of asceticism of the monks presents a saintly ideal that only could be reached by killing off the earthly nature of human beings. Consequently, it basically denies the full unfolding of human nature, the passage of the spirit through the sensory world with its blemishes, but also with its experiences which are irreplaceable, which can enrich and expand the human being. The stream of the Troubadours (we do not speak here of aberrations, which of course existed, as well as with the monks) confirms those forces reigning in the blood, enabling young people to love. This stream intends to purify and enhance it, not supress or kill it off. This was already taught in Plato's *Symposium / Banquet*, that Eros is a mediator towards the divine.

To recognize human personality in all its widths and depths and not to mutilate it, was the starting point of this mighty educational impulse that sought to enter Western culture. It presented an initial step on a new way to the spirit, which contained the Grail Mystery. For the certainty of this path rests on the knowledge of the high sacrifice of God, which wants to be taken up with inner feeling in the nature of the human blood. In the blood of Christ, which is saved in the Holy Chalice and carried through time, the Sun-power of transformation is at work. The Grail stream announces this, which is carried from the East towards the West. This does not derive from the Celtic culture but from the West, the Arthur stream and all those educational impulses meet it, which are borne out of the noblest forces of the declining Celtic culture, which is consecrated towards a new Christian ideal. Of this, the legends and fairy tales relate, which want to describe to us the paths of destiny of those who seek for the Grail.

5. Grail Seekers

The Breton fairy tale of Peronnik the fool

Let us take as an example the Breton fairy tale of 'Peronnik' [also spelt 'Perronik']. With its motifs, it presents a pre-stage of Parzival. The protagonists share the prefix 'Per', also found in the *Mabinogion*, the Celtic fairy tale of Peredur, closely related to the Grail narration but already appearing much subdued in many passages. This 'Per' characterizes such natures that cannot be deterred by any resistance. They penetrate where others find insuperable difficulties. The openness of their being, the complete simplicity, is to their advantage in the trials of life. This ideal is repeatedly found in many guises in fairy tales of the simpleton, a genre to be found in all collections of European fairy tales.

Peronnik travels like a tramp through Brittany, unhampered by schooling or professional training, until chance gives him the task for which he feels his forces are adequate. A knight who asks the farmer's wife where Peronnik has just eaten his fill, for the path to the castle Kerglas, tells him in passing what one could gain there—the golden chalice and the diamond lance. Both are kept hidden in a dark dungeon, to which there is no key, by a magician with the name of Rogéar. The chalice gives directly all kinds of nourishment and riches according to one's wishes; whoever drinks from it is healed of all ailments; even those who have died, if they just touch it with their lips, are awakened to life. The lance on the other hand kills and destroys whatever it touches.

These two things are more precious than all the crowns of the world. But the magician who possesses them is untouchable when with the lance on his black mare followed by a foal of thirteen months he goes for his daily ride. However, if he is in his castle, he cannot use the lance.

We already know the chalice and the lance from the Grail imagination when it was presented to the soul of Perceval when he enters the castle in the evening. The life-renewing forces, which radiate from the Sun-like vessel and the destructive forces that appear as the spear dripping with blood, embrace a double Mystery, which is completely inaccessible to human beings through their day-consciousness. The one is hidden in those innocent life-processes, situated in the vegetative nerve-system, with the organ of the solar plexus (the virgin takes up the sacred vessel); the other Mystery rises out of the instinctive drives that rage as selfishness in the blood and usually are held down by the awake consciousness (the spear wounds the Fisher-King).

The magician in the castle Kergals is the human being bound by his senses. He appears darkened when he steps out in his day-consciousness. For spiritual perception, he rides around the world on his black horse causing much damage. In falling asleep—returning to the castle—he loses his power over the deeper forces of human nature. 'God forbids him,' the fairy tale relates, 'to use the lance in the castle.' In this lies a protection for the healthy soul-life; the unpurified sensory human being would otherwise be destroyed in a short time.

Only the one who would be able to dive consciously into his own being's depths would find access to hidden, inner powers and being awake would learn to employ them. It is understandable that the soul on this path must meet the strongest opposition. The mystics of all time have reported on this. There are threshold experiences from which souls unprepared and unstrengthened would quail, if these suddenly confront them.

Peronnik hears from the knight what adventures have to be faced. More than one hundred knights have already failed on this path, but to him, he assures him, the hermit has given the right advice. To such hermits—we often meet the protectors of ancient spiritual knowledge—he lists seven trials. All of them are clearly drawn from an Imaginative psychology, a teaching of what today would be called the 'unconscious'. They present encounters with the impure and untamed powers within the soul which are to be recognized and mastered. First is the 'forest of dangers' through whose illusions one should not be led astray from the path. The one penetrating his own soul-depths has initially to learn to control his thought-life full of false illuminations; he is not to lose the calm direction towards his innermost centre.

What does Peronnik do? When he prepared himself for his tasks, he stole through cunning the magician's young filly that had followed the black mare. He rides this young filly, furthermore, he pulls his hat over his face ... the illusory pictures of his thoughts one does not need to fight but simply not become involved with them! The foal, which is only thirteen months old, indicates certain forces needed to free one from the compulsion of sensory life. They are those very young forces active in the bodily nature that have just completed the first year of life. What do they accomplish? They give the upright stance and teach us to accomplish our first earthly steps. Consequently, they are ego-forces, completely pure. In them is revealed what wants to lead us to our human status. To learn consciously to lay hold of this power of uprightness working in the depths means to entrust oneself to the power that gives inner direction. Nevertheless, this is only the most harmless stage that can be penetrated in this way on the inner journey. Any further encounter penetrates hidden depths, until the spirit-seeker meets the forces of death. One has to learn to overcome the dread of the ghostly woman in the black garment and learn to work with her.

How the 'simple' Peronnik prepares himself is characteristic. We read that the strong ones face the danger but frequently succumb to it because they misjudge their own forces. The clever ones avoid the onslaught; they forge weapons of cunning. Powers of passion and instinct are difficult to conquer when one faces them with force; one often increases them where one tries to suppress them. Peronnik uses his natural cleverness. Of the seven trials, the middle one is roguishly described. It would not be clever to face dragons in a cumbersome manner when they arise out of one's own soul. One would be completely overcome in the waves of the astral world into which one is cast. Peronnik carries with him his rosary of many prayer beads. He simply unfastens the thread and strews the beads into the water. The dragons devour the beads, but after each bead is devoured, one monster after the other lies on its back, breathing out its poisonous soul. For each bead within the rosary corresponds to a prayer exercise. Peronnik's simplicity is consequently a most mature inner stance. He knows how one can detox the soul when the mysterious evil begins to arise out of its depths. Although appearing simple, this young soul has achieved the power of prayer. Nevertheless, forces of prayer in this way are only able to unfold with those whose stillness of heart prevails. This means, however, one has first to have faced the threatening lion. Consequently, the meeting with the lion directly precedes the crossing of the lake of dragons. One has to be able to wrest from the lion the 'laughing flower'. But the true freeing of the heart leads back to the innocence of feeling. Naturally, for this some humour is required. The lion's self-importance has to be cut down; one has to get the better of him. Humour is the sign of gaining freedom over oneself. Only those who pluck the 'laughing flower', after conquering the great magician will be able to find access to the inner chamber where the golden chalice and the diamond lance have been hidden. Soul-forces of plant-like purity and floral tenderness have to blossom in the heart if the depths are to open up, in which the mysteries of life are protected from any impure access. All this breathes the spirit of genuine devotion, yet unsentimental and without otherworldly monasticism.

Bearing the most precious gifts, Peronnik sets off to the court of the King of Brittany. With this only King Arthur can be meant. For the city, which is in great distress, is called Nantes. Through the magic power of the lance, Peronnik frees the city from the siege of their enemies. With the life-giving chalice, he awakens the fallen back to life. Henceforth he goes through life as a redeemer and life-bestower.

The motif of the sword

The world needs somebody awakened in the spirit to the Mysteries of human nature that are revealed to the victorious one. In one of the prose stories of Parzival we read that 'the enchantment would have left Brittany', had Parzival asked the Grail question at the right time. After long excursions, the redemption of the Fisher-King, the 'enchantments' are indeed lifted from Brittany and the whole world.

The Celtic guardians of the ancient dying spiritual knowledge felt that a magic spell lies over all earthly existence. The British Isles, which once had to carry caring for the spiritual ordering, also for the peoples of Europe, is itself drawn into this magic spell. The Grail could redeem them, but its Guardian has succumbed to sickness. His full power is taken from him. Salvation cannot come out of care for the tradition; only out of the youthful forces of the world will the Grail regain its victorious power. Where are the youthful heroes able to penetrate and produce the Mysteries out of the strength of the utmost personal experience?

In fairy-tale pictures of the awakening power, such longed-for spiritual seekers are portrayed. Whoever can encrypt the language of Imagination, and knows the various stages and inner lawfulness, will have no doubt that such legends and fairy tales originated in the early Mystery schools. The most mature Celtic inheritance of wisdom still betrays the after-glow of a noble Druid tradition in the magic of its pictorial language, but now reborn out of a Christian illumination of the heart.

In the conventions of the bards, one can imagine how this language of the Imagination was practised; their laws were announced and passed on to the guilds of singers. Of course, as time passed and the spreading of intellectual education, the numbers of those able to reach authentic Imagination became ever smaller. In the place of visionary experience came the understanding of the feelings for the pictorial treasures. But these, too, not as a slavish repetition of what had been learnt; the sequence of pictures was assembled to a high degree with an 'exact Imagination'. Thus, legends and fairy tales blossomed in every new variation. With the decline of the singing guilds, an arbitrary element and superficiality became gradually mixed into the storytelling. Such phenomena of decline are clearly found in the later, often formless Grail stories. Nevertheless, some treasures still shine forth, strange pictures and events that can only be drawn from deeper insights. Moreover, if one disregards a certain level of story conventions, a background is betrayed that is formed out of a genuine knowledge of the laws of spiritual life.

If one day the decoding of the Imaginative language, the discovery of its real spiritual content, is moved logically into the centre of literary studies, one will find quite a different relationship to the poetic works on the Grail from the Middle Ages. A far more reverent appreciation prevails. Behind the works of the weakest writers and the cobbled together versions there are still hidden flashes of a glorious tradition. This can be uncovered for this sensitive observer with the help of a new knowledge of initiation.

Galahad

The carriers of the Grail's wisdom felt they were Knights of the Word. They had to wield the sword of the spirit [Eph. 6:17]. With their poetic work they were able to forge those weapons on which the victory of the Spirit on Earth would one day depend.

In a prose story of the thirteenth century, the [Vulgate] *Queste del St Graal,* this Mystery of the sword is expressively described. On a Whitsun Day, King Arthur gathered all his knights at the castle of Camelot. Hitherto, it was never possible for the heroes, involved in distant journeys or held back by a secret love, to be united in full number for the meal. As they just sat down for the meal, a servant entered and announced that at the riverbank beneath the castle a great block of stone was floating. Everyone immediately followed the king, expecting an adventure. They see a red block of marble washed to the shore. In it a sword is stuck, glorious to behold, the handle made of precious stone adorned with golden letters. When the knights draw near, they decipher the inscription, according to which there is only one who is destined to be able to draw the sword and wear it at his side. But he will be the best knight in the world. No one dares this, except Gawain at the king's behest, yet in vain. The sword does not move. Everyone returns to the meal, but hardly is the first course eaten, suddenly, as by invisible hands doors and windows of the castle are closing. An old man in a long white garb enters, leading by his hand a knight in red armour, without shield and sword. When he stands in the middle of the hall, he simply says, 'The peace be with you!'

We are reminded of the Easter report in John's Gospel, when the Risen One despite the locked doors appears amongst the disciples with the same greeting—as throughout this *Queste* strives to lift the story into the glory of legend. 'Galahad'—of the line of King David, and at the same time the expected redeemer, of the dynasty of the Grail guardians—is hero and saint in one. It is he—not Parzival—who is to complete the adventures of the Grail. He is led by the old man to the 'perilous seat' at the Round Table, on which until then no knight was able to sit without being punished. Full of tranquillity, he takes that place, and everyone present sees on the back of the chair a name appear—Galahad. While the old man in the white garb silently withdraws, the young knight remains with his red armour. In the eyes of the astonished people, he appears adorned with youth and beauty. Everyone expects of him that he frees the land from its spell and defeats the growing plight that gives so much concern for the king and his companions of the Round Table. Galahad is able to draw the sword out of the block of marble without trouble. He becomes the actual hero of the *Queste*—the seeker of the Grail to which the Knights of the Round Table in great number now set off.

A related sword motif from the Volsunga Saga is known, as Richard Wagner has told it in Act 1 of *The Valkyrie*. Here Wotan had thrust the sword of the gods deep into the tree trunk and promised it to the man who could pull it out. All the guests of the house attempted in vain, until Sigmund, the descendant of the Volsungs, who had been brought up by the god himself in the form of a Valsa, finally succeeds in his greatest deed. Here it is the power of the 'I', which until then was still held in the genealogical tree of the generations, that is, in the strength of the family. That power of the 'I' is to draw out of the family bonds, to gain the freedom of thinking and the autonomy of decisions. This, the calling of the Volsung tribe with all the tragedy initially involved with the gaining of freedom, tears off the bonds of blood-ties.

The sword of the Grail, however, does not need to be drawn out of a tree trunk; it is stuck in a block of marble. This does not concern the power of the 'I' connected with the tribal bonds, but it concerns that spiritual power connected to the rigidified part of human nature. For the human being striving for the spirit, the head organization with its expiring thinking nature appears like a block of stone within the stream of life-forces. The human intellect has become solidly mineralized, yet in it lies a supreme spiritual power—the free creating thought, pure intuition that waits to be rent from the hardened intellect. This is the sword of the Grail, which is to become effective in the spirit-word. During a Pentecost (Whitsun) celebration this Mystery is brought to King Arthur and his Round Table. His followers are not able to lay hold of the spiritual power, although the longing for it lives and burns in this circle. Like a messenger of the Holy Spirit, Galahad enters the Round Table. As the disciple of the Paraclete, the Comforter Himself, he achieves the deed of highest freedom. With his appearance, a high initiate is indicated who entered incarnation with the forces of most mature humanity. His presence among people invites the Grail. In the souls it releases forces of higher vision. Consequently, in the *Queste* a strange thing is reported. In the evening of the same Pentecost celebration, when all the company of the Round Table sit at their places with Galahad amongst them, a clash of thunder is heard making the palace tremble. A sunbeam, ten times clearer than daylight, penetrates the hall. The Grail enters, carried by invisible hands. It is wrapped in white silk; from it perfumes exude through the whole palace. The Grail moves from chair to chair; in passing it bestows on the tables an abundance of food. When it has carried out its gift of blessing, it disappears.

Gawain thinks that this mysterious feast has never happened anywhere in the Castle Corbenic (this is the name here for the Grail Castle), consequently, next morning he makes an oath to begin a search for the Grail. The point is to find the Grail in its actual realm, for here they could not see it clearly enough. All the knights arise and make the same oath. (9)

The Mystery of Galahad consists in the fact that he carries in his etheric body the forces of transfiguration, which in essence can be imparted to his environment, when this environment brings an open mood to the search for the Grail. In the Mystery-centres of earlier times, people knew blessed moments of a higher consciousness can arise through the presence of an especially mature individuality. Through an intimate living and working together, the members of the whole circle participate in the radiant powers of the ether-body, which that individuality can, as it were, share with them. Mystical brotherhoods of such a kind arose in the late Middle Ages, also within esoteric

Christianity. Similar things are reported of the meetings of the 'Friends of God'.[22] Moreover, in the initial Rosicrucian communities such ideals were fostered.

The Fountain of Lac

With Perceval it is quite different. His path of destiny leads through the depths. Through error and guilt, although it is brought on unconsciously, he fights for freedom and spiritual awakening. This is clearly shown in his way of taking hold of the Grail sword, or rather at first not really to lay hold of it.

The Imagination of the sword appears in the poetic work 'Perceval' by Chrétien de Troyes, and similarly with Wolfram initially in a nocturnal experience, when he allows the Mysteries of the Grail Castle to pass before his soul. As a present of the maiden who then carries in the radiant Grail, it will be given to the guest by the lord of the castle. This sword symbolizes what in the Grail Imagination wants to be communicated to the soul, which can become a strength in the soul if it penetrates in understanding the content of the sequence of pictures. But to achieve that, the soul would have to be able to live with it in the spirit. Then from it the full power of the Word will grow. Perceval did receive the sword, but one always wonders how little it is mentioned later, although the importance of this gift has been stressed with such weighty words. It seems that Perceval is not yet able to bring into effect in his soul-development what he has received.

Impressions of the spiritual world that are not laid hold of with the active understanding—and Perceval's failure to put the 'question' is indeed the sign for a clairvoyant experience which could not yet be intuitively penetrated—dissolve like dreams for the consciousness; they fall apart sooner or later, sinking into the soul's hidden depths. The sword of the Grail breaks.

That this could happen, although it is forged and hardened so well, is already pointed out to Perceval when he received it. The maiden whom he meets the next morning with the slain knight in her lap (with Wolfram she is called Sigune) warns him not to trust the sword

[22] *Gottesfreunde*, a medieval mystical group that grew out of the sermons of Master Eckhart, and especially his Dominican spiritual heirs, the preacher John Tauler and the writer Henry Suso. Several texts, including *Theologia Germanica* (later fourteenth century), discovered and published by Luther, are associated with the Friends of God. Many leaders of the group were executed for heresy for criticizing the corruptions of Catholicism.

too much; it will shatter. And when Perceval asks whether it can be reforged, if it should break, she names a blacksmith. He is called Trebuchet; only he would be able to reforge it. One should refrain from letting anyone else to undertake it. Yet one has to find the way to the lake near Cotovatre, in order to reach this master smith.

As the poetic work continues, which Chrétien left as a fragment, the trial of the sword plays a great role. Three poets worked on the completion of the epic. They were all concerned with the trial of the sword. During his second visit to the Grail Castle, Perceval is confronted by the Fisher-King with a broken sword, since he had previously asked the right question. When he is able to assemble the pieces, the king proclaims him as the best knight. He embraces him with the words, 'You shall be the Lord of my house.' This poetic work of the Grail that has remained fragmentary is itself the broken sword. To bring it to its right ending, means to penetrate to its innermost contexts, for the Imaginations want to be freshly produced each time in the soul. Where they cease they need to be completed in a creative manner. Only someone able to progress from the experience of the picture (from the Imagination) to the 'inner word' (to the Inspired consciousness), will gain the completed sword and be able to wield it.

Wolfram approaches the Mystery of the Grail sword in a different manner. When Sigune meets Parzival during the morning after the first visit to the Grail Castle, she believes—as one completely in the picture concerning the plight of the Grail—that Anfortas would have now found redemption, since she recognizes the sword Parzival carries by his side. She says to him, 'If you know the strength contained in it, then enter battle with courage.' But here the original wording is important.

> *'bekennestu des swertes segen*
> *du math ân angest stretes pflegen.'*

> 'Knowing the secret of the blade,
> You may fight yet be unafraid.'[23]

For, as she now explains to him, how it can be reassembled if it breaks, she adds:

> *'daz swert bedarf wol segenes wort:*
> *ich fürht, diu habestu lâzen dort.'*

---

[23] Tr. A.S. Kline, in the section 'He meets his cousin Sigune again and learns more'.

'A magic spell it needs, you'll find,
Though I fear you've left that behind.'

But when his mouth has learnt this word of blessing, then the healing forces will continue to grow in him, bearing fruit. His Grail kingdom depends on it. But as Sigune perceives him in his momentary soul-condition, she begins to doubt whether he really placed the question in the Castle.

People have pondered a lot what this blessing of the sword could be. It is obvious that it would have been the answer given to Parzival had he asked the right question. But for this, it would have needed the strengthening of his spirit-consciousness to come through contemplating the pictures to come to their meaning. In the spirit, the right question already contains the beginning of a recognition. The 'inner word' would have begun to speak. This is the 'word of blessing', which he missed to bring from the Grail Castle.

Sigune instructs him how the Grail sword can be renewed. Near Karnant there is a spring, named Lac. The shattered sword is to be taken to it.

'Doch brings du's zu dem Born zurück,
Macht es sein Wasser wieder ganz,
Schöpft es, bevor des Tages Glanz
Erschien, am Felsen deine Hand.'

'It may be rendered whole again,
If that far stream it can regain;
Go take the shattered weapon back
To the spring whose name is Lac,
Yet only draw its water where
Beneath the rock it rises there,
Before tis lit by light of dawn.'

No piece, however, may be missing, and it is to be understood that they are all assembled correctly. Then the sword will not only appear like new, but it will also have gained in strength. Nevertheless, this will not be achieved without the word of blessing.

Wolfram does not mean that it must be reassembled by Trebuchet, who forged it. Parzival himself will have to renew it at that mysterious fountain. That is:

'du muost des urspringes hân
underm velse ê in beschine der tac.'

'Yet only draw its water where
Beneath the rock it rises there,
Before tis lit by light of dawn.'

Where the source springs forth, where the Grail Imaginations are drawn, only there can the renewal take place. For this, one has to learn to grasp the moment of waking up in the morning. Before the bright light of day-consciousness spreads over it, the source or spring of the creative imagination has to be made conscious, which, active beneath the rocky bones of our skull in ceaselessly fashioning ideas.

In the first chapter of Novalis', *Heinrich von Ofterdingen*, the protagonist of the novel dreams of the 'blue flower'. After a play of magic or dream journeys, towards morning the pictures slowly clarify for the sleeper. They become calmer in his soul, clearer and more permanent. He reaches a high rock and finds an entrance into it. At the end of a long passage it broadens into a cave, from whence a bright light shines towards him. We read:

> On entering this expanse, he beheld a mighty beam of light, which, like the stream from a fountain, rose to the overhanging clouds, and spread out into innumerable sparks, which gathered themselves below into a great basin. The beam shone like burnished gold; not the least noise was audible; a holy silence reigned around the splendid spectacle. He approached the basin, which trembled and undulated with ever-varying colours. The sides of the cave were coated with the golden liquid, which was cool to the touch, and which cast from the walls a weak, blue light. He dipped his hand in the basin and bedewed his lips. He felt as if a spiritual breath has pierced through him, and he was sensibly strengthened and refreshed.[24]

Lac is the same spring as the one described by Novalis. At the same time, it means his awakening to be a poet, announced in these Imaginations leading him into ever more mysterious depths of experience. According to the novel, this dream upon waking up is dreamt in Eisenach, at the foot of the Wartburg. But this is where Wolfram von Eschenbach, too, was creating his *Parzival* for years, and according to legend where the well-known Singers Contest took place, in which as singer of the Grail he achieved victory over Klingsor.

Parzival was allowed to enter the Grail Castle as an evening experience. He was in the process of falling asleep. To be able one day

---

[24] Novalis, *Henry von Ofterdingen*, Dover 2015, p. 4.

to renew that broken Grail sword by himself, he must learn to add morning experience to the first awakening experience. In him there has to grow the ability strongly to carry over nocturnal impressions into day-consciousness, conscious penetration with the knowledge of the heart. Then for him the source of Inspiration will be opened.

This strength, however, can only mature for him through the trials of life. In Book 9, the heart-piece of his poetic work, Wolfram attempts to present how Parzival after long excursions again enters the realm of the Grail. Just prior he gives a short review over the hero's accomplished battles and victories. The Grail sword is broken in two, but at the source at Karnant it became whole again. That means, in accomplishing the trials of destiny, Parzival must have meanwhile received that power of grace, described as 'words of blessing'—the 'inner word'. What he was permitted to experience at that spring of Lac, the fountain of Inspiration, the poet honours with silence. He passes over it with a short sentence: '*Ver's nicht glaubt, der sundigt*', 'Whoever does not believe it is a sinner.' What is sacred does not bear to be much talked about. It is shown in its effects—in that deep change, which meanwhile occurred in the soul of Parzival. (10)

Perceval's youth

This soul is indeed uniquely prone to learn from experience. Distant from all conventional education, secluded from contemporary influences, Perceval grows up as the 'son of the widow'. In this way Chrétien introduces him. With unused forces, in the guise of the fool, he faces life. A storm of sensations, in which the transition to youth is announced, drives him from the arms of his mother into the world. He seeks the adventure of life, but he seeks and experiences it with a rare chastity of the heart. The poetic work of Chrétien, which we are following in this sketch, allows the stages of pure Imagination to shine through undistorted. During a morning in spring, when he, whom the mother had guarded with all care, becomes acquainted with knighthood (his father and two brothers had perished through it), he suddenly meets five knights emerging from the forest, their weapons reflecting the sunlight. The appearance overcomes him as a heavenly appearance. This must be angels; his mother had often told him of the most beautiful beings of the world. And the most magnificent amongst them must be God Himself. But God one should revere. And so, he throws himself on the ground before them, speaks his Credo and all the prayers his mother had taught him. The knights, who are pursuing some robbers, direct certain questions to him, but he is only interested in their armaments and, if they be knights, he too would become like them. If King Arthur, of whom they tell, makes knights, he wants immediately to set off to this king who lives in Carduel. Through this, disaster strikes. The mother cannot restrain her son, even if her heart breaks from it.

Like an angelic revelation, the calling of his life penetrates the soul of the young person. Each soul hears this call in its depths; it is the true experience of youth. But for a long time, thanks to the educators and conventions, youth has now learned to disregard this calling or make excuses to what is sounding in its depths. It is the breakthrough of the pre-existing human being, of that which the soul during its earthly descent was permitted to behold in mighty pictures in its heart as its life's task out of the sphere of the angels. Perceval completely undeterred carries as a whole the direction of his inner soul-development. This soul only requires a gradual awakening of the dreaming forces and their clarification.

All this, once released, occurs quite quickly. His mother gives good advice on his way, which particularly relates to dealings with women and visiting churches. But he initially obeys them somewhat foolishly. When in a forest, he sees a knight's splendid tent, he thinks this must be a house of God. Perceval has never entered a church; he received his religious education separate from it. He enters the tent as a house of God, finds a lady in it, kisses her and takes a ring from her despite all her struggles, since he has misunderstood the teaching of his mother, of how to behave with women. This fool's deed, carried out in all innocence, brings serious consequences. Destiny comes about.

However, he is driven further to Carduel. Arriving there, he sees a magnificent castle by the sea; he sees a knight emerging from the gate, holding a golden beaker. His weapons, which are completely red, impress the youth. These he wants to request from King Arthur himself. When he hears that his path leads him to Arthur, the Red Knight utters a challenge as a message to the king. Perceval understands nothing of this. Like a simpleton, disregarding all courtly customs, he arrives at Arthur's court. The king is sunk in deep contemplation; that Red Knight had demanded of King Arthur his land, which he said belonged to him. In his emotion, he had snatched his beaker from the dining table, so that all the wine had poured into the lap of the king. Through this the Round Table had been dishonoured. But where can the knight be found who can atone for such a misdeed?

Perceval, in complete ignorance of the conditions that could lead to a knighthood, is immediately prepared to fight for the armour of the Red Knight. This is what in a cynical way the king's advisor tells him to do; with this joke he wants to send the fool home. Perceval follows the advice. He rides back and after a short exchange of words, he pushes his simple spear, with which he was equipped, through the knight's eye so strongly that it went right through his head. Without more ado, he proceeds to take the armour of the fallen man. The page helps him, wanting to convince him that he should first take off his crude garments, if he wants to clothe himself in knightly garments. But Perceval vehemently rejects this; he does not want to take off the clothes originating from his mother; he simply puts the armour over them. Now he rides into the world on the horse of the slain Arthurian knight. He himself is called the 'Red Knight'.

These Imaginations are unmistakenly expressed. Young people seek adventures—that which comes towards them (Lat. *aventure*). Destiny brings him meetings with himself. That which in puberty rises from the depths of the soul as indignation, demanding its possession, is a lawless power. As the power of the blood, it rises courageously against the old order. The carriers of the old order are deeply upset, yet helpless towards it. Perceval slips himself into the armour of this Red Knight. He longs to experience himself strongly in the power of the blood. He experiences puberty, but innocently.

He has still not yet discarded the maternal sheath of the soul. This gives him the sheath of the young lad, which nevertheless in the moral world makes him appear childish and laughable. The next station on his way leads him to the castle of a nobleman who is pleased with him, immediately recognizing under the wild expression the noble nature. He manages to convince him to exchange the clothes his mother had made him for others that he offers him. This means he succeeds in educating Perceval into a young man. He also gains his spurs, the sign of knighthood, into the 'Order' of which, with all its honourable duties, he is now festively received. Gornemant of Gohort, as the nobleman is called here, makes him, as it were, fit for society. Quite quickly Perceval relinquishes the wildness of the boy, at the same time, however, the innocence making him always to think of his mother and to ask full of curiosity about everything.

Here the tragedy begins. Perceval needs education that curbs him, teaching him the world's conventions. It means for him a step further in becoming human; he would not otherwise see himself a member of his contemporary situation. But the certainty of the instinctive child-nature becomes disturbed. The elementary urge to ask questions, with which he seeks to know and lay hold of the world, has become lamed. Now he will be silent where *questioning* means everything. Seen from the side of his education, this is the reason of his failing at the Grail Castle. From the side of destiny's rule, however, there is another reason, already mentioned.

With the garments he had received from his mother, the nobleman also robbed him of a certain maternal inheritance. This became the reason for his restless search for his mother, which drove him on. Yet another station precedes the experience of the Grail. As a new knight, he arrives at a splendid castle, where he is received as a guest. The lady of the castle is called Blanchefleur, who conveys to him the plight of her whole town. Besieged by enemies, the inhabitants are dying of hunger; the streets and churches of Beaurepaire are deserted. The maiden, only dressed in a shift, over which a red silken cloak is laid—enters his room at night, to plead with him for help. He awakens out of sleep and takes her lovingly to his bed, yet without a passionate coming together. He becomes her warrior, succeeding to free the city. For this, she gives him her *Minne*, her innocent love. 'So sweet and mild, that she pressed the key of love deeply into the lock of his heart.'[25]

Perceval has become able to love. Only through this is he also able in his blood to experience the Grail as the Sun-power of cosmic love. But he would not have been able to experience the ability to love, had not the passionate nature overcome him at the same time. He put on the red armour as a victor, not as a conqueror. As a victor, who knew how to defend Blanchefleur against all enemies besieging her virginity, he is allowed to receive the purest love (*Minne*). What is here described is a nocturnal meeting, a becoming-awake out of the depths of sleep. The youth experiences the innocent soul-forces of his own being, the approach of his un-desecrated primordial image, which in unconscious depths in him wants to awaken him to love. The nocturnal approach of Blanchefleur, the 'white flower', wrapped in the red, silken cloak, is most tenderly described by Chrétien. From then on, love enters his blood as that soul's power of grace enabling him to

[25] The English translations (A.S. Kline / Burton Raffel) have no equivalent lines, unless we are to read between the lines 2032–2034 the meaning explained here by the author. Perhaps Meyer is conflating another episode (2638–2639)?

entertain ideals. The poet says of Blanchefleur, 'With her, God created an incomparable miracle; never did He create her equal, nor hitherto create anything similar.' A heavenly soul that had contained in itself the forces of the beginning of Creation has awakened in Perceval to its earthly consciousness. The name points towards the lily, always a mystical symbol—it is the flower not able fully to connect to the Earth; for in this exists the uniqueness of all flowering bulbs. This Blanchefleur-soul strives towards human becoming; she wants to be held by the 'Red Knight'.

Goethe mentions this symbolism, although in his time already deriving from a weakened alchemical tradition, by letting his Faust mock those arts of the adepts.

> Then a red lion, eager his love to claim,
> Was mated to the lily, warmly brewed,
> And both, subjected to the open flame,
> From bridal to fresh bridal-bower pursued ...[26]

With retorts the alchemist experimented with substances, from one process to another, finally to distil that elixir called *lapis philosophorum*, the philosopher's stone. Yet in genuine Rosicrucianism it concerned an inner process; the pictures attempt to describe it. The most intimate transformations of the soul were striven for; attempts to describe them are indicated in *The Chymical Wedding*. (11)

Wolfram characterizes the Grail as that mysterious stone that burns the phoenix to ashes only to let it arise rejuvenated. He wanted to point towards this 'chymical' mystery of the working of the Grail. His Parzival, although initially without understanding, perceives the '*Lapsit exillis*' for the first time during that evening when he came from Belrapeire. With the forces of Blanchefleur united in an innocent manner with his blood-nature, the youth is able to experience in himself the Mystery of the Grail. He first experiences it as a miracle of nourishment.

Perceval has crossed that threshold which, within the Christian soul-guidance, is always accompanied by the sacrament of confirmation. The young soul from now on is mature to receive the sacrament at the altar. It needs such nourishment, for with it the Blanchefleur-forces, which want to live in their tender feeling, are addressed

[26] Goethe, *Faust*, Part 1, 'Outside the city gate'. Tr. Philip Wayne, Penguin Books 1949, 65.

and gradually strengthened. To perceive the pictures of the Grail journey is a comfort for the young person's development. They mirror processes which, in crossing the threshold of youth, somehow always take place in the dreaming depths. Consequently, about this time they should be brought in the right way to young people to accompany in the innermost manner their youthful striving.

Around the turn of the twelfth to thirteenth century, these poetic works entered the European world and were received with great enthusiasm; through them a significant educational impulse was given. This impulse made a deep impression to Western spiritual development; the effect of it can be traced right into the present day. (12)

6. Wolfram's *Parzival*

(Sanctus Januarius)

This is no book: what do books matter!
To these coffins and shrouds!
The past is the prey of books:
Yet within lives an eternal *present*.

Friedrich Nietzsche, poem 'The Gay/Joyful Science' (1882).[27]

Characteristics of Wolfram's poetic work

With courage Wolfram placed his poetic work into his time—fully aware of giving with it that new educational impulse that was to go completely against the style of the Latin schools and all monastic educational ideals. He himself, although we are permitted to recognize a universal spirit, lives by his ideals, when at the end of Book 2, he says, 'I was born to the office of shield bearer', ensuring that he would find rather sickening the intention of a woman wanting to love him because of his song. Only with shield and lance did he want to earn love, that is, as a *knight*. But for him this means engaging his personality. Indeed, before presenting Parzival's path, he explains that this account should not be reckoned as a book:

Unkundig ist mir ganz das Lesen.
I'm not a reader in the least.

That he claims, 'no knowledge of a single letter', may be an exaggerated, ironical joke. He means, if somebody should think this poetic work is a 'book', he would not be more embarrassed than having to enter the bath naked.

Rather than have some wise sage
Take this for literature, I would
Choose to sit naked in my tub,
If only I failed not in my quest
For a bath-brush to scrub my chest.

[27] Translation by The Nietzsche Channel © 2009. http://www.thenietzschechannel.com/poetry/poetry-dual.htm#thisis/

Why all this? Because Wolfram sees a generation arise that will be intellectually overbred, and consequently will be stunted in its manhood. This method of education leads to a weakening of heart's courage. The Grail path is an initiation of the heart. Only as far as it can be freshly reproduced in the hearts of those who take up the message from it will it be understood. What in this poetic work out of necessity appears as a book has repeatedly to be overcome. Consequently, it is something that grows, can continue to be woven. There are pieces of art which summarize the content of an epoch. The Middle Ages produced two such works, Dante's *Divine Comedy*, and Wolfram's *Parzifal*. The former of an artistic completion, as only could be produced as a last fruit of the Spirit of the Age, a cathedral of architectural planning chiselled right into the finest detail and structured according to wonderful mathematics. In this will to build lives the courage of the young peoples, that also pulses through Dante's personality, but the maturity of the Latin race, endowed to this through blood and education, gives his poetic work laws and form summarizing the worldview of the ancient world and the Christian teaching on salvation, a memorial for future generations cast in bronze. Compared to this, Wolfram's poetic work is a stammering attempt. In it, too, if we analyse the sixteen books, we would no doubt find a structure of stages, and in the plot's mysterious weaving we would be able to discover deep mystical meaning, as in Dante. But whereas with Dante a wonderful static architectural balance can be recognized, Wolfram's figures and events live in a dynamic unfolding. Everything is full of seed potential. It demands of us to supplement and transform the poetic events, as it was the destiny of the Grail legend itself right into our time. On this, humanity itself poetizes further.

Dante, although rooted in the Earth of his time and its tasks, nevertheless devalued this whole earthly existence, by looking and judging it in the light of the heavenly cosmos. On his starry journey, under the leadership of Beatrice, he reaches the Saturn sphere. He looks back through all the planetary circles to 'this piece of land of which we are so proud'; it becomes clear to him that the truly wise are those who can already learn here to despise it.

On the other hand, Wolfram's *Parzival* lives in each moment out of the courage to become human. As we shall see, he too will finally extend his consciousness beyond the starry sphere. For the Grail itself has been a Mystery of the stars, as Master Kyot taught. But it has been carried from the heights of the stars down to the Earth. And here it is at work, and only in the experience of earthly destiny will it begin to shine.

For Dante's ecclesiastical Christian view, the great ascetics, who already had died in this world, appear as the inhabitants of the Saturn sphere, the highest of the planetary circles, according to which he had classified the souls of the redeemed. But Wolfram knows a life's ideal not interested in a premature annulling of earthly interests; to become human is the great adventure of the human spirit. We have not entered this earthly life to march on a prescribed route. Life with its rich destinies is to be explored, because only to those who dare will it be revealed in all its depths. Sigune, with the dead bridegroom in her lap, the maiden who early experienced the suffering of the Earth and for whom there only exists the path of renunciation, to transfigure the bond of love in eternal faith beyond death—she nevertheless encourages the youth towards the adventure of life: 'Indeed, your name is Parzival, / Which means, "passing right through".'

> 'Upon my word, you are Parzival!'
> She of the red lips cried: 'Withal,
> You shall "pierce to true worth," indeed,
> Through many a great and noble deed.'
> [tr. A.S. Kline]

Perce–val ('penetrate the vale'), is no personal name; it is the call of the divine powers that send human souls into the depths, that with courage they experience the meaning of the Earth and lift the hidden jewel out of a dark shaft, so that it can radiate in the light. But of course, to young persons the powerful impact of the soul must not be lamed through education and convention. Then they would become lost in 'the vale of Earth'.[28] They would be held fast in the low plains of earthly life. Only by entering the paths of youth with hearts intact will they be able to regain the heights.

Gamuret, the father

We already pointed out how that spirit-inspiration that seeks to point its pupils towards the path of the Grail began to be active in the eighth

[28] Cf. Shelley, 'This dim vast vale of tears' from 'Hymn to Intellectual Beauty', line 17 (1817), also Keats 'vale of Soul-making', letter to George and Georgina Keats, written from 14 February to 3 May 1819—*Tr.*

century in the Carolingian dynasty.[29] Rudolf Steiner describes how the pupils of this new path were called *Percevale*. They learnt to understand how the early paths of schooling, through the annulling of the sensory nature can spiritualize the human being more quickly, how individuals can free themselves from earthly entanglements, but would leave behind the Earth untransformed. This ancient path might lead to a self-redemption but does not engage in the world's redemption. To understand this Mystery was the task of an early Catharism. In it the stream of that Catharism, suppressed by the Roman Church, continued to flow, mysteriously penetrating the new burgeoning spiritual life.[30]

In Chrétien's poetic work, Perceval means *'li Gallois'*. He is a Celt. He is introduced as the son of a knightly dynasty fallen into poverty in Wales; consequently, the five knights who meet the young lad on the edge of the forest laugh about him, calling him a foolish *'waliser'*. The declining Celtic culture, with the Hibernian spiritual inheritance as we met it still glimmering in the soul, was predestined to take up the inspiration of a spiritual Christianity and to spread within the Western world. Out of this basis of an inner Celtic heritage those wonderful Imaginations could be produced, drawing on Perceval's path but also that of Peronnik, as it is reflected in the body of formative forces.

But a certain 'Perceval' once existed, whose destiny Wolfram decided to portray. His outer path in life is not described here; he wishes to portray his mystical biography. For this he has to use that Imaginative language drawn from the pictorial treasure trove of Celtic wisdom. This Perceval (Wolfram calls him 'Parzival') is not himself a Celt. He is a certain individuality who appeared in the ninth century within Europe. The poet was able to recognize this through Master Kyot, for Kyot researched the genealogical tree that was neither to be found in Britain nor in France. His father's family comes from 'Anshouwe' (even if the House of Anjou were meant, it concerns a Germanic family), although from his mother's side he is called *'Waleise'* (the tendency is to relate it to the royal family of Valois). But the mother only

[29] See Chap. 3, pp. 38, 51ff.

[30] The Cathars, who appeared later in history especially in the south of France, are known for their strict ascetic life. But in their connection with the Troubadour stream, which fostered the culture of courtly love, the *Minne*-culture in the south of France, it became apparent they also knew a teaching of the transformative forces of love and of the ennobling of the sensory nature through the arts.

took on this royal name '*Waleis*' inherited from her first husband Kastis, who died shortly after their marriage; she herself comes from the Grail dynasty. In her, Catharism is active, as we shall see. Through her, a stream in humanity, a human stream beyond nationalism is fostered.

From the tradition of Master Kyot, Wolfram wove this Cathar element into his poetic work *Parzival*. This is most clearly expressed in two extensive songs that precede the course of events, and two others conclude it, concerning which no indication can be found in earlier work. Through this alone his work became a poem of world literature; it breathes a cosmopolitan spirit that is completely missing with Chrétien's epic.

The first two songs concern Gamuret, the father of Parzifal. As the second son of the dynasty of Anschau, he does not want to spend his life as a servant of his brothers. He travels to the Orient with a group of knights and offers his service to the mighty Baruc, the Caliph of Baldag (Baghdad), who was at the time involved in some intense battles and to whom the help of Gamuret seemed highly welcome. Through his courageous deeds, Gamuret rises to ever higher fame within the extensive Orient. Baruc endows him with insignia of the anchor, which he exchanges for his panthers. But the poet says that this restless spirit would never be able to cast his anchor; everywhere on this Earth he remains a guest.

And so, it happened during a sea-voyage he lands at Zazamanc in the land of the Moors, where he frees the Queen Belacane from her plight. He conquers the enemy who besiege her town, gaining her noble love and her kingdom as a reward. She is beautiful, although her face is black. But he cannot be held for long in her arms, because he is hindered from carrying out knightly deeds. He secretly escapes, although under her heart she carries a child of his. With a ship that is ready to go to Sevilla (we can possibly imagine Zazamanc to be in Morocco) he steals away during the night, leaving behind a heart-moving letter. If she had been a Christian, he says, he would never be able to leave her. For he dearly loves her. Their son shall one day be enlightened about his father's lineage.

> 'He is of the House of Anjou.
> Love will be his mistress ever.'

Like Arthur, his lineage arises from Mazadan. We have already discussed the mystery of this genealogical tree—how the female ancestor was of the fairy folk who once took the ancestral lord into her realm.

It is this drop of fairy blood which will make him faithful to Minne love. The same can also be said later, about the other son of Gamuret, Parzival. When Ither, the Red Knight, meets him for the first time, he greets him with the words:

> 'A blessing on your handsome face!
> A fine woman, of noble race
> Brought you into the world, my lad.
> I've ne'er seen another who had
> So fine a form, and you possess
> Love's very glance, her success
> And her defeat, for joy entire
> In many a woman you'll inspire ...'

At that time Parzival had arrived at the threshold to youth, standing before the forces of love (*Minnekräfte*). This he inherits from his father, but what he inherits from his mother radiates from him as angelic purity. Through the latter, what he inherits from the Grail, he becomes the victor over the magic of the fairy folk in his blood. Consequently, he overcomes the Red Knight. Love enters him, yet he remains in command of its forces. It blesses him without making him unfree.

Gamuret, bearer of a worldwide knighthood, is able to offer mediating services between the Orient and the Occident. He is a Christian, without prejudices. He values the culture and humanity of the Arabic world. This exchange of cultural goods that had already taken place in France under Charles the Great in a generous manner with the Caliph of Baghdad shows a tolerant Christianity moving on quieter paths alongside a dogmatic, fanatical Christianity throughout the Middle Ages. It conveyed sublime treasures of wisdom that had still been preserved by the Orient, missing in the Christian West. Let us just recall how the Arabic scholars brought to Europe mathematics, chemistry, astronomy and medicine—especially via Spain. To these treasures belong the writings of Aristotle, especially his cosmological and natural-scientific knowledge that had been lost in the West. Such a messenger of spiritual life we can divine behind the figure of Gamuret. The name 'Belacane' may have derived from 'Balcis' (the Arabs say 'Bilcis'). According to old tradition, the Queen of Sheba was called this, who once went on a pilgrimage to Solomon. At the same time, the name 'Pelican' was found in it, of that legendary bird who nourished its young from its own heart's blood. It plays a special role in the symbolism of alchemy.

Gamuret became connected to the wisdom of the East when he married Belicane with a wisdom that came from Arabic sources not penetrated by the light of Christ. This causes conscientious scruples. Expressed in pictures, Belicane is beautiful with a dark face. Thus, he is driven back to the West. There he finds Herzeloyde, the young widow, whose hand he wins in a great tournament and with it the crowns of Wales and Norgal. The other soul speaks in his chest, speaking of inwardness. This strives towards the path to the depths of the heart.

But again, he cannot be held at home. A message from Baruc of Baghdad, asking for his help, drives him to the Orient, still before the expected son has been born. Gamuret falls in battle by the poisoned spear of a deceitful heathen. News of his death is brought to Herzeloyde by Gamuret's master-page. She receives the message two weeks before she gives birth to a boy. He is the 'flower of knighthood'.

Parzival enters existence already as 'son of the widow'. When Herzeloyde carries out her maternal duty, she always thought in reverence of another mother:

> 'The Queen of Heaven,' this her thought,
> 'Nursed Jesus, who in time was brought
> To the cross and a bitter death
> In human form, and his last breath
> He breathed for us, thereby to prove
> His true devotion, ...'

The young boy grows up surrounded by such thoughts and feelings. The mother relinquishes her kingdoms; in deep mourning she withdraws with a few faithful followers into the wilderness of Soltane, to dedicate herself completely to educating her son. She forbids all her servants ever to tell him anything of knighthood. He is to grow up without any regal finery; he is only allowed to shoot with a bow and arrow. The hunting instinct drives him repeatedly into the forest. The little birds whose sweet song moves his heart to tears, he shoots with his arrows. But when he hit them, he cries aloud and pulls his hair. Forces of compassion wake in his soul completely overcoming him.

This causes the mother to speak with him about the nature of God, Whose praise the birds are singing. When Parzival hears this name for the first time from the lips of his mother:

> 'Who is this God now?' asked the boy.
> 'My son, I'll tell you truth, without alloy;
> He shines more brightly than the sun,
> He who our human shape once won.'

The light-nature of the divine is the first thing she want to covey to him; moreover, this God Who is of purest light has out of pure grace become a human being wanting to unite with our destiny. His being is faithfulness. But she also speaks of God's adversary, 'the host of hell'. He is black; his being is unfaithfulness. Man is placed between light and darkness.

This is the essence of religious instructions perceived by Parzival during his childhood. Clearly Manicheism shines through. This teaching, epitomizing Persian culture, sees the world as the great struggle between light and darkness. To the early Zarathustrian tradition, however, Mani added the teaching of the great Sun-sacrifice, the devotion of a sublime being of light facing the darkness. Through this he 'Christened' the worldview of the Persians. From the third century onwards, this cosmically attuned Christianity fructified the Oriental cultures and extended its influence into the West, before it was suppressed by Rome in the most relentless manner. It continued to live in the Cathar community right into the Middle Ages.

Only now do we understand the opening verses of the poetic work. Wolfram begins with the Parable of the Black and White Magpie. With this, he wants to present the person torn between light and darkness. He is in the condition of division and doubt. This clash of opposites endangers the soul's eternal salvation. Yet whoever goes through such challenges with 'unwavering manly courage', may nevertheless live in hope when he has to pass from this world. It only depends on his keeping the '*Staete*'—steadfastness, keeping true to himself even in doubt. Whoever tend towards '*Unstaete*'—unsteadiness, characterless ['lukewarm' , Rev. 3:16], chooses the black colour. Their eternal being will succumb to the darkness. Whoever fosters steadfastness in the spirit will hold to the colour white.

Gamuret is someone who exemplifies the Parable of the Magpie. His soul was pulled hither and thither between two worlds. His marriage with Belacane, the black woman, and with Herzeloyde, the white woman, shows the division in his nature. But in his deepest strivings he was not faithless. At all times he remained a true knight, since in each situation he was ready to engage as a whole personality. Parzival inherits this from his father, moreover, he masters the division. This is clearly expressed in those moments when he feels caught in the deepest struggles of the soul. He certainly lives in situations of doubt. But just in this situation the hero appears; he rides towards the strife, clad in bright, white armour of iron, not as the Red Knight, but now as the White Knight. For even in doubt, he is able to keep steadfast.

This is not an ideal of the Church, for doubt makes the soul lose eternal salvation. However, it is a modern ideal; it is a stage that cannot be renounced for a true seeker of the Grail. Wolfram knows three stages through which his Parzival is led—foolishness, doubt, and certainty.

In foolishness he storms out to experience life. But in this foolishness there still lives a security of instinct he can trust. Led by the forces of the blood, which are dull yet pure, he progresses as the 'Red Knight'.

Yet he would not awaken to his earthly task had he not been shocked out of this being bound to his instincts. At that moment the world, as it had hitherto appeared to him, shakes to its foundation. His faith is shaken, doubt flashes through his soul. It is Wolfram's aim to show us how such an individuality can free himself out of the clutches of the power of doubt. How this individuality matures towards certainty—to the heart's certainty in the spirit, to divine blessedness. These are the stages of the path to the Grail.

His raising through Herzeloyde

In presenting the youthful experience of his protagonist, Wolfram's poem mainly follows the places we know from Chrétien's *Perceval*. Only here, everything is concretely described; colourful personalities appear in the place of Imaginative figures. The lady in the tent, whom Parzival surprises in her slumber and from whom he steals a kiss and a ring, is called Jeschute. Her husband, who suspects her of unfaithfulness and mistreats her abominably, is Duke Orilus. The maiden with the dead knight on her lap is his cousin Sigune with Schionatulander, who as we shall see, are deeply woven into the destiny-tapestry of the Grail seeker. Sigune knows him from his early childhood; early orphaned, she was reared by Herzeloyde in place of her own child. Consequently, she can tell him his name, which he did not know himself. At home, so he tells her, all the people only called him '*bon fils, cher fils, beau fils*'. With this, she recognizes him.

It is her task to lead him towards self-recognition. By telling him his name, explaining its deeper meaning, she is also the first he meets again in the morning after his visit to the Grail Castle. From her he hears where he had been the previous night, what the Grail and the Grail dynasty is about, to which she also belongs, and what he failed to do there. 'You didn't forget to ask the question?' But he answers, 'I did not ask.' Aghast, she turns away from him, for he is a marked man, laden with a curse, who in Munsalvaesche loses his knighthood and honour. Yet she will meet him again [a third time], under quite different circumstances, after many years of travel, shortly before his aim—as it were, at the border of the realm of the Grail, comforting him since meanwhile her anger has left her, and she feels pity for his deep suffering undergone for the Grail.

How does he find her now? In the figure of a anchorite, whom he meets in a newly-erected hut on the edge of the forest, completely given to prayer, from which she is startled by the stranger riding past her little window. She faithfully stayed here, at the coffin of her eternally beloved. Renouncing the world, she lives solely from the nourishment of the Grail. She tells her guest how every Saturday, Kundrie as the messenger of the Grail comes during the night to bring her food and drink for the following week. What Parzival initially finds strange with the recluse, is that she wears a ring. But she explains to him, if before God thoughts are equal to deeds, then she may feel married to the one so early taken from her.

> 'I am a virgin, yet every breath,
> Though I am unwed, cries that he
> Is my spouse before God ...'

Schionatulander suffered death for her and also for Parzival. For Orilus was his enemy, because he protected Parzival's inherited lands, defending them against anyone who wanted to take them. Moreover, there is another misfortune. In 'Titurel', that unfinished poetic work of Wolfram, the bond of love between Sigune and Schionatulander is most tenderly described. Signune demands of her chosen one a knightly deed, as this is the custom of Minne-love. A hunting dog, a Braque who had escaped his master, one day jumps into the tent of the two lovers. They discovered on the long leash, made with precious, colourful ribbons, a mysterious writing, beginning at the collar and continuing on the leash. It is a love letter that a noble woman had embroidered with beads of the most glorious precious stones. The name of the dog was Gardevias! ('Guardian of the Trail!'). In what is called the 'Younger Titurel',[31] the words of this letter are: 'Guardian of the Trail towards the Love of God. This is a command above all commands. Consequently,

[31] https://www.loc.gov/resource/gdcwdl.wdl_14681/?sp=2&st=gallery/

guard the trail so that you achieve the heavenly crown …' There now follow rules of courtly love, repeatedly interrupted by the admonition, 'Guard the Trail!' A path of the soul, drawn from the wisdom of the Troubadours is shown here. After a sequence of advice for life, there follows the graded path through twelve virtues, which are to be won on this path. They are like blooms that will be woven into a wreath. Patience is the eleventh flower; the twelfth is 'Minne', courtly love. 'Minne' is consequently more than a natural inclination of love, not to mention a passion that overcomes human beings. It stands at the end of a long path of purification. It is 'the flower that leads you towards the song of the angels'. For it opens wide the gates to the spiritual world.

Sigune and the leash called 'Brackenseil'

Wolfram now describes in the 'Brackenseil' (in the 'Titurel' fragment), how the dog runs off before Sigune can read the writing. She does not give up. The beloved is to return the dog to her. Until then, she will not give her hand in marriage. During this chase after the dog, after many confusions, it comes to a dispute with Duke Orilus, who meanwhile had gained the dog. Schionatulander is tragically slain by the duke. Parzival now enters this situation, when during that morning coming from the Grail Castle he encounters the maiden with her dead bridegroom in her lap. This destiny becomes interwoven with his—Gardevias! Like a continuous admonishing call from the realm of the dead, it mysteriously accompanies him on his life's path. That which Schionatulander sought with all the forces of his heart and for which he died, the path of stages towards the highest love—Parzival has to achieve. He, as it were, continues the search which had been commenced by Schionatulander. He never leaves the trail, however far the Grail still seems to him. Gardevias— the penultimate stage is patience. This brings him to the border of the Grail country.

Poetically, Sigune's destiny is completed. Wolfram narrates how Parzifal, after being made the Grail King, rides past the hut in which he once had found the mourning maiden. With his companions, he now meets her dead on her knees before the coffin of the eternal bridegroom. Parzival has the stone lid raised, finding in it the uncorrupted corpse of the bright Schionatulander. They place the virtuous maid with him in the same coffin, so that the lovers are also united in death.

The poetic work 'Later Titurel' adds that from the grave of those united in death, from both mouths, two vines grew intwined into high stems, ever green, never to be destroyed by frost and winter.

The vine is the parable of human nature, which can purify earthly forces into noble blood. Holy love that could conquer death knows no separation. It can bring about eternal forces. It was founded in the love of Him Who said to His disciples, 'I am the vine, you are the branches' [Jn. 15].

A deep law of destiny is revealed in how earthly suffering of faithful lovers ends at that moment when Parzival completes his path to the Grail. He had found the trail.

Parzival's first stage

Wolfram is a master of psychology. He fashions the Imaginations that delineate the Parzival path into many meetings of destiny. Mature soul-experience in meeting women—especially in the way love begins to bud in the heart, able to unfold into the richest blossom, is unfolded in his account. There is the figure of Liasse, the little daughter of that nobleman by whom the wild boy takes his first refuge and learns the rules of knighthood. Gurnemanz would have very much liked them to become a couple. In the company of this maid, Parzival experienced a youthful crush, but it remains in the bud. It is not the great love opening the whole human being. It is like a soft announcement that love is on the way to take possession of his heart.

What a miracle in delicacy and tenderness is the growth in stages of the great *Minnebund*, league of courtly love, which in the following canto the poet begins to describe. Blanchefleur, the young queen of Belrapeire, becomes here Kondwiramur. More than an Imagination, she is a human being of flesh and blood, radiating with all the virtues of a woman. And yet also an Imagination, as woman should always be for man's experience. When in her white silk shirt, she comes to his bed at night and in her whole helplessness entrusts herself to him—what daring poetic writing! The poet could only succeed out of a deep purity of heart, without in some way damaging virtue. And then, after the youth has fought for the pure one and gains the victory, the highest celebration of love—slowly blossoming out of innocence.

In Wolfram's epic, the life-bond Parzival enters is founded on the unerring faith of two hearts. Despite Parzival's short enjoyment of marriage, he has to ride into the world again, initially driven by concern for his mother's uncertain fate. After the maturing of this lover has been revealed, the more shocking is his complete failure towards the plight of the Grail.

Then there is the knightly concern for the suffering of Jeschute, the wife of Duke Orilus, who because of his youthful folly has now to bear shame. On a miserable mare, she has to ride in rags behind her proud husband, who despite her protestation of innocence does not want to believe her. Here Parzival has to make amends, but it has to take place in battle. For the honour of that woman, he takes up combat with the most feared Orilus. He conquers him, yet he is generous. For 'clemency' is the third flower in the wreath of virtues on the path of courtly love. Discipline and chastity, which he has already gained, are the two preceding virtues. This clemency Parzival has already practised with his enemies at Belrapeire; King Clamide and [Kingrun] his Seneschal, whom he overcame in the battle of life and death, he sent to King Arthur as an honourable prisoner. He does the same with Duke Orilus.

At the court of Arthur lives Kunneware; those who are conquered are sent to her for service. This noble maiden was in a certain sense the first soul who had recognized Parzival's mission, when he appeared in the fool's dress before Arthur's Round Table. At that time Kunneware had smiled at him with a loving, sweet mouth. This meant a lot, for she had made an oath never to smile until she sees the man who will gain the highest prize of all knighthood. When, with the appearance of the strange youth, she smiles, Keye, the Seneschal of the court, reprimands her before all eyes with his staff. For to him it seemed unworthy and completely unreasonable to give such an honour to this wild boy. But Parzival swore to revenge this insult. His first knightly deeds, consequently, he carries out all in honour of that lady. Kunneware is the first beautiful soul who believes in him and has to suffer for this belief. For him it is an obligation.

In the meantime, King Arthur had heard of the rising fame of the young hero, and he does not settle until he had received him in his Round Table as comrade. With his whole camp he sets out from Carduel, to seek the 'Red Knight'. They set up camp near the River Plimizoel. They are surprised by an unseasonal cold spell; thick snow falls overnight so that in the morning all paths are covered in white. Parzival allows his horse to find his own way to drift through the wood. Suddenly a falcon shoots out from the trees, to attack a group of wild geese. He hits one of them, who just escapes him, and flying upwards lets three drops of blood fall from its wound. Parzival sees the drops of blood glowing in the snow. In his soul there arises the picture of Kondwiramur. Her countenance shone with such purity penetrated by a red hue. Completely conquered by the power of love, the hero loses himself in contemplating drops of blood in the snow. The world around him disappears. A page sent out to reconoitre, discovering the strange knight with spear raised for battle, rides back immediately in alarm. For the Round Table will be disgraced if an intruder dares to enter its realm without receiving punishment. Segramors, greedy for battle, puts on his weapons and storms out to meet the enemy knight. But he remains as if asleep on the same spot. Segramors challenges him, but the other does not seem to hear him, until finally his horse, incited for battle, turns around. Through this, the hero's senses are momentarily released from the picture holding them in their grip. He lowers his lance and confronts the battle. But after the first clash he already unseats the attacker. The horse trots home without his rider, and the conquered one has shamefully to walk after it. But Parzival meanwhile turns back to the spot that conjured before his soul the picture of his beloved. The second knight fares even worse. It is the Seneschal Sir Keye, who mockingly challenges the dreaming one to a duel. With a broken arm and leg, he has to be carried from the battle ground. Now Kunneware's shame is completely atoned.

But now Gawain steps into action, the flower of knighthood. Without weapons he hastens out and rides close to the enchanted knight, who does not even respond to his friendly greeting. Then the thought comes to him, who knew the power of love as only one can know it.

> 'What if Love oppresses this man,
> As she did me,' was Gawain's thought,
> 'And his faithful heart, once caught,
> Has had to yield to her?'

He takes a fine silken cloth and covers the drops of blood in the snow. Then Parzival awakens. He certainly complains that the presence of the beloved had been taken from him, whose love, crown and country he had won in battle. Gawain gently leads him back to reality and invites him to the court of King Arthur. It is like a triumphal moment in his young life. He is received full of goodwill. The poet says he appears in his prime:

> Young Parzival, but for the wings,
> Seemed an angel midst earthly things.

What has happened? Gawain had offered him a great service, which was to establish a deep destined relationship between the two. It is not advisable to fight the magic of love. One must help the enchanted one to direct the gaze towards other things. In this way, being released from the enchantment, they are gently led back to the demands of the world.

The motif of drops of blood in the snow is not unknown in the world of fairy tales. Snow White and the Low German fairy tale of the '*Machandelboom*', 'The Juniper Tree'[32] begin in such a manner. With this picture the heavenly child announces itself to the expecting mother. The time of the growing hope begins. When the child is born, the mother dies of joy; the child grows up to describe a path of suffering (*Passionsweg*) leading through death to resurrection.

It is clearly a Christian Mystery that is sketched in pictorial sequence. With the Imagination of drops of blood in the snow, the soul begins the mystical path. In the depths of its being, it experiences the awakening of innocent forces of love. Thus, the fairy tale of Snow White contains the mystery of Blanchefleur.[33]

With the appearance of this Imagination, the spiritual path of development begins for Parzival. Mystical soul-forces are announced in pictures; they seek to draw him towards a path of inner meditative life. He rejects with elemental force everything from the outer world seeking to disturb him, wanting to pull him away from this powerful experience. 'Guardian of the Trail'—the trail that can point towards the Grail shines before his inner vision. But the seeker for the Grail would have to use his balance of soul if he only wanted to sink mystically into himself without awareness of the demands around him. Here Gawain proves to be a true friend. Instead to increasing mysticism, he helps the youth with understanding to find the healthy connection to social life, to become initially a 'contemporary'. Even the holiest feelings, if pursued one-sidedly, make one unfree. Gawain frees him from the compulsion of love. (13)

Meeting Cundrie

There opens for Parzival a brilliant field of activities. He becomes part of the Round Table, of the noblest knighthood. Will he be steered towards fame and the highest honours that the age can offer?

---

[32] The brothers Grimm, also translated as 'The Almond Tree', No. 47.

[33] In both fairy tales, the presentation of a mystical soul-path in a pictorial sequence, can be found in Rudolf Meyer, *The Wisdom of Fairy Tales*, Floris Books, Edinburgh 1995. [Meyer was inspired to study fairy tales by the example of Prof. Hermann Beckh, whose exposition 'Snow White' remains exemplary. See Hermann Beckh, *Collected Articles 1922–1938*, TL, Forest Row 2023, 118–30; also in *Alchymy*, TL, Forest Row 2019, 114–26. Beckh writes to Rudolf Steiner about this and other fairy tales, in *Hermann Beckh A Celebration*. TL 2025, 86–108.]

But the Grail is unrelenting. It makes demands of those belonging to it. Wildly riding, Kundrie la Surzière (that is, Cundrie the Sorceress) bursts into the midst of the festive gathering. She rides a dun-coloured mule, whose harness is preciously adorned, a being from whom all noble femininity is lacking; she even bears some animal characteristics. Her black hair appears like a boar's bristles, her nose like a dog, hog-like teeth protrude from her mouth; her ears are like a bear's, her hands covered with monkey's fur leading into lion's claws. Nevertheless, she is skilled in all foreign languages and experienced in such subjects as dialectic, geometry and astronomy. Of such a dual nature is the messenger of the Grail.

Her message is a diatribe. In her accusation she dismisses all honour and fame from the Round Table, since in their midst they harbour a Parzival. Then turning to him, she curses him who had sat with the Fisherman, seeing his suffering yet feeling no pity for him. It was hardness of heart that made him fail to question. There, silence was a sin. He who in such a way avoids the calling to the Grail has no honour.

Breaking out into tears, wringing her hands in pain, she rides off without any farewell. The poet is of the opinion that it is only her great faith that drives her to such events. Repeatedly looking back, she calls out, wailing,

> 'Ah Munsalvaesche, deep well of woe!
> Alas, that none doth solace you now!'

Wolfram's deep knowledge of the Mysteries of the inner path is revealed in the way he introduces this figure. Rudolf Steiner called him 'someone thoroughly initiated'.[34] What he described in *Knowledge of the Higher Worlds: How is it Attained?* (GA 10) about meeting the Guardian of the Threshold (initially the 'Lesser Guardian') provides a key to understand the Grail Messenger.

The spirit-seeker experiences a meeting of the self at the threshold to supersensory life. Out of the soul-depths, a figure emerges before the soul's vision, condensing the untransformed part of the human being. That part disregarded during the spiritualization of the striving human soul was indeed pushed back into hidden depths. Parzival had just then appeared to those gathered at the Round Table as an angel incarnate. But sanctity gained all too quickly often proves to be an illusion.

---

[34] See 'Reading the Akashic Records: Wolfram von Eschenbach', Berlin, 1 July 1904, GA 92.

True self-knowledge shows that one cannot skip over the stages of human becoming without consequences. It leads through the natural unfolding of inclinations and talents, as it can only be achieved in a constant involvement in all the widths and depths of earthly life.

Such self-recognition, however, produces deepest pain in the soul. It seems initially to want to destroy the human being's sense of existence, for it shows the unworthiness of all outer successes and recognition by the world. It wants to call him to be faithful to his deepest self. Wolfram says,

> 'Cundrie la Surziere, you'll allow,
> Has mortified the man. What aid
> Could a heart, as yet unafraid,
> And nobility, yet deliver there?
> And yet, regarding this affair,
> He has not lost his sense of shame;
> It may yet retrieve his good name,
> And reigns supreme o'er all his way.'

That which in normal life hides from the soul's view the figure of the Guardian is shame. What covers the self, one can call healthy instinct. The striving human being initially needs a certain still naïve feeling for the self, which can come out of a self-evaluation within the life of moral-religious tradition. Arthur's circle, with its intensified concept of honour, fostered in a special way this evaluation of personality, although it was very limited by its time with its social positions. Yet to enter the light of the spiritual world means to go beyond all evaluation measurements that the 'I' has gained from continuous reflection on the surrounding world. The soul must take courage to feel ashamed, right into the deepest grounds. The poet, consequently, has to present this experience as an exposure of the hero before the entire social circle.

Cundrie has hardly disappeared than another messenger rushes into the circle of the Round Table. Now Gawain receives an attack. An unknown knight, later revealed as Kingrimursel, brings a terrible charge levied against Gawain of assassinating his lord and king. Such a culprit would dishonour the whole Round Table. If Gawain, however, would deny this accusation, he would have to present himself within forty days to a battle of atonement. Mysteriously, the whole accusation later turns out to be erroneous. But it is Gawain's destiny to suffer under the slander. He has to learn to bear misjudgement, in order clearly to ground his 'I' in himself.

For every spiritual seeker, the meeting at the threshold appears in an individual guise. The reason why Cundrie bears these decisive traits of being—she will appear to Parzival at the end of his trial in a magnificent transformation—can only become clear out of the course of events. The two heroes recognize, at least for the time being, they may no longer stay in the circle of the Round Table. In such a situation, how little the comfort of well-meaning friends means is known to Parzival. 'A strict judgement has come down on me,' he confesses, and at the same moment he feels it would be pointless to try to justify himself here. With this is shown the deep modesty of his consciousness he has achieved. He has objectively failed, although without knowing it.

> 'I cannot show my wealth of pain,
> Where many, ignorant of my woes
> Treat me ill and mock my throes.
> I shall ne'er feel sound and hale,
> Nor know joy, till I see the Grail,
> Whether that sight be soon or late.
> My thoughts directed there, by fate,
> Naught shall keep me from it ever.'

What is his personal suffering? Compared to Anfortas' suffering his own pales.

> 'What help Anfortas, did I provide,
> By sitting, mute there, at your side?'

The matter here is the plight of the Grail. And yet, when Gawain offers his ongoing help for the difficult part of his destiny that now begins, and pleads to God that He may grant this, Parzival flares up:

> 'What then is God?' the knight replied.
> 'Were He all-powerful, at our side
> Working here, with His great might,
> He'd not have brought us thus to shame.'

Parzival quits his service; he cannot recognize a God Who brings the striving human being into such a situation. 'If He is angered, that will I bear.'

In complete doubt concerning God—today we would say, as an atheist—Parzival sets off to seek the Grail. It may be a contradiction, but life knows such contradictions.

7. Gawain's soul-path

Mysteries of the calendar

At the moment of highest tension, the hero of adventure disappears from our view. The poet thinks that it is not good always to present one's hero receiving the highest praise; one also needs how to present others without jealousy. Consequently, the story turns to Gawain's paths. Two extensive cantos glorify his deeds. Book 9 follows, the famous Good Friday instructions to Parzival that contain the Mysteries of the Grail. Once more, however, although we know the Grail seeker is close to his goal, the action passes once more to Gawain. Four further chapters are completely dedicated to him. Only the one that follows, which we count as Book 14, shows how the path of destiny of the two heroes meet, before the two final books in which Parzival is taken to the heights of life and becomes honoured as the Grail King.

Literary research is of the opinion today that Wolfram published the first six books around 1265, as it were, the first part of his work. The second part forms the actual Grail search, which begins with meeting the Grail messenger. Wolfram was only able to write about this in the ensuing years.

A decisive change can indeed be felt after Book 6; year after year goes by, before Parzival again becomes the hero of the adventure. Chrétien speaks of five years. Wolfram draws attention to the calendar calculation. On that Good Friday morning, when Parzival meets the hermit and is led by him into his hermitage, he once again recognizes the altar with the reliquary on which he had laid his hand to confess his innocence concerning Orilus. But this was in the morning after the visit to the Grail Castle. He had then met Duke Orilus, who in his rage had forced Jeschute to ride behind him in a lamentable outfit of rags. It came to a duel, and Parzival after his victory attempted to atone for the matter regarding the duke and his wife. Consequently, he made the sacred oath at the altar that between Jeschute and himself nothing had happened when he had surprised her in her tent. At that time, a painted spear stood at the altar. This he took—because on this morning he was distracted—and with it carried out many knightly deeds. But when did all this happen?

Trevrizent recalls the exact day when the colourful spear belonging to the 'wild Taurian' had been lost. With his Psalter containing a calendar, he works out when it must have happened 'five and a half years[35] and three days ago'. Only now does Parzival understand how long he had wandered without direction. According to sound spiritual tradition, April 3rd was the death-day of Christ; Wolfram shows especially in this Good Friday conversation between Trevrizent and Parzival that he stands within the best Christian traditions. Reckoning back from 3 April four and a half years and three days, one arrives at 30 September. Consequently, the entry into the Grail Caste must have taken place on the evening of 29 September. This means, the poet wants to tell us it was at a Festival of Michael [the Archangel]. Michaelic forces wanted to enter the depths of the young man's soul. It is a knightly Christianity to which Parzival felt called.

On the evening of that Michaelmas Day, when he was allowed to participate as a guest at the Grail meal, he had to see the spear dripping with blood carried past him. The drives working in the blood are presented in this Imagination before the soul's gaze. The next morning, he takes up the 'painted spear'. But it is not the day-awake human being; it is the dreamer in him takes up the spear with which shortly afterwards he unseated two Arthurian knights when standing at the edge of the forest, enchanted by the drops of blood in the snow. A young, impetuous force, a Michaelic will has entered his action. Although it is the gift of the 'wild Taurian', it was received from the sphere of the altar. This is the magnificence of this painted spear. Even if it still bears the colour of passion, nevertheless it is grasped in a moment of sacred self-knowledge. In it is mirrored the Mystery of the spear that is attempting to reach the dreamer in his nocturnal experience of the Grail.

The young Parzival seeks to establish himself in battling, confronting the world. After Cundrie's accusation has jolted him out of the circle of the Round Table, he swears from now on never to remain in one place longer than one night, before he finds out how the Grail and its Mysteries are faring. Fully conscious, he now enters the path of 'homelessness'. On this path he will not avoid any battle; each meeting with a knight will challenge him to measure his strength.

---

35 Meyer, who cited Chrétien a paragraph before, here writes 'five and a half', and a few lines later 'four and a half'. The readily available translators write '*viereinhalb*', Dieter Peschel, Bd. 9. 460. 22. Translators in English: Jesse Weston, A.S. Kline, Helen M. Mustard & Charles E. Passage, translate 'four years and a half'. A.S. Kline concludes his translation with a helpful 'Note on the Chronology of Parzival', pp. 707–11—*Trans.*

Apparently, this does not involve outer battles, at least not always. For where the Grail's sword is wielded it concerns spiritual challenges. The poet relates that Parzival crossed many lands by ship or on horse; with his spear he unseated any fighter who met him:

> He tipped the scales for his foe;
> For his fame rose as theirs fell low.

Then it is told how the Grail sword given him by Anfortas broke in withstanding the battles. Yet through magical power it was subsequently renewed at the will at Karnant, still gaining for him many prizes. Parzival is to achieve spiritual knighthood. He does not ride for national causes; it is a cosmopolitan attitude that meets us from this Grail search. Grail seekers were 'good Europeans', and their interest went beyond this Continent. (The account adds that Parzival also travelled by ship.) As we shall see, only with meeting the Orient can the Grail search be completed.

Nevertheless, the paths of Parzival are shrouded by the poet. Gawain moves into the foreground. But in the background, something takes place at the same time, whence the 'Red Knight' appears from time to time and—hardly graspable—quickly withdraws again. With this it becomes clear that the spiritual path that Parzival has to tread was at that time to be kept on the esoteric level.

Gawain's relationship to the Grail's path

Gawain's adventures are already related in the poetic work of Chrétien. There one experiences them even more as an interruption of Perceval's Grail search. Nevertheless, we do not know in which way they would have been woven into the whole of this work, since it has remained fragmentary. In any case, when in Avalon (with Wolfram, Askalon) after a heroic battle Gawain finds himself delivered into the hands of those who have betrayed the rule of hospitality; to make this good he is set free, yet under the condition that he 'goes to search for the lance, whose iron tip always bleeds, yet never so clean that at least one drop of blood is on it'. If he does not find it within one year, he will have to return as a prisoner to the tower. He makes a vow that he will put his whole strength to search for the bleeding lance.

After this, it seems that Gawain is to take over one part of the Grail tasks that Perceval failed to accomplish. With the first writer to continue Chrétien's poem, Gawain indeed enters the Grail Castle. He is allowed to take nourishment from the Grail and even places the correct

Grail question. Then the king imparts to him that the bleeding lance is the same with which the Crucified received the wound in His side. Now it will bleed until the Last Judgement. Here we see the motif of the lance connected for the first time with the Good Friday Mystery, similar to the chalice with which Joseph collected the blood of the Redeemer. But during the narration Gawain falls asleep and the king gives up telling him. Next morning the hero awakes, finding himself on the beach—but the castle has disappeared.

Wolfram does not describe this event, yet Gawain is commanded by Vergulacht, King of Ascalon, to seek the Grail within a year. Only through this can he retain his life, which in the eyes of Vergulacht he had forfeited. Here one consequently sees how the first law of guilt and atonement can be creatively interpreted by a person deciding to take the path to the spirit. The wisdom of the Grail wants to tell us that through this something positive is achieved, something that can be cast onto the scales where it is necessary to satisfy world justice. Initiatives exist that lead out of the prison of guilt, of human entanglements. Where human beings begin to pursue spiritual paths, old demands are resolved that the one person holds against another. Destinies strive to rearrange themselves. Gawain is repeatedly to experience this in his life of battles. Where people begin to seek the Grail, it always works as a transformative power between people. In its light the matters between them melt away magnificently. The greatest festival of atonement consequently stands at the end of all these paths and diversions.

This deep mystery of destiny is not expressed as an idea. Wolfram fashions Gawain's destiny in lively pictures, leading him through trials and tests. People became used to speaking of 'Gawain's episode'. But if one pays attention how lovingly these adventures are depicted and how they relate according to a deep lawfulness with the paths and aims of Parzival, one will value them completely differently. They reveal hidden laws of destiny, which were to be felt by the souls for whom the time had not yet come that they could be presented to the world in a rational manner.

Unlike Parzival, Gawain does not pursue the path to the spirit; his striving corresponds to a soul-path. His task is to purify and intensify his soul. In this already a Grail impulse is at work, although not one that leads into the heights and widths of knowledge. The poet expresses this by repeatedly mentioning Gawain riding on a horse of the Grail. He had received Gringuljet 'with the red ears' as a gift of friendship from Duke Orilus, who had obtained it indirectly. Without this warhorse he would never have accomplished his path, especially the leap over the 'Perilous Gorge'; he would have almost drowned in the rushing waters. This leap over the abyss was to have been the last and decisive deed that gained for him the wreath of virtues from the tree of Gramoflanz, and through it he achieved the aim of his striving for love, the grace of the beloved Orgeluse.

What does it mean, to ride a horse of the Grail? It means in one's depths of soul to be allowed to follow a spiritual leadership that guides the seeker on the trail to the spirit, even if it is only initially possible in an instinctive manner. This horse has 'red ears'—it is the voice of the blood to which it inwardly hears. For it is the power of love, which is Gawain's leader on all his paths. It drives him into danger and humiliation, but it also leads him on with unconquerable courage, which allows him to walk upright through any trial of the heart and plight of death.

> 'To aid a man against Love's pain,
> Well, I'm so fond of Lord Gawain,
> I'd help him and forego the pay.
> When all's said, no shame this day
> Is his that he is chained by Love,
> Love, that all defence doth prove
> In vain.'

And yet for him it becomes the grace of an initiation into life. For after suffering into the last depths, it leads towards the transfiguration of the heart.

Female figures around Gawain

For the poet to bring this soul-path into an intimate experience, he had to weave several female figures into the destiny of Gawain. Here Wolfram proves to be a true artist of the heart. Certainly, the poet had already found in Chrétien's presentation the three most important figures who make an impact upon Gawain's destiny. But how much soul-experience had to be condensed into poetry to give these female beings flesh and blood!

First there is the moving presence of Obilot, a girl around ten years old, who with her mother and sister in their castle are surrounded by enemies. Looking down she sees the train of Gawain's riders at the walls of the stronghold. The older sister believes he is a salesman come to sell some weapons. But Obilot immediately recognizes the knight in him. Despite all the ridicule she has to bear from her sister, she is determined to choose him as *her* knight. And Gawain, who is able to hear this conversation from the castle—although he is just on the way to Ascalon where he is to re-establish his honour in a duel—is driven to become involved in the battle occurring here. For how could he disappoint the young, sweet Obilot—she, who believes in him, while he has been banned from Arthur's circle and has to follow his path in shame? He, the proud one, used to fame, is now looked upon just about as a salesman. But a *child* sees in him the knight and at the same time the saviour! And now coming to him and bashfully confirming that he is the very first man with whom she has spoken, how she so movingly speaks of her love and how she entreats him by this sacred love to come to her father's side in his greatest need—here Gawain is already drawn into this adventure. Still unsure, since he had given his word of honour as a token, whether to offer himself in battle to the king of Ascalon within fourteen days, he had to think of Parzival's farewell words:

> 'My friend, when battle you prepare,
> Let a woman work for you instead,
> And by her guiding hand be led.
> Let the love of one, whom you know
> To be virtuous and modest, show
> The way, and so watch over you.'

Words of innermost inclination of the heart are exchanged between Gawain and the little girl, as if they want to exchange their souls. The hero goes along with the love ideals of the little girl, which are not yet confused and weakened by any life-experience. The romanticism of a first love speaks out of these words.

> 'Let my sword be in your fair hand,
> And if any would joust, understand,
> You must attack them, forge ahead,
> And fight them bravely in my stead.
> The folk will see me fighting there,
> But 'tis you who'll order the affair.'

With a language increased into highest belief and courage, love gives him wings to battle. As a sign in whose service and whose protection he knows himself, he needs a token of his beloved. Thus, she sends him the right sleeve of her precious garment, which he fastens onto his shield. Adorned with this talisman, he leads the host of those besieged towards victory.

True love (*Minne*) is a mystical fact. It is the penetration of one's own soul with the radiant archetype of another; it is the calling in of heavenly forces of this other soul into the presence of wrestling and struggling; an acting out of love's full power.

We see later how Parzival in highest need calls the name of Kondwiramur, to effect the final decision that brings him to the threshold of his Grail kingdom. But here it is Gawain who is encouraged by a child towards a renewed knighthood. A rejuvenation of his being takes place. The one who was unjustly accused and shamed begins to be penetrated with the forces of innocence.

And now the second meeting of souls—Antikonie, the heroic lover. While Gawain in Schampfanzun, the capital of Ascalon, intending to engage in a duel to cleanse himself from the accusation of assassination, he is invited by King Vergulacht as a guest into the castle of his royal sister, but is then deviously attacked. Hereby, since as a guest weapons are discarded, he would have been defencelessly killed, had not the king's sister, the maid Antikonie, stepped manfully to his side, placing herself with him in the tower room. A wild, desperate battle ensued. But from the moment he beheld the woman who stood for him, Gawain always gained new courage. In this raging storm, he grows so much beyond human stature that he elicits high respect from his opponents, which ultimately leads to a settlement.

Not in vain did Wolfram name this maiden 'Antikonie'. She loves, where she according to the demands of family law should hate; for Gawain is the (assumed) murderer of her royal father. The noblest figure of Greek poetry, Antigone, found herself in a similar conflict. Out of the courage of her pure heart, she decided against the law to stand for love, although she had to atone for her deed with death.

Sophocles, pre-empting a Christian element, puts into the mouth of his heroine: 'I am here not to join in hate but join in love.'

Orgeluse and Klingsor's castle

The most significant trial of his knighthood came to Gawain through Orgeluse, the Duchess of Logroys. He was certainly able to prove his innocence in that matter with which he was accused at the Round Table. He also had sought for the Grail throughout the world as was his duty; he fought hard, because—as he believed—'Whoever longs for the Grail can only approach it fighting courageously with spear and sword.' In this way Gawain meets the world counter to the Grail. He has to face the adventures of Schastel Marveile. Cundrie had already mentioned this magic castle at the Round Table. She had challenged him to face these adventures that await the courageous one longing for love (*Minne*). Four queens are imprisoned there with four hundred maidens. In this, too, Schastel Marveile seems to be a counter picture to the Grail Castle, for there Parzival found four hundred knights gathered for the meal. But whereas in Anfortas and the ancient Grail King, Titurel, he meets his own relatives, although at first not knowingly, Gawain, when accomplishing the adventures at the magic castle, finds this in the imprisoned queens. They are Sangive, his mother, Arnive, his grandmother, who at the same time is mother of Sangive and Arthur, also Gawain's sister, Itonje, and Cundrie (not the Grail messenger). It is curious that initially he does not recognize his relatives; they, too, do not recognize him. This can only be explained by understanding it does not concern meetings in the sensory world. Gawain has entered a magical dream sphere; astral imaginations meet him. His maternal inheritance he finds again in his own soul, enchanted. The masculine element is a picture of spiritual forces—this Parzival beholds in the Grail Castle; the feminine element pictures the soul-forces. The latter have become enchanted for him, but not only his own soul-forces. It is the destiny of the times that the soul-forces appear as if imprisoned. The way the poet describes how in this magic castle they all do not know each other, that is, they vegetate in an isolated existence, is characteristic for that condition into which human development strives with increasing strength the more the soul succumbs to the magic spell of sensuality. They can only lead a shadowy existence imprisoned in their own bodily nature. Whoever knows how to break this spell also paves for many other souls the path to freedom. Gawain is a fighter for the awakening of the soul.

How does this occur? It is indicated in a picture. When Gawain had made himself the lord over the realm of Schastel Marveile and the hour of release for all who inhabit the castle has come, out of the 'rich stuff' that fell to him, he chooses a harp. This he gives to the daughter of that ferryman who in the night before the adventure had hosted him so kindly and given him an initial explanation concerning the magic castle. The name of the humble maid is Bene, who serves him in selfless love while his search for courtly love was for the proud Orgeluse. Bene deserves his first gift. Wolfram remarks that this precious harp still during his time was well-known in England under the name 'The

Swallow'. In the song entrusted to the simple soul of the people, what had been achieved through Gawain's victory will be carried on—free as the swallow. Through the art of poetry, this soul-freeing power, during the course of time is witnessed to, awakening in the heart as a counter-force to the evil magic which through Klingsor spreads over the world.

It is Klingsor who had built Schastel Marveile and within it had imprisoned many souls. After the accomplished deed, Gawain has the facts about the evil magician explained to him by Arnive, whom he calls his wise helper. We hear that Klingsor was the Duke of Terra de Labur (near Naples). He gained great fame, while still working in his main town Kapua. But then he fell into disgrace when he went with Iblis, the Queen of Sicily, into an extramarital relationship. Surprised by her husband, who found him in the arms of his wife Iblis in his castle, Kalot-Embolot, he made him a eunuch. From then on, Klingsor had to bear the shame of losing his manhood. A hate against man and woman filled his soul, no longer able to engage in *Minne*, courtly love. He particularly pursued with his hate the people who still honoured virtue. To rob them of joy as much as he could was the greatest pleasure in his heart.

Wolfram describes the soul-condition of a black magician. For it was always the first degree on this dark path, to suck pleasure for oneself out of the destruction of another's joy. Forced denial of sexual love prepares the soul for this. It is a mystery of human development that unnatural asceticism, this, however, means drives not purified but suppressed, can often transform into dark hatred against everything human. Much evil has been conjured up through this connection of Klingsor with Iblis, and his castration. In the town Persida he learned the art of magic and spells. He studied black magic. Klingsor gained power over all evil and good spirits living between the Earth and the firmament, except those who stand under God's protection.

When Wolfram approaches the stronghold Kalot-Embolot, he points to a certain place in S.E. Sicily, Kalta-Bellota. From 827 onwards, the Saracens conquered this island, founding places of Arabic culture. From Sicily great Arabic wisdom shone over the West for centuries, but also everything that killed souls and made hearts thrust thorns against the Christian element. The Normans, who in the following centuries established themselves in Sicily and Southern Italy on their raids, lived in continuous dispute with this Arabic culture, but also in the partial acceptance of it. Consequently, it will not be by chance that Gawain, who from his mother's side comes from the Arthurian dynasty, that is, belonging to the Celts, is the son of King Lot of Norway. The Norman element is a characteristic of his being. With this Nordic stream, a world-courage was manifest, radiating out of an unbroken strength of the heart in confronting the soul-laming intelligence exuding from Arabism that threatened to engulf Europe. Without the continuous curbing of this Arabic, Oriental stream, which in various scientific and cultural realms was far superior to European Christianity, the development of the West would have been accelerated into materialism. All this is mirrored in Gawain's battles around the magic castle of Klingsor.

Arnive now reports that this magician, from his realm of Terra de Labur carried his 'miracles' into other countries. However splendid and soul-enchanting Schastel Marveile, the magic castle he built may be, it is still small compared to his other magic deeds. It concerns a place of this activity that has moved into the northern regions. It is characteristic how Klingsor has come to take possession of this place. The king of this country, Irot, the father of Gramoflanz, offered it to him. He was afraid of Klingsor. To keep peace with him, he laid all his goods at his feet. Klingsor's method is to spread fear around him; through this he lames resistance in the soul. He disarms through fear. Consequently, forces of courage that have to link with knowledge of the situation are the only defence against his magic.

In this realm Gawain has to withstand the utmost tests of courage. His entrance into the magic castle is described in imaginations that mirror a diving into the mysteries of one's own bodily organization. Such an imagination is the '*litmarveil*', the 'Lit Marveile'. He has to enter the magic bed that glides along the chamber's floor, smooth as glass. Gawain succeeds to jump into it.

> ... Dear Lord,
> No such speed could aught afford
> A bed! It crashed from side to side,
> Spared not a wall, as he did ride,
> Hurtling against the stones, until
> The castle echoed to the thrill.
> In this manner, my Lord Gawain
> Rode many a charge, and, again,
> If all the thunder that ever roared
> Were in a room, and all the horde
> Of trumpeters from all ages past
> And the future, from First to Last,

Blowing away to earn their hire,
No greater a din could it inspire.

The magic bed had finally to stop. It comes to rest in the middle, between the walls of the chamber. A process of initiation is described here. The diving into the activity of the formative forces, into the gliding, fluctuating and over-welling life of the ether-organization that works through the physical human being, building it up, is initially an experience of elemental power. It threatens to numb the soul. Only a soul held by the divine can withhold the shock imparted to the inexperienced by the seemingly bottomless, ever-moving nature of the body of formative forces. Through the inner forces of calm, such a person has to gain mastery over these forces.

The battle with the lion is another Imagination. In meeting one's own heart-forces, the mystic learns to know the untamed power of his hidden will-nature. They want to overwhelm his full humanity. After this terrible battle, covered with wounds, the hero sinks down, his senses dulled. His head rests on the lion whom he had overcome. He has gained peace of the heart. A mysterious protection covers him. Without the help of his forebear Arnive, the mother of King Arthur, who has secretly observed the battle, he would be unable to come back to life. She hastens to his aid with medicines. Through the magic power of her ointments, Gawain is healed. She tells him how she was only able to gain these unique medicines through Cundrie's teachings. During her repeated visits, the Grail messenger had taught her the healing art. The ointment, which can lead back to life the one near to death, comes from Munsalvaesche.

When Gawain hears the name of the Grail Castle, he is filled with joy. His senses return. Now strengthened he feels how the Grail is very close to where the soul has to wrestle in danger of death. Only now do we understand why Cundrie, when she voiced her complaint against Parzival, at the end spoke of Schastel Marveile, communicating she had to be there that very same night. What radiates out of the heights of the spirit, has to sink its forces into the depth of the bodily nature, to wrest the soul from the fettering power of material existence. Only when the magic world of the senses begins to recede, do the noblest soul-forces become free. Love is refined from sensory greed. It returns into that purity of heart which beholds God, of which we hear in Christ's Beatitudes [Matt. 5:8]. The heroic act is now raised to the love-feast in Schastel Marveile, since Gawain is finally allowed to unite with Orgeluse.

One only slowly gains orientation in this jungle of Imaginations by seeking to live into Gawain's adventures. They gradually reveal a deep lawfulness, revealing itself ever more strongly the more openly one can give oneself initially to the pure human feeling in the poetic situations. One has to be able to wait until a gradual path of soul-transformation begins to be revealed. Gawain was able to gain riches of the heart on his life's pilgrimage before he was allowed to behold purest beauty. Thus, one day before his gaze Logroys arises, the high castle, artfully built, that winds around the mountain ascending to the pinnacle. It is impregnable to onslaught. In the same way is its lady, the proud Orgeluse, whose distain Gawain very soon experiences.

A sudden vegetation spreads out around the mountains—fig trees, pomegranates, olive trees and wines grow in abundance. But amid this miraculous world, 'the most beautiful flower of nature' appearing at the rock spring, Orgeluse of Logroys.

> But for Kondwiramur, no fairer
> Woman was born in this world ever

the poet exclaims here. We divine that she will be for Gawain the aim of all love's longing, as Kondwiramur became for Parzival. But how different everything is here compared to what Parzival found in Belrapeire! The beautiful lady disdainfully answers Gawain's first veneration. Here no heart is taken by storm. Orgeluse is beyond any sentimentality. Her rejection goes so far that she would deign to touch the harness of a horse, as in one situation she has to do, only at that place where his hand had not yet touched. Her coldness of feeling goes so far that she despises Gawain, as if he were a physician selling salves when she sees him digging out a root with which he wants to help a wounded knight he had met on his way. This contradicted the knightly ideal; again, Gawain has fallen under suspicion of being a salesman. Undeterred, however, he bears the ridicule; he is not swayed from his will to heal.

Gawain is no conventional knight. He has learned to alleviate the suffering of others. He is on the way to become a helper of humanity. However, in this case Orgeluse was right. For when Gawain returns to the ailing knight and binds the root onto his wound, the knight begs him to help him to the nearby sickbay. While he tenderly attempts to assist to lift the knight's accompanying lady onto her horse, the wounded knight suddenly jumps on Gawain's noble steed and rides off with his lady. Gawain had succumbed to a rogue.

Orgeluse's enjoyment of ridicule pours even more over him. She believed him to be a healer of wounds, but now he is at most a foot soldier. If we think that in addition to this, it was Gringuljet, the Grail's horse, taken from him in this deceiving manner and who will return to him in a difficult way, it can become clear to us that Gawain has still much to learn in spiritual wakefulness to gain an inner counterweight to his warm heart-forces. Orgeluse seems to be a strict teacher. Consequently, the poet advises one ought not to judge her too quickly for her coldness, but silently wait to learn this Lady's heart.

The one strong of heart has to undergo trial after trial. His love-wooing remains unerring; yet the beautiful Duchess seems to remain untouched, despite all his achievements. Gawain, in whose blood lay honour and self-esteem, has to undergo schooling in humility. He has to suffer through love, but Wolfram makes us understand that this love is not yet the true one, which Amor and Cupid, with sharp arrows and flaming torches, plant into the human being.

> If I the marks of love reveal,
> Then they derive from faithfulness.

Gawain does not yet know true faithfulness. He still stands under the 'compulsion of love'. Consequently, he has to go through all the suffering in Schastel Marveile. Orgeluse herself leads him there, where that magic castle can shine before his gaze.

In Gawain, the archetypal picture of an artistic soul stands before us. He completely succumbs to the vision of beauty. But he first has to learn that beauty in its purest form can never be gained in the storm of passion. He does not yet know the calming of all passions in beholding beauty itself. Gawain here experiences what Nordic artistic natures have often experienced, when for the first time they went on a pilgrimage to Italy. Gawain dives into a southern landscape; the sensual magic of Klingsor's world lays hold of the soul, and the picture of complete beauty continuously moves around him, only giving itself to the one who succeeds in calming all longing. This is the aim of the trials Gawain must undergo. Several kings, we learn, have already wooed the proud beauty; they all failed. Only one came to Logroys a short while ago (the ferryman says he only brought him over the river yesterday), who fought so mightily against Orgeluse's army that she agreed to give herself to him. She offered her lands, hand and body to the hero in the red armour. But he refused her, explaining he has a more beautiful wife at home. This speech hurt her very much, when he confessed to her:

> 'She is the fairest of the fair,
> And is the Queen of Belrapeire,
> And my own name is Parzival.
> And I seek not your love, withal.
> My pursuit of the Grail demands
> That I meet trouble in other lands.'

We see again that Parzival moves, as it were, in the background of the action. The poet wants to point out that the true seeker of the Grail also has to know those experiences, with which Gawain has to wrestle in his soul. Parzival goes through the world of sensual magic without becoming entangled in it. In his soul lives another ideal picture—the glory of a Sun that only begins to shine where all sensory experiences pale. Parzival, the inset is to show us, has meanwhile grown beyond all 'compulsion of love'. He stands at the threshold of his Grail kingdom. We shall meet him again, wearing the light-filled wreath on his head, taken from the tree of Gramoflanz. He too has passed the trial connected with achieving the wreath of virtues.

Gawain can regard Parzival's path without jealousy. It is said that he and the Lady of Logroys during this conversation looked deeply into each other's eyes. For she is completely changed since he jumped over the 'perilous gorge' on the Grail's horse and thereby had broken off the branch from the tree of Gramoflanz. Now she confesses to him what pain of heart she had suffered for him during this daring adventure, as only a faithful wife can feel for her beloved. All her pride melted in the Sun of this love, which from her heart breaks forth in confession. His manly virtue appears to her like gold purified in the fire. Now it is *she* who woos for his love, and under tears she recounts her destiny of suffering. During this occasion, we also hear that Anfortas, the King of the Grail, once on his knightly travels had come to woo for her love. But his bond of love ended in pain; she points out that Anfortas received the wound he now has to carry as an eternal pain. Thus, at this place, the deep connection of Orgeluse with the suffering of the Grail is mysteriously indicated. At the same time, Klingsor is mentioned here. She confesses, as soon as the protection of Anfortas was taken from her, she had to fear the art and cunning of the great magician. Out of fear she made a contract with him, only for the sake of peace. This is connected to all the trials Gawain has to undergo. Since he emerged from them victorious, the magic gifts of the Orient become free again, that is, that 'stuff', which Anfortas had given to Orgeluse as love-jewels and which in her plight she had given to the magician. Klingsor's power over those treasures in now broken. Gawain and Orgeluse are allowed to receive them as their possessions. Of what kind these treasures are, the poet leaves one guessing, when Gawain chooses that harp named 'the Swallow' out of the rich stuff and has it given to the devout maid Bene. The richness of the Orient falls to the victor. In Gawain a freer of souls has emerged, who is able to found an extensive kingdom of beauty—not a kingdom of cold forms from which the soul has departed. Thus, it appeared in Orgeluse herself, as long as she had to live in Klingsor's grip. Her castle winding up above the human world and the glory of her captivating beauty without goodness threatens everyone who venerated her, to be led into a realm far from life—into the world of aestheticism.

When we hear the story of Gawain's blessed union with the much-praised Orgeluse, the scenes with Helen, the pure archetype of beauty, in Goethe's *Faust* Part II, Act 3 can arise before our inner gaze. With that 'classic-romantic fantasmagoria' he seeks to demonstrate the mystic marriage between Faust who thirsts for beauty and Helen of Troy. Cultural realms mutually penetrate. The Nordic hero dives into the ripe beauty of form of the South, but he does not become enchanted by what he sees. He penetrates it with soul. He releases it out of its fixed form. The ensouled beauty frees the hearts. Goethe describes Euphorion arising out of the bond of love between Faust and Helen. He is greeted as 'blest soul of poetry' as he ascends. Where beauty becomes productive, new forces of genius want to communicate themselves for the life of the future.

In his Gawain poetry, Wolfram does not directly speak of such mysteries. At the end, he brings together Gawain's soul-path with the path of the Grail seeker. For in the Grail Temple and its Mysteries everything comes together, that which the Christian Middle Ages was able to fashion as ideals for the future.

8. The Mystery of Good Friday

Parzival's threshold experience

The way Wolfram has woven Parzival into Gawain's story is noticeable. When the latter, after the farewell from Arthur's Round Table, completed his first adventure in Bearosche, he hears during the exchange of the captured dukes after the battle that on the opposite side a Red Knight had fought and captured them. From the description of his weapons and his stipulation that they become committed to seek for the Grail, Gawain guesses that it could only have been Parzival. He thanks God that they did not come near to each other during the battle. It seems mysterious that the Grail seeker here fought on the side of those in whom rebellious forces were at work. Here he is still shown as the 'Red Knight', although when he was leaving the court of Arthur he still appeared in bright armaments.

Something else of significance appears here. In this battle Parzival gains Gawain's noble horse that had run away from him, 'Ingliart with the short ears'. On this horse he now rides through all the years from adventure to adventure. One realizes an impulse has entered him from meeting Gawain. That is how deep is the connection between the two destinies.

The 'short ears' seems to indicate that this horse is good at 'pricking up its ears'. Its qualities include awake perception. For, when Parzival had forgotten the world over the drops of blood, did not Gawain pull him out of the mystical trance? The Grail seeker does not travel the lands and sail the seas as a mystic but as the observer awake to the world, until one day he arrives at that still hut, in which he can meet Sigune again. Pointed by her towards the trail of the Grail messenger, Cundrie, who only a short while ago has left her, Parzival approaches the border land around Terre de Salvaesche, which is strictly guarded by the Grail knights. He enters a thicket in the forest and loses the trail.

In this forest a man rides towards him challenging him to a life-or-death combat, for, as he explains to him, Salvaesche is not used to anyone riding up so close. Now he would need to atone for what 'in such a way that outside the forest one would call life'. That means, outside the forest—in the sensory realm—what is called 'life' in the realm of the Grail hardly any longer means that; at the most it is felt as a shadowy existence. Parzival has to undergo a wild battle with lances. With his horse in full onslaught, he succeeds in unseating his opponent, who falls into a deep ravine. But because Parzival's horse was charging so intensely, it too falls down and is shattered. Parzival, however, was able to take hold of a cedar branch and soon gains the ground under his feet. The Guardian of the Grail retreats on the other side of the ravine, having to leave his horse on this side. Parzival mounts it. Now he rides a Grail horse. 'Ingliart with the short ears' has to be sacrificed at this meeting.

This is the great turning point that occurs in the soul-life of the Grail seeker. The thick forest in which one gets lost is like the one Dante sung a hundred years later; he too becomes lost in it and has to see his life threatened by three animals, until help is sent to him from the realm of the dead. Through this he found trustworthy spiritual leadership. He became a mystic to whom the other worlds opened.

Parzival, who hitherto had completely given himself to observe the world, continuously using up his strength in worldly events of confrontation, sees himself placed at the abyss of existence. What confronts him here comes from beyond the threshold of death. Although the warrior is not yet able to cross this threshold, yet something in him—the instinctive force, which hitherto had carried him through the world of appearances is hereby shattered. He must achieve an inner turnaround. The poet speaks in pictures—he was forced at the ravine to change his horse. If Parzival did not ride a horse of the Grail, he would never find the path to the Grail again. Through this a mysterious force from beyond the threshold of death has entered him. Someone who had died had from then on taken on guidance of his unceasing striving for the spirit.

We already pointed towards the mystery that the Guardians of the Grail are those who have died. In a later chapter we shall meet an important example, how they can influence the soul of somebody living on the Earth. For Parzival reached the Grail Castle for the first time when looking for his mother who had died. We then saw how under the impression of Sigune, who held her dead bridegroom in her lap, he gained the first inkling of the missed opportunity of his calling to the Grail. How he began to walk the gradual path of true love, which Schionatulander had sought out of the strength of a full heart and evermore pursued.

But now a spiritual ear awakens in his soul. Now he not only listens with 'short ears'. With ears which are no longer closed against sacred matters but are open to the voices from the other world, he perceives the message of the God Who descended to Earth to go through death for humanity's guilt. In Parzival's soul the Mystery of Good Friday begins to shine.

The initial doctrine of Good Friday

These events are heart-moving. The poet is fully aware how he has now to appeal to quite different soul-forces of his listeners and readers. He opens the new Book [9] festively, which is to show this turning point in Parzival's destiny.

> 'Open up!' calls a voice, and the poet asks, 'To whom? Who goes there?' 'To enter your heart thus, I would dare', answers the voice. Once more, the human being resists—'Then you try too narrow a space.'—but that which is wooing entrance cannot be denied.
>
> 'How so? Can I not seek a place?
> I promise not to jostle and press,
> I would tell you wonders, no less.'[36]

It is almost like the voice of One who says, Behold, I stand at the door and knock [Rev. 3:20]. It is not the same, but His messenger.

> 'Is't you, Lady Adventure? Pray
> How does he fare, your knight, this day?
> Tis noble Parzival I mean,
> Whom, with words harsh and lean,
> Cundrie drove forth to seek the Grail ...'

Homer invoked the muse, to sing of the troubles of the divine, suffering Odysseus. The Christian poet has to converse with Lady Adventure. In the adventure of life—in that which approaches the soul when it fully consciously lays hold of the daring to become human, He is present Who in love connected Himself with all earthly destiny, to bear it with us and to give us the strength to raise it transformed towards the spirit.

In the light of the Good Friday Mysteries, all earthly destinies receive a new meaning. They are ordered according to the world-context; in this light the human soul can experience a broadening of viewpoint. Nevertheless, the human heart is initially much too small for

---

[36] Another translation:
'Open!'—'To whom? Who is there?'—'I wish to enter your heart.'—'Then you want too narrow a space.'—'How is that? Can't I just squeeze in? I promise not to jostle you. I want to tell you marvels.'—'Can it be you, Lady Adventure?' Trans. A.T. Hatto (Penguin Classics).

this comprehensive [event]. The poet experiences the content of what he has now to relate as something that would burst the heart. The proximity of the Grail touches us from these verses. Wolfram wants to indicate that he himself has to be different; he had to undergo a transformation of the heart before he could present these Mysteries. One is not able to describe the meeting at the abyss in such a way as he does without having oneself stood at this abyss. In this Book [9], he also speaks extensively of his Master Kyot and his Grail research.

The poet says he does not want to count the weeks which, after the threshold experience, Parzival still had to ride without a path, suffering that he still was kept from the Grail. One spring morning, however, when a thin covering of snow had fallen bringing a fresh chill, deep in the forest he met a group of penitents. An old knight with his wife and two maidens, all dressed in grey cloaks, wandering barefooted in the snow. He seemed to be a Duke, for a train of knights and pages follow him on this pious pilgrimage—quite the opposite of Parzival. He appears, riding along in the splendour of his rich knightly armaments and has now to listen to the complaint of the old penitent that he on this holy day does not observe the custom to ride without weapons, through this honouring this day.

Parzival answers that he is completely ignorant of the season, that he does not follow the weeks and days. He does not know it is Good Friday. He openly admits:

> '… I used to serve
> One called "God", till He did reserve
> Such shame for me, …'

and yet he had remained true to Him, of Whose help had always been spoke, yet he had to experience how this help had failed him.

> 'Unseemly the armour that you wear,'
> Said the other, 'if you should mean
> Our Lord born of the Virgin Queen,
> And, thus, believe in his Incarnation,
> And the remembrance of the Passion
> Which we are observing on this day!'

And now he instructs him that the greatest devotion has been revealed that this God agreed to be nailed to the cross for us, for in this devotion right into death He had saved humanity from debt and the distress of hell.

Parzival had not yet experienced the Christian recognition of God. Like many people, he sought a God Who, as it were, protects us from above and serves us exactly according to our needs and as we believe to deserve it. He thinks of the Almighty God. He must become disappointed, feeling deserted by Him. But *that* God, Whose unshaking faithfulness is revealed in His sharing earthly destiny with us—experiencing powerlessness in order to unite for all times with human guilt and human weakness. Him he does not know. Although he received baptism, he actually knows nothing about the Crucified.

Parzival has become an unbeliever, because he had sought God in a wrong direction. He wanted a 'faithful' God, but he did not understand of what this highest faith consisted. And now the presentation becomes deeply Christian because of a deeply human trait. The poet narrates how the ancient knight wants to point Parzival to a holy man who can instruct him about atonement—but also how the two daughters plead for the homeless knight, who wanders about in his steel armour, cold to the marrow.

> 'Why give him such chill counsel?
> Lead him where, for a goodly spell,
> He may warm himself. However
> Fine he looks in his steel armour,
> He must be cold, three times over.
> You have tents and warm shelter,
> If even King Arthur came here,
> You could feed him, now appear
> As a good host should, and take
> This knight with you for pity's sake.'

The old knight immediately understands this and ceases speaking of the atonement. He warmly invites the erring one. And as Parzival sees the red lips of the girls and perceives the warm invitations of the parents and children, he becomes aware of the miracle, that despite the cold they do not freeze. A different kind of warmth obviously lives in them. Nevertheless, he does not manage to overcome his prejudice to take up their invitation. How could he spend time together with those souls who with their whole heart can love him who only feels hate. Painfully they take leave of each other.

Whilst he continues to ride on without a path, the experience continues to work in him. The chastity and mercy—virtues which his manly education has gained, penetrate his being. And the heritage from his mother, the young Herzeloyde, begins to work—faith. He begins to feel regret; thoughts about the creation of the world and the power of the Creator move his soul for the first time. Should not the One Who can accomplished such works also find the help of a human being worthy, whose manly carriage in life has only known the shield and the sword?

This he wants to put to the test. If God's power is really so great, then He will be able to point the right way to animals. Parzival foregoes his conscious seeking. At this moment, for the first time he entertains a soul-mood of *serenity*. He allows himself to be led by his horse. It is a Grail horse he now rides—until now he had not entrusted himself to the hidden wisdom living in it.

Trevrizent and the plight of the Grail

He strongly spurs on his horse, which carries him to Furntane la Salvaesche. He had been here once before on the morning after the Grail experience when he swore an oath to Orilus at the altar and as in a dream had taken the mottled spear with him. Here he finally finds his Grail teacher, for Trevrizent lives his holy life here as a hermit in strictest renunciation. Fasting he disputes with the devil, striving towards the heavenly Host. As we will hear during the conversation, he too was once a worldly knight, the younger son of Grail King Frimutel, who died young. But his older brother Anfortas, to whom the Grail crown came, sinned against the laws of the Grail. He rode out for love: '"Amor!" was ever his battle cry.' He rode through the world in the service of a noble woman (it was Orgeluse), seeking and surviving adventures, until the poisoned spear of a heathen hit him in battle, who in this way attempted to gain the Grail. He was hit in the groin; the wound could never heal. But when the king in his pain was carried before the Grail a second misfortune occurred. Now he could not even die. Trevrizent lists all the medicines that were used for his healing. Remarkable things are reported here, which lead deep into the occult wisdom of the Middle Ages. (6) It is obvious that it cannot concern a bodily wound. It is a deep poisoning of human nature that has made Anfortas sick. It has spoiled the blood through untamed indulgence in love, the blood that was destined to allow the Grail to shine forth. Anfortas is the human being who was to awaken to that which is immortal and yet indulged completely in what is mortal, who had already been touched by holy love yet had succumbed without resistance to the drive that people call love. It is this unfortunate mixed up nature, the conflict in himself, which caused the unspeakable suffering condemning him to powerlessness.

In this plight, his brother Trevrizent swears an oath before the power of God to forbear forever the service of the sword. In strictest asceticism he was to atone for the guilt of his brother. In the realm of the Grail strict laws are operating, but the law of substitution also exists for those who participate in the Holy Blood of the Redeemer, standing for each other in brotherhood. This deed of Trevrizent, nevertheless, is insufficient for full atonement. The healing of the illness can only take place through something completely different.

Trevrizent tells his guest that once gathered in prayer before the Grail they saw written on it that a knight is to come. If he could place the right *question* to the Grail, then the plight will cease. But nobody is to prompt him to this question, for then it would remain ineffective, indeed, the suffering would increase.

We see that this question has to be a free deed of the one who is led to behold the Grail. It is a testing of the heart, the answer to that which can be revealed out of the spirit. It means an awakening of the highest moral forces, a uniting with the one who suffers. Only an individuality can give himself completely to serve the Grail who is not limited through any selfish interest, not caught in his own destiny through any unatoned guilt (even if unconsciously occasioned). This unconditionally involved individuality, through this is called to become the Guardian of the Grail. Consequently, the Grail crown would pass from Anfortas, who through this would find his healing, to the one awakened in the spirit.

Expressed differently, the Grail calls for a new initiate, since the old forces of initiation no longer suffice to purify human nature from its selfish drives and urges that it can become a fully conscious carrier of the spirit. The esoteric stream of Christianity has reached a point where it has to seek for completely new ways to the spirit. Western human beings, who dive ever more deeply into the material world and there unfold their forces of personality can no longer pursue the old path of denying the sensory nature and depersonalizing the personality. They have to find a way to ennoble the sensory forces and the personality, without weakening it, to let it grow in devotion beyond the self. The wound heals. A stream of holy love enters the circulation of the blood; it renews the blood. But this gains the power to excrete by itself the poison of the cunning spear.

Parzival is the personality found mature enough for this deed. In beginning his earthly path, a prophecy already lay over him. He is the hope of the spiritual world; the Guardians of the Mysteries watch his development. Out of his purest youthful forces he arrives at beholding the Mysteries of the Grail, but he is not yet able to lay hold of them out of the strength of a fully awakened humanity. He still has to complete a difficult path of destiny, on which—cut off from spirit-beholding—he gains in standing up to the powers of his time, but also in the unerring faith in himself, those forces that make him capable of the strongest engagement for the sacred aims of the world. This moment is soon to arrive when on a Good Friday morning Parzival stands before Trevrizent.

Parzival's confession

Again, he has first to experience the accusation that on this holy day he carries weapons. The hermit relates to him that one rides like this for adventures and love's favours, but today is the day to feel the highest love within oneself. And now Parzival jumps immediately from his horse and humbly steps before the 'good man'. He is on the way to let the highest love, the love of God, work on himself. He says: 'Sir, give me advice; I am a man of sin.' It is a confession for which he pleads. But Trevrizent is not a priest.

One is made aware that here a tradition is involved, placed outside the Roman Church with its practice of confession. The Albigensians rejected—this was a major point of contention—the Roman priests who take confessions. Within their ranks they had '*bonhommes*', 'good men', as the hermits were called in the Old French poetic works. Wolfram frequently calls him the '*guote man*', yet Chrétien veils the situation. Besides him a priest appears who reads Mass and to whom Parzival, through the holy hermit, confesses. He is told in his absolution he should whenever he can visit churches and chapels and join in celebrations of the Mass. At the end of making his confession which he makes on Easter Day, he then receives Holy Communion. [Towards the very end of his fragment, *Tale of Perceval*,] Chrétien writes:

> Thus Perceval came to know again
> That God, upon a Friday, was fain
> To meet His death upon the cross;
> At Easter-tide thus Perceval was
> Granted communion, blamelessly.

Yet Wolfram's Trevrizent acts out of his own spiritual calibre. Clearly, he represents the Cathar communities. (5) In them, the 'good men' carried out a sacrament that was to convey spiritual comfort—the '*consolamentum*'. Slowly, by being permitted to look into humanity's deepest situation, Parzival is led in this extensive conversation of confession towards an understanding of his own situation and with it a full confession of his guilt. Only quite late, after Trevrizent had described to him the plight of Anfortas in detail and talked with him about that guest at the Grail Castle who had neglected to ask the question does he overcome himself to admit the great guilt of his life, weighing on his soul.

> 'That man who viewed the suffering
> At Munsalvaesche, never asking
> The saving question, that was I;
> Such the error that makes me sigh.'

He says, it happened out of 'youthful foolishness' and if he could not find pardon here, he would have to move on without comfort forever unredeemed. At first deeply shocked, Trevrizent nevertheless encourages him that he should not accuse himself too heavily. Even grief over his failing has to be viewed in context. He wants to see his youthful forces sprout, restoring heart and vigour to change the prize again.

We clearly see that here an atonement for the wrestling human 'I' is not undermining self-confidence and thus weakening future development. Trevrizent once more places before him the whole seriousness of the situation, through which the penitent's will for atonement is to be ignited. He brings out of Parzival's soul in detail the memories of his youthful experience of the Grail. He also speaks with him of that double sin he also carries—that he blindly slayed Ither and that he broke his mother's heart. After the misdemeanours are recognized and clearly expressed, he should 'leave the matter', Trevrizent advises.

Fifteen days he is allowed to remain with his host. With him he has to share his hard bed of straw and eat herbs and roots with him, but he is content. In this way they live through Eastertide. When saying farewell, Trevrizent once more places before his soul the picture of the noble ancestor Titurel, his immortal life and knightly youth. The ideal of the true Grail guardian shines out. For his knighthood, he advises the one departing always to protect those who are defenceless on Earth, 'woman or priest'. And now follow words describing the position of priesthood for the one who seeks to be a Christian called by the wisdom of the Grail. What Trevrizen underwent with Parzival was a festival of recognition in the spirit. After this a deep veneration of the sacrament is awakened in him. Trevrizent concludes:

> 'Naught like to a priest can you find,
> Naught can compare, to my mind,
> For his lips pronounce the Passion,
> That doth save us from damnation.
> Into his consecrated hand,
> He takes the highest pledge that can
> E'er have been granted for a debt.
> If he doth not true virtue forget,
> And performs his office chastely,
> Where is there a life more holy?'

Here the problems of the Church are not mentioned, as we find frequently in that time, not just in the communities of the heretics; simply the ideal of priesthood, the responsibility for the sacrament in its purity is upheld.

Then the absolution can take place. 'Yield me your sins,' says the confessor. 'I'll vouch for your being penitent, before the Lord.' With a word of encouragement for his future strivings, he lets Parzival return to the world.

The cosmic aspect of the sacrifice of Golgotha

From the instructions he received on Good Friday, some aspects may be emphasized, which can show the characteristic element of the Grail wisdom. A first, Parzival begins to explain to the hermit why during all these years he had completely stayed away from churches and cathedrals. What kind of God is this Whose help one cannot perceive during greatest plight and tribulations? Against Him on can only carry hate in one's heart.

Here Trevrizent takes his start:

> 'Though I was a layman I could read,
> And copy, the sacred truth indeed:
> That, as the Scriptures say, to gain
> Help, His service we must maintain,
> He who is never tired of granting
> Aid to the soul at risk of plunging
> Down to Hell ...'

Although only a layman, from out of the 'true book' (he means the Bible), he was able to gain the following. Humanity should never waver of the service of the One who can help, Who never withheld His help when there was a soul to be rescued.

> '... Be loyal to Him then,
> Since God is forever loyal to men,
> And steadfast in scorning falsity.
> We should grant Him our loyalty,
> For His sublime nature did take
> Our form, for humanity's sake.
> God is Truth [*Treue*], and is e'er named so;
> Of falseness, He was ever the foe.'

Here Parzival receives again the essence of that teaching his mother Herzeloyde tried to plant into the heart of the young boy. How does this faithfulness (*Treue*) manifest? That He has come from His height to us and taken on human form. In this deepest union with human nature and human destiny, one has to seek Him. In this the true help is given.

Why did this become necessary? Because Lucifer and his heavenly hosts, which once had been innocent, had come through jealousy to strife with God and had to descend into hell. Only after this has occurred was the human being created. He consequently takes the place of Lucifer. God creates him out of earth. But when He took Eve out of his side, all the misfortune of the human race came. For Eve did not listen to the word of the Creator. From this human couple humanity was engendered. But one of the two sons was led through selfishness to rob his ancestral mother of her maidenhead. This happened when Cain slew Abel. Then the blood of the brother flowed into the Earth and the Earth who innocently had produced Adam was tainted through this. Thus the Earth, Adam's mother, was robbed of her maidenhead. Since then, jealously and strife began to prevail in humanity. The Earth herself was involved.

In this account the cosmic wisdom of Manichaean teaching shines through, which speaks of two conditions of the Earth. It is *'Terra Lucida'*, the Earth of light from the primordial beginning as it had arisen unspoiled out of the hand of God, and the *'Terra Pestifera'*, Earth carrying pestilence that became involved in the great cosmic Fall and on which we now have to live.

Trevrizent says that two human beings are virgin-born. Adam, as the son of the still virginal Earth, was the first; but when God Himself, to take on a human countenance, underwent birth, it again occurred through a pure maiden. Through His becoming human, He bequeathed Himself to us in faithfulness (*Treue*). Thus we, who are related to Adam, are also related to Him. And now once more His light-nature is described, which can completely penetrate us; it lights up all darkness. Trevrizent describes the nature of human thinking into which this light wants to enter. In these rays our most secret thoughts are judged, but on the other hand, as far as they are pure, they are also protected by God. Yet the human being, because he is empowered to *think*, has received the freedom to choose between love and hate.

These thoughts are developed with a marked sensitivity. Joy enters Parzival's soul, when in this way he begins to understand God's nature. He learns to understand how God's steadfast faithfulness (*Treue*) manifests. Steadfast faithfulness was his ideal from his youth, although faithfulness caused him much pain. From this life-experience, however, he gains a key towards the Mystery of God. Now he can also speak of the twofold nature of his great suffering—the highest suffering he carries for the Grail and that other suffering for his wife, from whom he had to be absent for many years. Twofold faithfulness produces in his soul the deepest suffering. But now suffering no longer darkens his soul. It begins to become for him an organ for higher knowledge.

Through this he also initially understands the suffering of Anfortas. It is humanity's suffering; on him the mark of Cain is revealed.

> 'At Munsalvaesche, now, did you see
> The lance? ...'

Thus Trevrizent seeks to awaken his memory. A cosmic Mystery is announced—the influence of the planet Saturn. Each time Saturn completes its course, returning to its starting point, the suffering of Anfortas is renewed; the pain of the wound is increased. The influence of Saturn means hardening forces; one can also speak of the effects of lead that lay hold of the organism. Then the body of the sick person is penetrated by coldness of ice. Only through a counter-effect, although of a painful nature, can this pain be softened. The spear, which contains a poison producing a burning heat in the blood, has to be inserted into the wound; through this the pain of the frost is removed from the limbs. But thereby a layer of ice begins to cover the spearhead. The crust is so hard that it can only be removed with the two silver knives that the smith Trebuchet had forged. What are these silver knives? In literary criticism it is believed they appeared in Wolfram due to a mistake in translation, that he did not understand the 'silver plate' of which Chrétien speaks. In the forces of silver, cosmologically seen, Moon-forces are always revealed. Two silver knife edges, that is, the sickles of the waxing and waning Moon, work in a specific rhythm in our bodily nature. Through this inner rhythm of the Moon, the circulation of fluids repeatedly experiences a rejuvenation. Through this the hardening forces leading towards ageing are balanced out. Nevertheless, they affect the instinctive forces, which glow through the blood with the poison of hot passion. Where these forces have to counteract those that freeze, the suffering is not yet healed. There are momentary reliefs, but they drive the Anfortas-nature into ever deeper suffering.

In these Imaginations, physiological mysteries seek to be expressed from the cosmic aspect. Healing cannot be brought by the spear with the dangerous poison, which fires through the blood, but only the Sun-power of the Holy Grail. It alone is able to gain victory over the hardening power of Saturn, over death within human nature. An element overcoming death has entered humanity through Good Friday. He Who shone like a Sun, when He was transfigured before the disciples on Mount Tabor has gone through the death on the cross to transform the effects of death into higher life; Saturnian rigidification shall be dissolved through the radiance of the Sun, of holy love. Ageing humanity cannot be rejuvenated through the hot poison of the spear; the Christ-spirit, as the Light of the World, wanting to enter human nature, leads the blood towards transfiguration. It is no longer the selfish instinctive drive but holy love that renews the blood. The Son of the Virgin as the new Adam, enters as eternal life into humanity. He wants to give the old Adam who had succumbed to the forces of death a second youth.

Those wanting to understand the supersensory human nature have to learn to regard their nature as involved in the cosmic activities. Then the suffering of Anfortas will appear before their soul. Parzifal, through a disposition bestowed by grace, already in his young years, was led to this Mystery. He perceived it clairvoyantly, but did not yet penetrate it with that understanding that can only arise through the deepest moral forces. Trevrizent tells him that at the moment when Parzival entered the Grail Castle, the pain of Anfortas had increased more than ever. Saturn had approached more closely; the sudden wave of coldness, which during the next morning brought the heavy snowfall, of which we read in Book 6, was a sign of this.

Consequently, Parzival especially on that evening had to behold the shocking suffering. However, one could now ask why did he enter the place of the Grail precisely in the sign of Saturn? Because Saturn is not only the power of death, but with these death forces in us the consciousness-awakening forces are brought to us. The destructive, ageing effects within the bodily nature are the basis for the awakening of Spirit-Man, whereas the up-building, regenerating effects that occur within the rhythm of the Moon are forces that dampen down consciousness. Human nature needs the effect of Saturn. Dying forces have the task to awaken the spirit. And so, it is emphasized that Parzival entered the realm of the Grail in the sign of Saturn. But only now does he know how from death—whom we need to become spirit—a higher life can be wrested.

Trevrizent initiates him into the Good Friday Mystery. He speaks to him of the Dove which year after year on this most holy day renews the effect of the Grail—it carries the Host down from heaven and places it on that stone which allows the Phoenix to burn to ashes, to let it arise to new life. In the Sun rhythm of the year, the force of the overcoming of death full of grace wants to enter human nature. It awakens in us the immortal human being. Parzival had completely lost his sense of time. He no longer knew of the Christian festivals and the calendar. Through the teaching of the Grail, he learns to recognize the activity of Christ over the year. He begins to feel 'Who' had in faithfulness united with life on Earth—that mother soiled by fratricide—to sanctify her anew. A Christianity of cosmic breadth shines forth here. (14)

9. The Fulfilment of the Grail Path

The meeting at Joflanze

In the glory of Easter's grace, Parzival travels on his further way. He lives for the Feast of Pentecost. Everything still to report, according to Wolfram's unique time indications left as exercises in calculation, we can relate to the calendar. We have heard how Parzival rides through the realm of Schastel Marveile; the ferryman took him across the river one day before Gawain stayed with him. This occurred during the Easter week; he must have jumped then over the 'perilous gorge' with his Grail horse, to pluck a branch from the tree which Gramoflanz protects. With this branch wound into a wreath around his head, he appears to Gawain outside, before the camp of Joflanze—at the edge of the wild Sabbins—when Gawain rode out to meet Gramoflanz for the arranged duel. The latter had challenged Gawain for a battle of life and death, since he had dared to break a branch off the protected tree. Through a messenger, Gawain had invited King Arthur to this spectacle at Joflanze. The latter gives the honour to his beloved nephew Gawain, who had remained so many years away from the Round Table. With his Queen and the whole court, he sets off to Joflanze. It becomes a Feast of Pentecost as had never before occurred within the circle of the Round Table.

But most bitter battles still threaten and have to be contested. When Gawain, in the early morning, sees the lonely knight appearing, riding adorned with the shining wreath, he initially imagines this can only be Gramoflanz who wants to challenge him to the dance of weapons at an hour too early and not on the public plain as agreed. It comes to a fight and Gawain is about to succumb to the mighty blows of his opponent; his pages, who ride past, call in dismay the name of their badly harassed lord. When the winning knight hears the word 'Gawin' he throws away his sword. He feels again miserable and dishonoured; God once again is not with him.

'Misfortune has taken to the field,
Good Fortune herself must yield,
Misfortune's coat of arms I bear,
As in the past; to think that there
Tis not Gawain whom I attack,

But I myself, and at my back
Comes Misfortune; Fortune fled
On the instant, and honour's dead.'

In this way he has to think, for he was just about to slay his beloved friend, to become once more innocently guilty. Parzival feels, in measuring himself against Gawain he has overcome himself.

Both rode horses of Munsalvaesche, as the poet emphasizes. Consequently, a mysterious guidance must stand behind this meeting. Was it not that in this victory Parzival had to conquer that element which hitherto had drawn him into the threads of Gawain's destiny and which he had to follow on his path? For he too bears the branch of the wreath of virtues and is emerging from the magic of love.

Parzival is now invited to a festive meal and is led back into Arthur's circle. A feast of happy reunion commences. The freed ladies of Schastel Marveile, including Arthur's mother and sister, are joyfully received; Gramoflanz, who meanwhile arrives with his army and insists on the arranged duel, is appeased through Arthur's wisdom and married to Itoneje, the sister of Gawain; the radiant Orgeluse is welcomed into the circle of the Round Table as the spouse of Gawain. Four weddings are celebrated at the same time. Only Parzival, although honoured and lovingly received, cannot feel happy in this exuberant festivity. Only now he feels the whole pain of loneliness.

When morning approaches, the one 'fleeing happiness' prepares himself; by his own hand he harnesses his horse and secretly steals away.

Feirifis

Now, says the poet, the reader will discover through him 'the true end of the adventure' hitherto unknown (for Chrétien's Grail narration remains a fragment). He introduces a figure, who is completely unknown in other Grail traditions. This is Feirifis of mixed race, the [half-] brother of Parzival, Gamuret's son, to whom Belacane, the Queen in the land of the Moors gave birth after Gamuret had secretly left. He appears as the heathen king with mottled skin both black and white; with a great army he comes over the sea to claim his father's heritage, the realm of Anjou.

He had just arrived in a far-off haven. The fleet of twenty-five armies made up of various Saracens and Moors could not understand each other because of their different languages; they still wait hidden behind a forest. Without his followers, he alone has ridden towards adventure. The poet comments that the Earth is so large; do the brothers have a chance to meet and fight without a reason? With the appearance of this heathen king, one is reminded of the three holy kings with their riches, the Wise Men from the East. As in a fairy tale, they were a favourite subject in the Middle Ages. Feirifis rules not only the Arabic world. Queen Secundille, to whom he is connected in love, has given him Thrabonit, an Indian kingdom. The treasures of this golden country at the Caucasus under the rule of his beloved are at his command. Through Secundille's love which acts as a shield in battle, and through the jewels with which his armour and weapons are adorned, he feels unconquerable. Feirifis appears with the whole magic of legend; fully to understand this figure and its adornments one would have to draw on the Middle-Age wisdom of precious stones as well as all sorts of other Eastern wisdom traditions. What is brought to our experience in this clash between Parzival and Feirifis is the meeting of the Occident and the Orient. The youthful force of the Christian European is initially overcome by what meets him from the ancient wisdom and overripe cultural tradition. The Infidel fights with gigantic strength. His battle cry, recalling everything Queen Secundille has bestowed on him, makes him appear superior. The Christian already tires in this measuring of strengths. Only in his last plight Kondwiramur comes to his mind; through this Parzival regains his strength. The purest love saves him—the battle-cry of 'Belrapeire' charging at his opponent, forces him to his knees. Then his sword shatters on the helmet of the Infidel. It is not the sword he gained in Munsalvaesche. With the Grail one would never want to fight the representative of Eastern wisdom. It is the sword Parzival once took from the dead when he had slain Ither.

Now he stands there powerless. The Infidel jumps up with the power to subdue one unarmed. But his noble mind does not allow him to fight someone defenceless. He offers peace. Now they discover they are both 'Angevins'—sons of the same father—but representing two worlds. Feirifis offers to address him in the familiar 'thou' form. But Parzival, out of shame, cannot initially respond. He feels the superior dignity of the mighty ruler to whom the vast realms of the East are subject.

Here the noblest attitude is revealed of a cosmo-political Christianity as it has been formed out of the experiences at the time of the Crusades in many Western souls who, in the meeting with the elevated culture of the Orient, learnt to regard with awe and often felt ashamed by the greater humanity of their Moslem opponents. With Wolfram we find no arrogance of a dogmatic churchmanship; we sense nothing of the fanaticism of Christian missionary zeal.

The experience of brotherhood initially breaks forth with elementary power out of the Infidel soul. Although with pain he hears that Gamuret, the father he had never known, to seek whom he had come to the West, had fallen honourably in battle a long time ago. However, the joy to have found his brother—lost and at the same time found—shines over everything.

> 'Truly, I, my father, and you,
> Were one; though ever seen as three,
> No wise man deems them so. In me,
> You fought yourself on this field;
> I came to battle, not to yield
> Myself, indeed, rather to slay;
> By fighting fiercely, in that way,
> You defended my life from me.'

Feirifis' words lead to a prayer of thanksgiving to a god here called 'Jupiter'. His 'infidel eyes' are filled with tears; the tears could witness well to someone who had been baptized.

> His infidel eyes began to scatter
> Water-drops, in no small manner,
> (As if sprinkled to the glory
> Of the Baptism, whose story
> Teaches love and loyalty.
> Christ is love and loyalty;
> And our Rule takes its name
> From Christ, in whom that same
> Was witnessed).

It is a Christ-experience, although initially unconscious, which at this moment passes through the soul of the one who had found his brother.

For Parzival, another thing is important. For the first time, he has emerged from battle not as victor. The moment the sword of Ither broke in his hand, his life was forfeited. This atoned for the guilt of his youth, when he bad blindly slain Ither and robbed him of his armour. But his life, since it is spent, is given him anew. It is a sacred law: only a spent life—an existence, which no longer lives out of the force of self-awareness—can be called to the Grail. By rights he already belongs to the realm of the dead. Cain's nature, which through murdering his brother had soiled the Earth, has been led through death in Parzival. His name shines from the Grail.

The calling of the Grail and the riddle of Cundrie

Feirifis is immediately led to the tents of Arthur's court and received into the Order of celebrating Knights of the Round Table. The poem leads the reader to a Pentecost celebration of the Spirit. The great harmony of religions and the reconciliation of the races is symbolically shown.

The poet praises this dawning day. For now, the messenger of the Grail appears again in the festive circle. She is recognized by the emblem of the Grail, the golden turtle dove embroidered on her garment. In noble array, her face behind a long veil, she rides along ceremoniously as if transformed, although she is recognized as the same Cundrie la Surzière, whose appearance once caused great dismay. In a disciplined manner she stands before the gathering and greets the son of Herzeloyde. She announces to him the epigram that can be read on the Grail—you shall now become the Lord of the Grail. Kondwiramur, his wife is chosen with him for the Grail.

Only now he hears that she has born him two sons while he had been riding in the world. Parzival has become a father, unknown until now. The twins' names are Loherangrin and Kardeis. One shall be brought with him to the Grail and the other shall be educated to rule the worldly kingdoms.

Let us look at the communication of this fact first as a picture. The unification with the archetype of the soul, the awakening of the 'ideal human being' in oneself, remains not without fruit where it has been fostered. The seed of a higher life matures in the depths of the soul, although at first unconsciously. This new humanity is revealed as a twin being—the one side of which develops the faculty to live fully consciously in the realm of the spirit; the other is to give itself full of strength to the earthly tasks and gain mastery over the earthly duties. The initiate of the Grail must be able with the same dedication to live in both worlds, doing justice to their demands.

Cundrie, furthermore, communicates to him that he is now able to place the right question to the Grail. Through this he will redeem Anfortas from his suffering. Parzival has reached the stage of '*Saelde*', steadfastness; 'doubt' has completely disappeared from him. No word of judgement is spoken. The Grail messenger says to him that from youth onwards he has always been concerned; through this he was robbed of the joy in life. But he has fought for equilibrium of soul.

'The Grail denies a false companion,
Its power forbids. Cares and fears,
You nurtured in your tender years,
But happiness, approaching now,
Will banish such; I here avow,
You shall win to your soul's peace;
Joy, in this body; woes will cease.'

Cundrie in a unique manner describes of what the Grail kingdom consists. She lists the names of the seven planets in the Arabic language, in the order of early astrology, beginning with Saturn that forms the outermost boundary, via Jupiter, Mars, Sun, to Venus, Mercury and Moon. Feirifis, it is emphasized, knew their names well. The Orient had preserved a starry wisdom, although in a pale guise, and transferred it to the West through the Arabs. But it is said to Parzival,

'All that these famed lights embrace,
Within their orbit, every last place,
All that they shed their light upon,
Marks the scope, as they move on
Of what you may win, for, indeed,
Your woe is doomed to pass, tis greed
Alone can deny you your portion.'

From now on, he may penetrate the starry world, to become a citizen of the macrocosm. Before our soul the picture of the heavenly human being can arise which was once revealed to the seer on Patmos. He is the one Who holds the stars in His right hand—He has made Himself the Lord of the planetary forces. No longer controlled by the stars, He is free.

Early astrology looks to a cosmic connection of human beings and their destiny. It was known that they are not only earthly citizens. Astrological knowledge, drawn out of a clairvoyance of the characters of the stars, seeks to interpret human destiny out of the effects of the stars. It was able to lay hold of the human astral nature and how the human being was urged to act and suffer out of these astral influences.

If humanity is to develop towards freedom, these astral effects have first to be dampened. The 'I'-being is to learn to act out of itself; it has to be released from starry control. Consequently, young Christianity as it developed in Europe did not possess any starry knowledge. Through the Arabs, astrology increasingly penetrated the medieval world. Wolfram narrates how Queen Secundille heard about the Grail kingdom and in her admiration sent Anfortas presents from her realm; the Queen of Sheba heard of the wisdom of Solomon and went to Jerusalem to honour him. Amongst the gifts of Secundille were two misshaped beings, Cundrie and Malcreatiure. The latter appears as the male counterpart to Cundrie; he was passed on by Anfortas to Orgeluse when he was seeking to gain her love. Once he was called, 'the son of herbs and stars'; he approaches Gawain with derision when the latter sought to gain a root he wanted to use as a remedy for the wounded knight. We already heard how Orgeluse took him for a medical doctor and tried to mock him. At this opportunity the poet teaches us about the descendants of Adam. He tells the reader how Adam, our ancestor, still possessed the all-embracing starry wisdom and knew the healing forces of roots. Through greedy misuse of certain forces, however, his descendants could not avoid producing creatures completely disfiguring the picture of the human being. Shameful deformations came about; Cundrie and Malcreatiure belong to this. Astral figures, not physical people, are meant here. But in them the early clairvoyant inheritance of humanity continues. Consequently, in an archetypal sense they are still wisdom carriers, simultaneously penetrated by an animal instinct. Terrible animalistic characteristics are shown by Cundrie and her brother. Such astral beings gain power over people, when they get hold of them, and begin to work in them like 'doubles'. Gawain had to meet such a being when he sought to live into the nature wisdom used for healing.

When he first meets Cundrie, Parzival is confronted by an astral Imagination. At the same time this being conveys to him some painful self-knowledge, for she shows him what still works untransformed in his deeper instincts. But it also calls upon him to overcome these retrograde forces, which he too carries in himself—as an inheritance of earlier earthly lives. For everything we unconsciously carry over from earlier stages of existence into the present one becomes a hindrance in one's development; we have first to learn to lift it into the light of recognition and transform it. Parzival is an individuality who carries an elevated inheritance of wisdom out of early incarnations. On that stage of development, when the young human soul struggles to become free from the maternal reins and learns to take hold of its own destiny—this took place with Parzival with an abrupt force—that astral figure begins to take hold of him which has protected for him the inheritance of his past earthly life. Parzival has to learn to unite with this part of his inheritance, and yet it cannot be used in its past form. He has first to transform it completely in going through his earthly destiny and in conquering all dull instinct. Then his inherited wisdom is given him in a new form. This is the key to Cundrie's mysterious being.

Untransformed, she reigns like a curse over Parzival's path of destiny; lifted into the light of recognition, she becomes a blessing for him. Only now, does she become a true messenger of the Grail. She leads him on the way to Munsalvaesche.

His 'I' has battled through to freedom. It stands no longer under the compulsion of the stars. Consequently, he learns to penetrate the starry spheres on a new level as an awakened spirit. It is said of Feirifis that he knew planetary wisdom. His god is Jupiter; cosmic wisdom is a gift of Jupiter to humanity. In being with him, Parzival, who was blessed to experience the Sun-Mystery of Christ, gained the knowledge of starry wisdom. The poet wants to convey that the Orient is to bring a rich inheritance to the Christian Occident.

The healing of Anfortas

When Parzival is allowed to begin on the path to the Grail Castle, Cundrie says

> 'My dear lord, choose one
> To go as your companion.'

And Parzival chooses his brother. Feirifis, who out of his own constitution could not have found the path to the Grail, is allowed to go on it as Parzival's companion. One cannot appear before the Grail unless one brings *one* human brother. Parzival understands this now.

In a festive procession under Cundrie's secure leadership they reach the Grail Castle. Temple Guardians rush towards them. Uncountable hosts of poor, suffering souls welcome the arrivals. The long-expected one is festively received. But Parzival urges to be allowed to step before the suffering man. On his sickbed the tortured man receives them. In tears Parzival throws himself to the ground, pleading to the Holy Trinity for the healing of the sufferer. Then he gets up only to say, *'Oheim, was wirret dir?'*, 'Dear uncle, what afflicts you so?'

This is the Grail question. Only the one can ask it who himself has experienced *afflictions* of destiny. Consequently, we read that Parzival, because of the unatoned guilt he brought to the Grail Castle earlier on, was hindered in his asking. Only the one awakened to freedom, who could solve the afflictions in his own destiny, can see through the afflictions of the human condition. He begins the work of ordering destiny.

In the sphere of the spirit, the question is at the same time one of recognition. A physician would say, in the right diagnosis the beginnings of therapy already reside. Knowledge, or recognition, proves to be a healing force. Pentecost is the festival of 'the healing Spirit'. And the poet wants to celebrate Pentecost Mysteries in the last books. This he points out in a parable, reminding the reader of Saint Sylvester who once had to undergo a trial before the Emperor Constantine. The latter awoke an untamed bull who had collapsed dead through the magic spell of a rabbi.[37] He was re-awoken through invoking the name of Christ, and the bull walked away tamed. It is an Imagination for the transformation of the bull nature in the human being—this nature is led into death through the strictness of the law, but through the grace of Christ is called to a higher life. This is connected to the sickness and healing of the Anfortas aspect of human nature. Another picture is given by the poet, when speaking about the healing of Anfortas. He speaks of the raising of Lazarus; the same Person who awakened this disciple out of the grave at Bethany to new life also healed Anfortas.

Further on, it is described how the whole being of the convalescent began to blossom. A youthful glow exuded from him, compared to which the beauty of Parzival was but a gust of wind. The ether-form of the supersensory human being wrests itself triumphantly from the fetters of the selfish instincts which confuse it, and from the powers of death which lame it. It appears in its bright undimmed nature. Parzival is now called to take on the kingdom of the Grail as had been determined by the writing on the Grail.

In a rich report Wolfram brings all this before the reader, which is important for the completion of the path of salvation and for the future of the Grail dynasty. Seeds of future poetic writing, as, for example, the whole saga of Lohengrin in swift strokes and the one of the priest-king Prester John, are contained in this final chapter. Some of it may be summarized here.

---

[37] The story is in *The Golden Legend* of Jacobus de Voragine—Ed.

Meanwhile, Kondwiramur, to whom the Grail messenger had come, set off with a large company from Belrapeire and is accompanied by her followers to the borders of Terra de Salvaesche, there Parzival meets her, informed by a Guardian of the Temple of the Queen's approach. He finds her tents pitched besides the Plimizoel, where five years earlier the spots of blood had shone in the snow and enchanted his senses. The poet emphasizes that Parzival during all those years never received the comfort of love in his longing for *Minne*, although it was offered by several women. It is a song of praise in marital faith. Very touching is the description how the Queen's Court Marshal leads him into the tent, where he awakens her from sleep and the two recognize each other again. Then he sees his sons for the first time and lovingly kisses the two as they wake up. In a blessed festival of love, Parzival and Kondwiramur renew their bonds.

Above all, it is still significant that the destiny of the black and white brother is fulfilled. Although an Infidel, he is allowed to participate in the radiant celebration of the Grail, held after Kondwiramur's entrance into the Grail Castle. With awe, he beholds the procession of the twenty-five maidens that ushers the Grail into the hall of celebration. Repanse de Schoye, the pure maiden, is the last of the train. The Grail can be carried by no other, for she possessed the purest heart. Now the miracle of the feeding occurs again; the Grail provides in abundance what each person longs to eat and drink. But the Infidel does not understand how the vessels on the table are repeatedly filled. Nowhere can he perceive the source of the miracle of feeding. He only sees the crowned maiden in green silk standing before him—but he does not see the Grail lying on its cloth. But the gaze of this maiden goes to his heart, filling it with the deepest pain of love. His whole being is drawn to this carrier of the Grail. When Titurel hears of this, he explains the riddle—an eye will never be able to behold the Grail without baptism. A barrier remains.

The Christening of Feirifis

Now the moment has come when Feirifis is advised to receive baptism to earn eternal salvation. 'Does baptism help me toward love?' is his first question. Now he confesses to his brother what is happening in his heart. For him, Parzival is to woo for the hand of the Grail carrier. But he explains he can only do this if Feirifis first obtains baptism. The Infidel is so naïve—and here the poet seasons the description with humour to take from it any fanatical note of Christian zeal that he asks whether one can gain baptism in a knightly combat. He would willingly joust for it and win a sword fight. His mind is not yet attuned to the Mystery of the grace of baptism.

We have to observe how Wolfram proclaims a religion of comprehensive tolerance. The heathen brother brings the rich inheritance of wisdom from the East. Parzival needs this completion on his path to the Grail. Through him, Feirifis without Christianity finds access to the sphere of the Grail. He even receives revelations of the spiritual world with great openness. He perceives Christ's activity, he feels deeply drawn towards human souls illuminated by Christ, but the source of the radiance remains closed for him. A barrier has still to fall; it concerns an awakening of awareness.

Concerning Grail wisdom, it is important to understand that Christian confession is in no way a prerequisite on the path to the spirit; moreover, the deepest community with someone who has not confessed to Christianity is not rejected. Yet in going further on the spiritual path a situation occurs in which the seeker becomes aware of facts that through their own nature lead him beyond what he has hitherto gained. He learns to understand that he himself would bar access to the deepest sources of power, if he remained stubborn at this border. Effects of grace are revealed to him, the origin of which he is not initially able to perceive.

Somebody like Feirifis is not interested in Christian truth as such. It is the Christ-filled human being himself who convinces him. This is a fact in life we may repeatedly meet in many forms. It gives the highest responsibility to the person who in a conscious sense wants to be a Christian. Early next day the Infidel is led into the Grail Temple. He is to receive baptism in the presence of the Temple Guardians. The baptism vessel is a ruby that rests on a circular stone of polished jasper. By inclining this stone towards the Grail it fills with water, 'not too hot and not too cold'—that is, in body temperature, for its flow is received in the human blood. The ruby takes into itself the pure stream of the Grail, by inclining towards it. A supersensory fact is indicated, in which life on Earth is continuously at work. There is an etheric stream of cosmic love radiating from Golgotha; it connects with the streaming of the blood in the heart when it inclines towards Christ.

Before Feirifis received baptism he was blind to the Grail. Baptism enabled him to see the Grail. It is described to us as a sacramental event that directly leads the soul towards enlightenment; it releases in the blood a completely new clairvoyant force.

What precedes this act of baptism is significant. Parzival initially poses the serious question to the one to be baptized, whether he will foreswear his old gods. This means he has to forget Jupiter and also Secundille. Through this a law of human development is expressed, which the wise people in the Middle Ages knew—the earlier starry wisdom has for a time to be sacrificed. Only through the complete denial of that which is given through earlier astrology to humanity can the forces of freedom be born in the soul, can the 'I' be confirmed. The soul experiencing itself in the starry grid of forces is determined by them. Islamic believers brought to the West the art of making horoscopes [Arabian astrology]. They also denied human freedom. They saw human beings as determined, their god was almighty, the rigid cosmic law. Theologically expressed, they only knew the God the Father; God the Son was still not visible to them. But those who cannot find the Son within the soul, cannot wrest themselves from the burden of the past. For them there exists no unravelling of destiny through the atoning, sacrificial Deed of Christ. As a result, they cannot in freedom lay hold of the Spirit, the Spirit Who allows the human 'I' to grow beyond all earthly fetters, allowing it to live from the realm of nature into the realm of grace.

Anfortas did not find the path of unravelling [destiny]. He was unable to carry out the fully conscious transition from God the Father towards the divine Son, and consequently unable to release in himself the Holy Spirit.

After Feirifis had denied his whole inheritance of atavistic wisdom, able to lead him into the vicinity of the Grail but hindering him from perceiving the Grail itself, he is now instructed into an understanding of the Holy Trinity. An ancient, honourable priest now comes forward to baptize him. He speaks to him of the God Who had become man and Who is the Word of the Father Himself. If the divine Son enters the human soul, everything traceable to primordial times is led through a rejuvenation—it must undergo a complete smelting process. This occurs in the Mysteries of the Grail; they intend to foster the Spirit in a new form, proceeding from the *Son*, because the spirituality, which as an inheritance is fostered in humanity, has become rigid in tradition. This struggle for the rejuvenation of the spiritual life is expressed in the dogmatic controversies between the Eastern and Western Church. The Councils wrestled for the formulas in the Creed, whether the Holy Spirit proceeds only from the Father or also from the Son—'*filioque*'. The West decided for the latter formulation [one of the main causes of the East-West Schism of 1054]. This meant—if it does not remain dogmatic but effective in life—that in human beings who receive the Son, the source of the living Spirit begins directly to flow; the Christ-filled human being becomes able to receive revelation. (15)

'He who believes in me,' Christ says (John 7:38), 'out of his heart shall flow rivers of living water.' John's Gospel adds (v. 39), 'Now this He said about the Spirit, Which those who believed in Him were to receive.'

After the priest in festive words has proclaimed to the person being baptized the Mystery of the Holy Trinity, he continues the Mystery concerning water:

> 'By the Trinity's power,
> He, from whom Adam, in dawn's hour,
> Took his likeness, entered the water
> For His baptism.'

He Who originally fashioned human beings in His likeness, joined Himself to human nature through baptism in the River Jordan. Through the element of water, He entered earthly life entire:

> from water trees gain their sap,
> Thus, water in their leaves they trap.
> All things are made fecund by water,
> All those things that we call 'creature'.
> By means of the eyes' waters we see.
> Water grants souls a majesty,
> That with the Angels' doth compare.

These are the words inviting meditation. Only to deep meditation will they open their innermost meaning. Speaking in modern words, water is more than H_2O. It is the mediator of etheric formative forces at work in the circulation of saps in nature. This etheric force of life awakened by water and effecting its circulation, passes over to the human soul that immerses itself into the pure weaving of plants in nature. It then releases vision in the human self. The gaze becomes clairvoyant in the intimate participation of the pure processes of growth in the life of plants. In this etheric illumination, the human soul is transfigured; it becomes akin to the angelic nature. Moreover, with the ascending and descending of liquids, at work in natural life-processes, it then understands how that divine Being could be connected to sacrifice Himself to the Earth and to penetrate it with His Son-glory.

Through birth we are led into the darkness of earthly matter. With it, we become connected to its dying part. Through the grace of baptism, we are to be lifted to that stream of forces of the etheric Earth that allows us to participate in the future life of our planet, allowing us to become akin to the Sun. Through physical birth, we enter '*Terra pestifera*', as Manicheism would say. Through the grace of the Spirit, we become seers of the '*Terra lucida*', the shining Earth of the future.

When the ruby vessel inclines towards the Grail, it receives that 'stream of living water', of which John's Gospel speaks. For this stream penetrates the community of those who are united around the Grail. It is the stream of the Holy Spirit, into which Feirifis enters the moment he decides to relinquish the stream of the ancient forces of inheritance.

And, as soon as he'd been baptized,

> ...
> And as to viewing the Grail there,
> Till the water had covered his eyes
> He'd been blind, but did realize,
> Thereafter, the sight of the Grail,
> Brought as if from behind a veil.

The Grail allows the baptized person to see it. When he now wants to take Repanse de Schoye as his wife into the distant East, Feirifis has first to go to the harbour where his army is still gathered on the ships, anxiously waiting for the king. There he learns of the death of Queen Secundille. Only now is he free for the new destiny he has chosen. But with Secundille, everything is extinguished that still reigned as atavistic spiritual inheritance, as redundant faculties. Although it gave breadth and richness of spirit, it also fettered him to the past.

After his return, Feirifis now begins to spread Christian life throughout India. The son born to him by Repanse de Schoye receives the name John. He, and all the succeeding kings, is called Prester John, 'John the priest'. This legendary figure, behind which indeed stood the carrier of an Eastern Christianity, which still contained early Apostolic traditions, was mentioned with veneration right into the Middle Ages. The Crusaders sought his land; tidings of him even reached the West. But with this, Wolfram wants to point out the comprehensive human connections of the Grail stream. It concerns [the] Christianity of the Holy Spirit, that Christianity which even the furthest

East can perceive. The poetic work ends, as it were, in Goethe's confession: 'Orient and the Occident are no longer to be separated.' [38]

The conclusion of Wolfram's poetic work

We already heard that the poet accuses master Chrétien de Troyes of being unjust to the story, not because he was unable to finish it but because he did not free the legend out of the narrow bounds of the Celtic tradition. He did not attribute to it the world perspective that belongs to the Grail. He was unable to recognize the 'Grail dynasty', to place it in cosmo-political contexts. For it fosters concern for the salvation of humanity entire; it has to govern, following the guidance of the Holy Spirit. Wolfram acknowledges:

> The true tale was sent complete
> From Provence, to us, to greet
> Its audience in German lands.

These words we must take against the background of events of the times, the threatening clouds gathering over the south of France and shortly afterwards to be discharged over the Cathar community, leading to their destruction.

> He claims he has taught,
> … what the bard himself has said,
> And so, with honour crown his head.
> I've named Parzival's sons correctly,
> And his high lineage too, directly,
> And have brought him to that end
> A glad dispensation did intend,
> Despite the trouble he's endured.

The Grail Guardians should be known by the historic period, for the soul from now on shall gain an insight into the hidden leadership

---

[38] Allusion to Goethe's (1749–1832) *West-östlichen Divan* ('West-Eastern Divan'), a body of lyrical poetry in the Persian style, a dialogue between East and West (1819). Versifications of the Koran are included:

> God's very own the Orient!
> God's very own the Occident!
> The North land and the Southern land
> Rest in the quiet of His hand.

(Trans. Edward Dowden, West Eastern Divan, p. 5.) https://ia800400.us.archive.org/14/items/westeasterndivan00goetuoft/westeasterndivan00goetuoft.pdf of humanity. This should be increasingly revealed, for in no other way could souls striving towards the spirit free themselves from old authorities.

Wolfram, consequently, did lead the Grail seeker to his goal. In spirit he went on the same paths that lead to the vision of the Holy Grail. How could he otherwise describe the path with such certainty?

10. The World Mission of the Grail

The rapture of the Grail

The message of the Grail and its Guardians ends repeatedly in a tragic mood. At one time the West could proclaim this sanctuary in its midst. But it withdrew. When they appear, its messengers are no longer received in the right way.

In the French Grail Story, we read that the Grail has been taken back to Sarras, that is, into the land of the Saracens. (9) Galahad boards the 'ship of Solomon' with his two companions Perceval and Bohort, following the command of a heavenly voice, and lands after a long sea-voyage at the city of Sarras. After several deeds and sufferings, Galahad is raised to become king. He has a special shrine made for the holy vessel. Out of the realm of the dead, Josephe appears, who according to this tradition is the son of Joseph of Arimathea. He reveals to Galahad the Mysteries of the Grail. After this vision Galahad longs to be allowed to enter Paradise. His soul is loosened from the Earth, but the Grail and the Lance are removed by invisible hands to heaven. Perceval dies as a hermit; Bohort returns to the court of Arthur to report. King Arthur has the history of the Grail written down for the recollection of those coming after.

Another account, how the Grail withdraws from the West, is to be found in German literature. The 'singers contest on the Wartburg' arose as the poetic work of musicians around the 60s of the thirteenth century. In it, we read that King Arthur with his whole court was transported in rapture to a mountain. Parzival and the Grail sanctuary are also with him. We see how these two Mystery circles increasingly melt into each other. The Grail stream, which from the East had to bring over the Christian Mysteries flows together with the Celtic stream, which from the West moves towards Christianity.

Barbarossa, too, was presented as the emperor who had been transported into the interior of the mountain. At the end of the twelfth century, he had undertaken a crusade, as was the longing of the times, to find true Christianity in the East. There, however, he met death. Yet his spirit, as was felt, had returned to the West. If one could penetrate the depths of the Mysteries, one could meet him in his activity as an inspiriting, leading spirit behind the outer events. This is expressed in the transporting into the mountain.

In the poem of the Wartburg, which is directly followed by the narration of Loherangrin, it is reported how this son of Parzival is sent by King Arthur out of the interior of the mountain to Brabant, because Arthur's knights remained true to the custom of sending their hero everywhere in the world as a protection and shield for the innocence that is under siege.

Later, in a continuation of this poetic work by a Bavarian author, the legend is harmonized with the Grail narration of the great Titurel epic. Here the hero is called Lohengrin. When forced to reveal his heritage, he reports: In the centre of India a high mountain range had taken into itself the Grail with all its heroes; King Arthur brought them with him. There one can also find Munsalvaesche, where stand temple and palace adorned with precious stones …

Prester John

Albrecht von Scharfenberg is the only writer who, at the end of his *Titurel*, gave an accessible description of the translation of the Grail into the Far East. When the nefarious neighbours around Salvaterra increase and it seems evermore impossible for the Grail Guardians to stem the fall of sinful human souls through prayer and fasting, the Grail no longer wants to remain in the West. It turns from an unworthy world towards the land whence comes the light of the bliss-giving Sun. The Temple Guardians journey with the Grail; in the harbour of Marseille a ship lies prepared for them, which the Guardians of the Sanctuary board with Titurel and Parzival at their head. Wherever they arrive on their journey, the Grail feeds their hunger, easing all pain, when the Christians approach it with reverence. They travel, led by favourable winds, through wonderful heathen countries. Through the power of the Grail, they pass without harm the Magnet Mountain, which draws all iron from the passing ships so that they have to fall apart. The Liver Sea, of which sticky fluids otherwise fetter the keels of ships, becomes fluid like ice in the fire through the power of the Grail. These and other adventures they must undergo on their travels.

There are miracles of nature, sufficiently known from medieval narrations, for example, from the legend of Duke Ernst von Bayern. Such strange experiences were perceived in their souls by the elemental clairvoyance of certain medieval people. One would need an ether-geography to interpret them. When people with such abilities travelled through the various zones, be it as pilgrims or as seafarers, they experienced unique impressions from the Earth's radiations, or the streams in the air. The journeys of the Grail take place in an Imaginative sphere, and it is shown that the sanctuary proves to be the master over the realm of the elemental beings. Thus, the brethren of St Columba, the monks of the Scottish Church, in their early Celtic hymns and prayers called Christ 'the King of the Elements'. On such journeys souls were permeated by the power of Christ, were able to experience how the atmosphere became brighter when the transformative power of the Grail began to penetrate it. The Earth itself with the elemental beings inhabiting it will be involved in the great transformation.

The poetic work now relates how Feirifis with his wife Repanse de Schoye come to them from the East when he perceives the approach of the Grail. The Grail Guardians are received by them in the most cordial manner. All the countries subject to the rule of Feirifis have meanwhile been converted to Christianity. But he gives immeasurable praise to a king in India, of whose wonderful treasures and deepest piety we hear. This king over 'The Three Indias' goes by the name of 'Prester John' ['Priest-King John']. His country lies close to Paradise, which God had separated from the world through the glass mountain, yet from the heights of which a stream pours into the countries, which in its gravel carries the most varied precious stones. The poet indulges in a fairytale-like description.

Descriptions of battles with the Tartars follow, pointing towards conflicts of Gengis Khan with the Ong Khan or Toghrul, the ruler of the Keraites [† 1203]. He was called 'Prester John' by the Nestorian Christians, who as heretics since the fifth century had to withdraw to the Far East and here missionized various tribes.

In the high Middle Ages various letters came from this Prester John to Western leaders. The Crusaders, too, had received messages from him. Without doubt, many reports of this Nestorian Church working in the Orient were fantastically exaggerated. However, it cannot be denied that these splintered Christian communities who were pushed towards the East had world-historic tasks to fulfil. They penetrated the Eastern cultures with Christian spiritual substance. With this spreading of Christian Church life, it does not concern numbers and quantitively fixed organizations, but with this dream. It concerns a mysterious fructifying of the Asiatic world with the impulses radiating from Golgotha. This, in the language of legend, is meaningful for the future of humanity and consequently, in matters of the Grail, thoroughly worthy of the radiant pictures with which they are clothed. Here the 'land of St Thomas' is mentioned, reminding us of the mission of that Apostle whose legend is always associated with the finding of the Three Kings in the Far East.[39] This favourite legend known in the Middle Ages clearly contains Manichaean spiritual traits. It serves the same humanity-embracing ideal of a Christianity of the Holy Spirit. Consequently, Goethe in his old age was particularly attracted to this legend, working hard to make it known.[40]

Parzifal, and with him the Temple Guardians, now entered these legendary countries. After fervent prayers of everyone, the holy mountain of the Grail and its consecrated Temple in a wonderful way are removed to the East from the corrupted folk of the West. When the morning Sun rose again over India, its first sheen falls on the pinnacles and cupulas of the Temple of Munsalvaesche.

The mysterious flowing together of the deepest Christ-knowledge with the life of wisdom of early India can now begin. It is a process in the supersensory worlds in which this mutual penetration takes place; consequently mirrored in radiant Imagination whence something has been perceived. That which between the Asiatic and Christian spirituality began to enter into an exchange during those centuries may of course, from the viewpoint of outer history, have been something proportionally insignificant.

It is said that Prester John wished to learn about the sanctity of the Grail. Titurel instructs him that the Grail had been a precious stone that a host of angels in early times had brought to Earth. Here Wolfram's teaching of the stone once more appears, which awakens the Phoenix to life after it had been burnt to ashes. But now this esoteric, alchemical teaching is for the first time smelted with the sacramental teaching from the French Grail tradition. It is said that out of the stone a chalice was formed. From this chalice Christ with His disciples had taken His last holy meal. Joseph of Arimathea, the lover of Christ, was allowed to take care of it after the Lord's crucifixion, but an angel brought it later to Titurel, calling it in the language of the angels 'the Grail'.

Titurel, after he was allowed to behold the Grail for half a millennium and was its guardian now longs, as he admits, for a rest from earthly existence. For nine days he was not to be shown the sacred vessel, then he would be able to die. And this it happens. Prester John, deeply impressed by the sanctity and dignity of Parzival, offered him

[39] The legend is recorded by John of Hildesheim in his *Historia Trium Regum*.

[40] Discussed in jstor.org/stable/43626770.

the crown of his kingdom. Yet Parzival is only prepared to do this when the writing appears on the rim of the Grail: he should become king, yet he should change his name to that of Prester John.

For ten years he reigns as Priest-King John. Then, when he too had returned to God, he is followed by the son of Feirifis and Repanse de Schoye. From now on all the Guardians of the Grail succumb to the law of death since they are no longer rejuvenated by beholding the Grail. But their pure soul no longer needs purification in Purgatory. The writing on the Grail always shows the name of the one who is to become the next Prester John.

Since then, whoever travels through the world looking for the Grail, in the first instance the Knights of the Round Table, returns without success. In the distant East near the sources of Paradise, the Grail remained hidden with its Guardians.

We should understand how the possibilities of visionary experience have withdrawn. Nevertheless, in the Orient places still exist where elevated masters guard the Mysteries of the Grail, without being able to bring the light of full revelation to it. The Grail poetic work of the end of the thirteenth century sounds like a call of longing for what has been lost into the spiritual world.

In view of the dogmatic rigidity of the Western Church, its threatening demand for power that everywhere found out the streams of the free spirit by means of the Inquisition, seeking to wipe them out with fire and sword, it is like a contemporary recalling, a call for the presence of the Grail to enter the plight of the age. The legendary Grail Guardians, who long ago had moved to the East, some have thought to find again in the Knights Templar Order. But it took only a few decades until the noble figures of the Templar, with Jacques de Molay as Grand Master, under torture were forced to admit the most terrible crimes. But they recanted and under constant insistence of their innocence had to go to the stake. With this tragic event, darkness spread over the West.

*

The Singers' Contest in Wartburg Castle

Behind the splendour of courtly culture and the heavenly striving of the Gothic [age], a spiritual battle takes place raging for the soul of the Western world. The impressive Moslem civilization had in Spain its strongholds of science and the arts, but it also extended to Sicily and south Italy. Here the Hohenstaufen Emperor Frederick the Second [1090–1147] connected strongly with it, and through the many contacts with the Crusaders in the East, it entered ever more strongly into Europe. This civilization seemed to be victorious in the Christian souls of the Western world. The progressive spirit beheld with admiration what came to them as an Arabic striving for wisdom. Where could one find in Christianity a medicine, chemistry, mathematics and astronomy that could measure with that science spanning the world? But this science, particularly star wisdom, shows it knew nothing of the freedom and the eternal value of the individual human soul. It knew Allah, the mighty God, but not the divine Son, Who had sacrificed Himself on the cross and through it had redeemed humanity from its chain of guilt, releasing it into freedom.

The other Klingsor

In the poem of 'the Song-contest on the Wartburg' this wrestling for the spirit is mirrored. Here in the Knights' Hall of the Wartburg which the Duke of Thuringia had made into a court for the Muses, the famous singers enter competition with each other. Heinrich von Ofterdingen challenged them to a contest for which he gave his head as a trophy. When the contest finally goes against him and the henchman is already called, the Duchess Sophie pleads for his life. But the sorely set-upon Ofterdingen calls on a mightier person, whom he recognizes as his master. It is Klingsor, 'Master Pastor from Hungary' who enters in the guise of a merchant, offering his wares to the Duke. But his wares are riddles, which he can give. And now a contest begins between Klingsor and Wolfram von Eschenbach—Wolfram, although he had died only a few decades earlier, in this poetic work already grows into a legend. It was felt that this singer of the Grail presents a spiritual power. In its individuality, the contest of the Christian West concentrates against the powers that want to deliver the striving spirit to a cold intelligence. But with these powers the greatest power of the heart arises.

Wolfram is now able to solve the riddles Klingsor poses to him to test his wisdom. It concerns the Christian truths of salvation, the mystical teachings of God and immortality, of sin, grace, and redemption. But with the tenth and last riddle, Klingsor lets loose the devil Nasio, who tempts Wolfram with the most difficult astronomical questions. Here it should prove that Wolfram is only an 'amateur' and will fail in the realm of starry wisdom. But Wolfram sees through what is brought against him. He calls on God Himself and the Virgin Mary to help him. With this the magic of the devil is expelled. Wolfram bans him with the sign of the Cross.

Klingsor attempted to lead the contest as a magician. He had been initiated into black magic. At Paris, so we hear, he found a good school; at Constantinople he learned, but also in Baghdad and Babylon he was in the service of Mohammed for three years. There he studied alchemy and astrology. He was called '*Meisterpfaffer*', 'Master Parson', because he had the knowledge of a 'parson' (theologian), but he pursued a worldly position. On different occasions he tells us, his ancestor who already bore the name Klingsor, according to that ancient magician of *Terra de Labur* ['what is now Southern Calabria', R. Steiner[41]], was once sent from Rome to the King of Hungaria. This name, too, he had inherited from him. A mysterious line is drawn from that magician, who ages ago built the castle Schastel Marveile, the mighty counter centre to the Grail Castle, through the centuries to this other Klingsor, who brings his influence into the group of Minnesingers. Even in the ancient Minnesinger manuscripts verses are contained, the authorship of which is ascribed to him. Of course, literary criticism also seeks to deny this, although a chronicler of the thirteenth century reports on Klingsor and his role. It could even be the case that Wolfram, who very freely and yet significantly had named the magician of the ninth century (through whose realm Parzival strides unerring and whose power Gawain is able to break in a certain realm) had named 'Klingsor', to point with this towards the spiritual relationship of the great black magician with that Master Parson of the thirteenth century. Then with this a tremendous challenge towards a contemporary person would have occurred; one can well trust this to the spiritual knighthood of Wolfram von Eschenbach. It was important for him in his poetic work *Parzival* to demonstrate the great contrasts which mutually wrestled in the spiritual life of his century. In particular, the Minnesong and the knightly epic of his time were threatened by the *Ungeist*, the evil spirit, of the lower Minne; to raise it towards the divine Minne, to climb up by stages given in the *Brackenseil*, was the deep meaning of his powerful work. How, besides all the admirers, he should not also have found some enemies—even a Gottfried von Strasburg, who in his poetic work *Tristan* knew well how to extol the 'noble hearts' but was not able to

---

41 R. Steiner, 'The Mysteries of the East and of Christianity', GA 144, Berlin, 7 Feb. 1913.

lead the souls out of the compulsion of the Minne towards freeing of the hearts, became involved with the opponents of Wolfram. He mocked him as an 'inventor of wild stories'.

The 'song contest in Wartburg Castle', even though lifted into a legend, is the echo of a spiritual battle at a turning point at which, indeed, Wolfram knew he had to fight with the newly smelted sword of the Grail. (16) Wolfram unmasks the starry wisdom, which is of an Arabic spirit holding souls in unfreedom. He confronts it with the wisdom of faith out of the courage of the heart given to Christ. In comparison with the great Arabic spiritual tradition, this may at first appear amateur. Yet it carries the seed of something for the future. In the unification of Parzival and Feirifis that future form of Christianity shines forth, which will one day have found harmony with the wisdom of the Orient. For in no way is Christianity to disregard the striving towards cosmic wisdom. At one place in that Wartburg poetic work, a sublime wisdom of the history of the Grail shines forth, as has never been expressed by any other poet.

> 'Shall I bring forth the crown?
> It was freely fashioned by 60,000 angels.
> They intended to oust God from the heavenly realm,
> Behold, Lucifer, then it became yours.'

At the primordial beginning, the sum of all wisdom had been fashioned out of the working together of unsurveyable angelic powers. It was fashioned into a radiant crown; Lucifer, however, grabbed it for himself. But we read that Saint Michael, when he saw God's wrath concerning this, took up the battle with Lucifer and knocked the crown off his head. Thereby, a stone flew out of it. Titurel, the one wrestling for highest honour, found this stone, the same stone which one day Parzival was to gain for his own.

Here the cosmic Imagination of the Grail Mystery is given. Its description is given again by the poet to Wolfram. With this stone a highest treasure, the extract of all wisdom of the angelic world is entrusted to humanity. But this stone had to become the vessel to take up a still more sacred content. It had to be wrested from the falling Lucifer, to form the vessel for the Blood of the Redeemer, Who wanted to give Himself for us from the root of the Cross. For divine Love, if it is not to stream away unrecognized, needs a vessel in which it can be held. This vessel is formed out of the forces of wisdom. Wisdom is the gift of Lucifer; Michael wrested it from him in the cosmic Fall. Lucifer's gift is to establish the *form*, but from Golgotha, the *content* is to stream into it. Through this the gift from Lucifer's realm is to become sanctified.

Lohengrin in the Middle-Age epic and in Wagner's music drama libretto

This mysterious poetic work of the Wartburg Contest is followed by the narration of the Swan Knight, Loherangrin. This too has been put into the mouth of Wolfram, for already in the last song of his *Parzival*, he had described the mission of Loherangrin in brief outlines. Klingsor challenged him to continue what was indicated there. It is significant that into this battle of the time a great spiritual comforter is placed. For the world in its greatest plight repeatedly needs the proximity of the Grail, and the Grail—this is made clear in this legend—perceives the prayers of innocence under pressure. It sends its champions into the world.

The poetic work written in the Thuringian dialect remained incomplete. But through a Bavarian poet it was continued, although heavily overlaid with the description of many battles, yet through this most recent poet, placed into a clearly defined historical situation. It concerns the epoch of King Heinrich I, that is, around the dawning of the tenth century. This is the time of those defensive battles against the Hungarians, who with their horsemen coming from the East brought the realm into unrest. The military situation demanded the building of solid towns. Many souls during this century had to take the transition into a town life. With this they were completely jolted out of their connection to nature, becoming estranged from the divine powers working in it. They became citizens, but through it were led to that inwardness into which the Christian impulse could enter ever deeper into the soul. In his Lohengrin libretto, Richard Wagner was able dramatically to lay hold of this turning point, by adding to Duke Telramund the figure of Ortrud, the carrier of magical heathendom. She still calls upon the old gods to take up the battle against the forces of the Grail.

Through Wagner's romantic music drama, the radiant figure of the one sent by the Grail has become widely known despite the dramatic intensification and through it the shortened action, he brought out in an exemplary manner the essence of the legend. Consequently, we need only to mention the Middle-Age poem in a few broad strokes.

Elsam, the daughter of the Duke of Brabant, is given to prayer in her great plight of the heart. Friedrich von Telramund, to whom the dying

Duke had entrusted the protection of his daughter, insists that Elsam had promised to marry him. Since she obstinately refuses, he took his complaint right up to the emperor. Now a divine judgement, set up by the decree of the emperor, shall bring the decision. Yet no champion is found to take up the battle for the innocence of the duke's daughter; that's how much Friedrich is feared. Then Elsam whilst kneeling before the altar as a sign of her greatest plight, rings a little golden bell she once had taken from an injured falcon. The sound grows into the distance beyond the clouds, swelling into a thunder and sounds continuously before King Arthur, who with his Grail Knights had removed himself into the mountains. Writing appears on the Grail, announcing how in Brabant a noble, pure maiden, in her plight begs for a champion. Lohengrin is chosen to be her knight. Parzival himself armours his son. When he already has his foot in the stirrup to mount his horse, a swan comes swimming trailing a small craft. Lohengrin leaves his horse and steps into the little boat. When his provisions for the journey are brought, the swan denies it. 'Nourishment is due to the Lord for Whom I travel.'

A quick current carries them out into the high sea. For five days Lohengrin fasts, then the swan dives into a wave and carries a Host out of the sea. He offers it to the hero, who wants to share it with him. Then the swan begins a sweet angelic song and sings the hero to sleep. They enter the mouth of the River Schelde and the knight is brought to shore in Antwerp. There Lohengrin places himself before the astonished gathering, to fight for Elsam, gaining victory over Friedrich von Telramund. For we know—and Wagner had built up his dramatic action onto the motif of the forbidden question—how the Swan-Knight only places the one condition, that he has to remain unrecognized amongst people.

What is the mystery of such a swan-knight? In that connection already mentioned in describing the Guardians of the Grail, quoting Rudolf Steiner's words that it concerns 'specially chosen living people who have already died', who gathered around the Grail, the swan-knight is also mentioned. We read further, the people of the early Middle Ages still knew that in the highest sense one can only be effective by taking up in oneself what the living dead are able to give. For those who have died to accomplish deeds on the Earth, need the sheaths of such earthly people who completely give themselves to their activity. In this sense, Rudolf Steiner continues, there existed at that time an Order of the Swan.

Those dedicating themselves to the Order of the Swan wished that the Grail Knights could work through them here in the physical world. Such a person through whom such a Grail Knight worked in the physical world, was called a Swan. It is the Swan who took on a companion out of the circle of the Holy Grail that appears here:

> One may not ask him about his actual Mystery. The most fortunate in that century did feel—but also still in the following centuries—even those kings like Heinrich of Saxony, who during his battle with the Hungarians could include this Swan Knight, this Lohengrin, within his host.

When the legend wants to describe how an earthly personality is to be permeated with the being of a great one who has died, it speaks of the sea-journey of the knight, of his fasting for days and how he nourishes himself miraculously from the power of the Host until he reaches the land. The process of incorporation of a high initiate into the sheath of an earthly human being is thus clothed in legendary pictures. A special body of formative forces must first be built up to allow the one sent by the Grail to enter into an earthly body. For this, the most holy substances out of the etheric world have to be gathered. The feeding through the Host, as the Swan brings it out of the ocean, is the expression for the mysterious build-up of an etheric organism corresponding to the life-conditions of a great figure who has died. The body of a Swan-Knight has to be permeated by the life-forces of Christ, when he wants to make himself worthy for the indwelling of a second, higher human being. Such transformations as occur in the depths of soul of a personality, are something much too tender to be laid hold of by earthly concepts to be talked about in human words. They are to be honoured through silence. But personalities working on Earth may never announce that they work out of the forces of somebody who has died, or that they do their deeds commissioned by the community of the Grail. What they do should convince on its own merits. The Middle Ages demanded from the one who wanted to be active in public life either the legitimizing through the bloodline of the aristocracy or through the priestly succession, as in the Church hierarchy. Whoever serves the Grail may not rely on such authorities. The effect of the Grail itself, how it continues in a free manner from one human being to another, awakening purest spiritual forces in the souls, witnesses to the Grail messenger. Nothing else.

Swan legends always point towards mysteries of birth. The heavenly wingbeat of a soul in process towards incarnation was seen in this picture. The imagination of peasants has made of it the stork who brings the children. When Helena is praised as the one begotten by the Swan, because Zeus approaches Leda once in the figure of a swan, our gaze with this is led towards a divine soul, which out of the Zeus- or Jupiter-sphere, has been entered into this particular body; Jupiter-souls brough the ideals of all Greek striving down to Earth.

Who was this Lohengrin, whose swan-birth is described by the legend? In a letter to Mathilde Wesendonck (August 1860) Wagner writes of his opinion about it.

> Yesterday I was very struck by 'Lohengrin' and I can't say other than believe it to be the most tragic poem, because atonement can only really be found when one casts a terribly far-reaching view over the world. Only the deeply meaningful belief of soul-travelling could show me a comforting point onto which in the end everything comes to the same level of redemption, after the various courses of life which in time run separately side by side, meet each other out of time in understanding. According to the beautiful Buddhist belief, the stainless purity of Lohengrin is simply explained that he is the continuation of Parzival—who had fought for purity. In the same way, Elsa in her re-birth would reach up to Lohengrin ... Thus all the terrible tragedy of life would only be found in the separation of time and space.

And he thinks, the complete clairvoyant who knowingly overcomes this separation, sees through with this the deepest tragical pain as an illusion.

In Wagner's soul, the thought of repeated earthly lives is working towards consciousness. Initially he found only the Eastern-Buddhist form of this concept to be able to form into concepts his view born out of deepest pains of life. Thus Lohengrin became for him 'the continuation of Parzival'.

One can also say, Parzival in his world mission, in his becoming effective within European history, is presented in the radiant figure of Lohengrin. This incorporation appears in that realm which in the division of the great Carolingian realm between East and West forms the middle realm, the kingdom of Lothar. From the south northwards, via Alsace and Lothringen up to Flanders and Brabant stretching to the North Sea.

According to another version of the legend, after he has to bid farewell to Elsa, Lohengrin moves on to the country of Lyzaborie and worked there. But this was later called Lotharingen after him. The name Loherangrin is interpreted as Garin the Lothringer. True legends always contain certain historic figures and events.

Once more, in the fifteenth century, a mastersinger reworked the Swan-Knight legend. The mysterious hero is called here 'Lorengel'.[42] When he steps on land in Antwerp, he first visits a citizen named Calebrand. There he meets a knight who had still known Parzival; he tells him how once with the help of the Grail had made an end of the rage of Etzel. Through the similarity to Parzival he recognizes Lorengel as the latter's son.

Etzel, too, the great Hun king Attila, is indeed a legendary figure active over centuries. He who threatened the existence of the Christian Occident with his hordes, was still felt behind everything that up to later times gave unrest with the attacks of the Hungarians onto European culture. Parzival, and his presence in Lohengrin's mission working beyond his death, stands as the guarantor for the destiny of the Christian West. This Western realm may expect leadership and protection out of the realm of the dead. The Guardians of the Grail are the mighty protectors of the Christian mission of Europe.

With the fact that around the middle of the thirteenth century the Lohengrin legend was made into folklore, one can see a direct parallel between the wars of the Huns and the Hungarians of earlier centuries and the Tartar onslaught of that present time. In 1241 the Christian knighthood of Silesia faced the onslaught of the great Mongolian army. Thereby, in the Battle of Liegnitz, this knighthood was completely defeated, but the Mongolian army retreated. It was a mysterious process, behind which people believed they felt the wielding of invisible powers.

The Lohengrin poetic work with its explicit descriptions of the heroic battles against the Hungarians and Saracens could have encouraged the knights whose sacred task it was to hold the shield over the Christian culture of the Occident. After following the law of the Grail and having to bid farewell to Elsa and the children after she posed the forbidden question, Lohengrin leaves behind three gifts—a sword, a horn and a ring.

We have described the Grail sword; it vouches for victory out of the purest spiritual forces. The horn is able in greatest danger, to summon helpers out of the realm of the dead. But the ring is to be the sign of constant memory of the one who once in greatest plight appeared, a token of the ever-present nearness of the Grail for all who know how to foster faith in the spirit.

---

[42] 'Lorengel' is an anonymous fifteenth-century epic. See Elias Steinmeyer, Zeitschrift für deutsches Alterthum, 15. Bd. (1872).

11. In the sign of the Rosy Cross

The crisis in the thirteenth century

There are times when the spirit gives itself abundantly to humanity. But there are also times of expectancy. Then the soul, thrown back on its own sources, lives on the afterglow of the past times of revelation. The thirteenth century found itself in such an ebbing away of earlier spiritual abilities. Through the poetic works on the Grail, the whole glory of a lost Mystery-world was to shine out once more, awakening yearning in the hearts, at the same time fostering the expectant mood necessary to precede the return of spiritual revelation.

At that time, with scholasticism choosing Aristotle as its master to lay the foundations of a Christian worldview through cognition, the striving for knowledge was raised into courageous structures of concepts. At the same time, in narrow towns the Gothic Age built towering cathedrals, striving towards heaven. The foundations for Cologne Cathedral took place around the middle of the century through the famous theologian and alchemist Albertus Magnus. This building was to be erected in honour of the Three Wise Men, whose sarcophagus was kept in the walls of the town. Barbarossa had their bones brought to Cologne. For with them was not a token given that the Oriental wisdom, which in Caspar, Melchior and Balthazar had brought its gifts to the child of Bethlehem, would now also shine in the West? Should not the wise kings also become godparents, when the mystical miracle, the birth of Christ in human hearts, is to take place? The thirteenth century can certainly be characterized by severely criticizing the powerful political unfolding of the Roman Church and proceeding from it the threat against a free spiritual striving. We had to speak of those Crusades against the Cathars of southern France, which were crimes against a culture ignited by the Holy Spirit. But this culture, too, was nourished by spiritual forces that were only still a dying light compared to the mightily surging new spirit of the time. At the same time the other side of the truth is evident, to do justice to the plight of the spirit of the age. Within the Church, too, especially in the Orders of the Dominicans and Franciscans, efforts of extraordinary intensity were made to counteract the onslaught of Arabism. This rising culture of an intellectualism opposing Christ was to be countered by well-founded doctrinal truths and Christian, sacramental forms of life, right into artistic style.

A new faculty of consciousness was to be fostered in the human soul, like the force of seeds, waiting in the Earth for the awakening spring Sun. The ego-force, strengthened by innermost concentration, would one day learn to lay hold of the spirit again in quite a new manner, free from all traditions. In his *Titurel*, Albrecht von Scharfenberg has Sigune say to Parzival, when after much travail he meets her again, 'Be pure and foster manliness, and *do not seek the Grail*, but be assured, at the bottom of the Liver Sea God would choose you for the Grail. Oh, how quickly Cundrie would find you!' Now, the imagination of the Liver Sea, in which the keels become stuck because of the thickness of the water and the ships have brutally to sink, does not seem so far-fetched to us. How many, setting sail to begin their travels in life, eventually enter regions that become congested, and nothing seems to move any longer! But even there, so Comfort speaks, the messenger of the Grail can find the individual, if the starry hour of spiritual awakening has come. He might have disappeared into anonymity, faithfully pursuing the challenges of everyday chores; he had become nameless. But now his name shines on the chalice of the Holy Grail.

The beginnings of Rosicrucianism

When Albrecht's *Younger Titurel* poem appeared before the end of the thirteenth century, the moment meanwhile had appeared—the gate towards the spirit had gently begun to open again. The Rosicrucian stream had commenced. That which in historical research is regarded as charlatanism—and unfortunately is often mixed up with questionable occultist pretentions—has been described with its true foundations by Rudolf Steiner. In his lectures on *Rosicrucianism and Modern Initiation*, Dornach, Jan. 1924 (GA 233a), he presents in great detail Rosicrucianism and the beginnings of a modern initiation principle—the extinguishing of the earlier Christian initiations in the West and its rebirth in the humble brotherhoods who gathered in the sign of the Rosy Cross and who were arduously striving to achieve a first stage of a spiritual path as it is suited for the soul-faculties of contemporary people. Here too, that mood of expectation was fostered, which is only able to arise out of deepest devotion, out of a serenity in giving oneself to Christ.

What was the characteristic element with this new path of knowledge? That the spirit was not sought in realms removed from the world but initially in its working and weaving within matter. The Gothic Age ultimately removes the soul from the weight of matter and lifts it towards a blissful beholding of God; through this it comes into danger of leaving the Earth behind, to give it over completely to the powers of the adversary. When a divine being was able to link so inwardly with human nature that it completely merged into earthly destiny, to atone for the guilt of the Earth, then within earthly substance something must exist that persists receptive for this divine seed. A condition of matter must exist which still bears the un-desecrated source of its divine origin—virginal Earth, '*terra sancta*'. In Wolfram's *Parzival*, the reader has heard Trevrizent's teaching concerning this:

> for Earth, she was
> Adam's mother, and because,
> Though she nourished Adam, she
> Was yet whole in her virginity.

Only through Cain's fratricide, when the blood of Abel soiled it, did the Earth lose its virginity.

Through this matter itself has becomes something else. It is permeated with the forces of selfishness. It carried the effects of death in itself; through the selfish actions and greediness of human beings, this has been constantly carried into the Earth. Trevrizent says, the virginity of the Earth has been desecrated.

In an Imaginative form, the primordial world-condition is mentioned here, in which our planet itself still carried such substance necessary to fashion a human body in an innocent way; at that time the Earth itself could still be the mother. Propagation through the human sexes did not exist at that time. The alchemist, who followed the Rosicrucian path, sought to re-find that '*prima materia*'; a substance which is still enlivened and ensouled, completely pure. Once all matter—at the seed stage—was still contained in the ether. It was then expelled from it; it fell from it. Thus, out of the weaving of warmth, there consecutively arose the gaseous, liquid and solid states of substance. But that archetypal substance contained (potentially) all these forms of matter, undivided.

From this archetypal substance, human beings alone carry something in themselves, which is the reason why they can take up the spirit in themselves, can become mediators between spirit and matter. Rudolf Steiner describes this fact from which all genuine alchemy has to proceed, in the following way.[43]

---

[43] Rudolf Steiner, *Anthroposophy, an Introduction*, lect. 2, Dornach, 20 Jan. 1924. GA 234.

> You see, we may regard our physical organism as organized for taking in external substances—present-day substances—and excreting them again as such; but it bears within it something that was present in the beginning of the Earth but which the Earth no longer has. This has disappeared from the Earth leaving only the final products, not the initial substances. And so, we bear within ourselves something to be sought for in very ancient times within the constitution of the Earth. It is what we bear within ourselves, and the Earth as a whole has not got, that raises us above physical, earthly life. It leads man to say: I have preserved within myself the beginning of the Earth. Through entering physical existence through birth, I have ever within me something the Earth had millions of years ago but has no longer.

In the human being, the *prima materia* has still to be found. It is 'the stone' known to the Knighthood of the Grail, which each Good Friday is enabled to renew its strength when on to it the Dove of the Holy Spirit carries down the Host. Into this substance, the seed of the incorruptible body can be received, the resurrection body that wants to be formed out of the regained *prima materia*. This was also called the *Lapis philosophorum*, the philosopher's stone. In the lecture cycle, *From Jesus to Christ*, Rudolf Steiner explains the Pauline teaching of the resurrection body through modern means of knowledge: 'Consequently, the alchemists always emphasized that the human body in truth exists of the same substance out of which the completely transparent, crystal-bright philosopher's stone exists.'[44]

The 'Fama Fraternitatis'

The genuine Rosicrucians sought the 'Chymical Wedding'. By this, they meant—to learn to look at the material processes in such a way that in them one can see the revelation of the creative spirit. But this is only possible for the one who knows initially how to find these processes in oneself. They are at the same time moral processes in ourselves. If we form pure thoughts, we set into motion in ourselves the same process as if salt is precipitated out of a liquid. It is a process of crystallization but at another level. When in sacrificial devotion we allow our self-centredness

---

[44] In these lectures (*From Jesus to Christ*, Karlsruhe 5–14 Oct. 1911, GA 131), the pure body of form is described, the blueprint of our physical body, which in the Resurrection of Christ is wrested from matter falling into dust—the latter is the archetype of that form of the body that as a seed can already be received into ourselves and in which form we shall one day resurrect.

to be consumed, a similar process takes place, as if sulphur is ignited in warmth and is consumed in the flame. Seen in the right way, natural processes are preliminary steps to that which takes place in human beings. They are, as it were, checked on the way to a full human creation.

> *Nichts ist drinnen, nichts is draussen:*
> *Denn was innen, das ist aussen.*
> *So ergreifet ohne Säumnis*
> *Heilig öffentlich Geheimnis.*[45]

> Nothing is inside, nothing is outside,
> for what is within is without.
> Make haste, then, to grasp
> this sacred mystery which is the 'open secret'.

In these phrases, Goethe summarizes the impulse of the Rosicrucian worldview. Nature with all its processes—which are on the way towards the human being, which urge towards the human being because only there do they find their self-fulfilment—is the 'open secret', or public knowledge. Nature reveals the same laws that in a hidden way take place in ourselves. In an age that with all its forces today aims towards the exploration and mastery of the world of matter, we need such a view of substance through which we comprehend its coming from and its striving towards the spirit. If one devotes oneself to explore matter in the sense of a true natural science, one does not need to become a materialist. However, on this path trials are to be undergone. Temptations approach the soul of the person striving to fathom nature; loss of the human dimension is threatened. The pioneers of the age of natural science felt a knighthood of the spirit is to be practised. They knew that one needs to wrestle with the deceptive pictures of matter. Whoever can behold the substance of the spirit in an illuminated manner, however, is no longer susceptible to the deception. He becomes a 'Knight of the Gilded Stone'. In the well-known writing, appearing under the titles of *The Chymical Wedding of Christian Rosenkreuz* in an Imaginative language, the soul-paths were shown that can lead to such a new 'knighthood'.

The 'chymical wedding' is clearly conceived to stand to contrast with 'the mystical wedding'. The latter had been the high aim of all

[45] Goethe. *Epirrhema. Gedichte letzter Hand.* 1827. http://www.zeno.org/Literatur/M/Goethe,+Johann+Wolfgang/Gedichte/Gedichte+(Ausgabe+letzter+Hand.+1827)/Gott+und+Welt/Epirrhema

medieval Christian striving. The mystics sought a path leading to the depths of their own souls. By striving to purify themselves, to loosen the soul-forces from the entanglements with the nature of the senses, they prepared the soul for union with the spirit. At the end of this path, they could celebrate the marriage of the soul with its higher self which they found in Christ. The killing of the sensory nature led towards a mood for life denying the world; mystics leave the Earth untilled and untransformed when they rise towards a pure realm of soul-existence. But the Christian West would never have been able to gain spiritual victory over the rising materialism had the noblest spirits given themselves to a mysticism directed to one side.

In the '*Fama Fraternitatis*', a Rosicrucian text written by Johann Valentin Andreae in 1614 addressing the 'heads, leaders and scholars of Europe', we are told of a youth who, after a monastic education, longs for a pilgrimage to the Holy Grave. Following his intense pleading, he is taken by an older brother of the Order. But since the latter dies on the journey, the youth has to continue alone and is held up in Damascus. There he meets a community of wise people, to whom the mysteries of nature are revealed. They live together in such an exemplary harmony of spiritual activity that this becomes a new ideal for him. We read: 'Through this the high and noble genius of Brother Christian Rosenkreuz was awakened, so that to him Jerusalem no longer appeared as esteemed as Damascus.'

For years he is initiated by these wise people regarding their comprehensive knowledge of nature. They are Arabs. Through them, however, he learns the ideal of true tolerance in spiritual things. When he returns to Europe, his inner concern is here too to found a community of spiritually striving people, who in the attitude of genuine tolerance, in mutual furthering and supplementing of their forces, devote themselves to the mysteries of the world. The Middle Ages did still look with deepest fervour to Jerusalem. The Crusaders looked for the Holy Grave. But Christian Rosenkreuz looked in the spirit towards Damascus. It is the place where Paul could meet the Risen One. With this a step is indicated what Christianity, as it were, had to achieve from Good Friday towards the Easter Mystery. The light of Christ, which has arisen in the soul, shall from now on permeate all world situations; it shall lead to world illumination. But on this path the Christ-Impulse takes on a character beyond all the confessions. Spoken in a picture of the Grail Legend, Parzival unites with Feirifis, the black and white brother, in the light of the Grail. The

Christian begins to learn something essential from the Guardian of spiritual treasures of the Orient.

This mysterious exchange between the Christian West and the distant Orient with its Arab-tinged wisdom, already begins in an earlier time. We have mentioned the Carolingian Age, when a lively exchange took place with the court of the Caliph of Baghdad, the leader of the Abbasid Caliphate. Gamuret's journeys into the Orient are pictorial descriptions of this spiritual contact between the cultures. In the legend of Flore and Blanchefleur, we find a poetic reflection of those fervent searches for the lost archetypal wisdom for which many people undertook pilgrimage to the East. This legend takes place in Spain at the time of the intruding Islam, the eighth century, and became known at the beginning of the thirteenth century as an epic poetic work. But this was around the same time as the great poetic works on the Grail appeared. We hear of Flore, the son of the Spanish King Fenix, who out of his unlimited love for Blanchefleur begins his adventurous journey into the East and does not rest until he brings the imprisoned maiden home. The alchemical trait of this legendary picture can be felt as a pre-stage of Rosicrucian wisdom. Who was this son of King Fenix, with whom clearly the carrier of a Phoenix Mystery is indicated? Rudolf Steiner says, the same soul 'appeared reincarnated in the thirteenth and fourteenth centuries in the founder of Rosicrucianism, to found a new Mystery School, which in a new way, corresponding to the new age, fostered the Christ-Mystery'. Of this Rosicrucianism it is said that in it at that time the initiates were educated, who could become the successors of the early European Mysteries, 'the successors of the School of the Holy Grail'.[46]

'The Chymical Wedding'

It is the conviction of that '*Fama Fraternitatis*' that God 'on the last days (meant is the dawning seventeenth century) pours out His mercy and goodness so abundantly over the human race that the knowledge of both His Son and of nature is increasingly extended'. Hidden worlds begin to open to human beings; here one thinks of the journeys of discovery of Columbus and his successors as well as the discovery of supersensory spheres. The time is ripe that 'finally human beings understand their nobility and glory'. For they themselves are each a

---

[46] From Rudolf Steiner, 'The European Mysteries and their Initiates', lecture, Berlin 6 May 1909 (GA 57). Concerning the legend of Flore and Blanchefleur, see Additional Note 11.

'microcosm' or, as Goethe later expresses it, 'within there, too, is a universe'.

This writing, the *Fama*, pointing with an emphasis on its own time, sought to induce a gathering of striving spirits in Europe. Today it appears like an ultimatum, for especially Central Europe was a melting pot of forces striving against each other in fantastic religious landscapes. It was sent to those bearing responsibility, shortly before the outbreak of the Thirty Years War [1618–1648], that civil war of Christian confessions destructive of culture. A group of spiritual persons who knew they were guardians of sublime Mysteries, who believed they were protecting a golden hoard of wisdom they deemed more precious than all the golden treasure the Spaniards brought home from America, decided to bring the Rosicrucian wisdom into public cultural life; hitherto it had been held secret, only cultivated in most intimate societies. 'For Europe is pregnant and will give birth to a strong child. This requires a great gift from the godparents', claims the author of the *Fama*.

In the dawning age of natural science, the soul of Europe appears in the apocalyptic picture of the woman struggling in childbirth [Rev. 12]. A strong spiritual child is to be born, but the dragon from the depths rises at the same time before the woman, to devour the fruit of her spiritual striving. This was the tragedy of the Western development. Their noblest spiritual fruits, beginning to ripen out of the womb of a thousand-year-old culture, were in their tendency diverted and one-sidedly developed into a materialistic civilization and technology. The spiritual impulse, in the way the Rosicrucian writing expresses it, 'the gift of the godparents' to be laid at the cradle of the new-born child, was not accepted. It was only recognized in its true value by very few striving for illumination. Jakob Boehme belonged to these few. Only after the great stormy flood with the release of religious fanaticism had spread over Middle Europe, there slowly arises in the eighteenth century the ideal of a spiritual-religious tolerance paving the way to reconcile true natural knowledge with the light of Christ. Goethe became the effective flag-bearer of this spiritual stream.

From a letter to Frau von Stein (1786), we know that he was familiar with the significant writing of the Rosicrucian stream, the *Chymical Wedding* of Christian Rosenkreuz. This writing that arose in a mysterious way (it was written down c. 1603 by Valentin Andreae, who was then only seventeen years old; later he became known as a Pietist Swabian theologian), a spiritual seeker is presented to us, who in a progression of seven days has to undergo a sequence of deep impacting life-trials. In transforming his whole being, they lead him to that illumination presented in the picture of his participation in the chymical wedding.

The description begins on the eve of the Easter festival. In an intimate way it describes a meditation experience of the one searching fervently for the spiritual mysteries of existence, who bears the name Christian Rosenkreuz. This personality appears here at a ripe age; the action, moreover, is dated 1459. A spiritual researcher is characterized who lived from the fourteenth to the fifteenth century; he is endowed with certain high spiritual abilities that yet seem to be an inheritance of the world of the Middle Ages, but he has to experience how humanity from now on has to seek completely new ways to the spirit.

He is pulled out of meditation through a storm-wind that shakes his quiet hut. A wonderfully beautiful woman enters his hut in a blue garment, sprinkled with golden stars. She brings him a short letter in which he finds the festive invitation for the king's wedding. She departs to strong brazen sounds that resound in the mountains. As if it would be an awakening call of an apocalyptic kind, a call of the times by the spiritual world, thus the invitation touches his soul drawing him to a pilgrimage extending over the whole Easter week. We are convinced that Goethe under the impression of this writing placed the first monologue of his *Faust* on Easter Saturday. In the first version of his work, this detail is still missing. Only when Goethe in his fifties again took up the work on his *Faust* fragment, did he give the first scene that meaningful background through which the drama could become a journey of the soul from Easter Saturday to Easter morning and consequently could become a great awakening event.

Already from the great French Grail story, he became acquainted with the visions of that holy hermit who during the Passion Week received a little book from Christ that disappeared on Easter Sunday. He had to set off on a long journey until he could find it again lying on an altar. This pilgrimage was placed into the Easter week and allowed the soul to grow into the world of resurrection. In a similar sense, the seven-day pilgrimage of Christian Rosenkreuz is characterized as one of a Grail seeker.

Out of the abundance of Imaginative experiences received by the Grail seeker, after he had found entrance to the mysterious Spirit Castle, only some motifs may be mentioned here. He reports how during the tour of the Castle he is also shown the grave for the Kings, 'where

I received more wisdom than that written in all the books. I also found the magnificent Phoenix.' The Three Holy Kings from the East were always venerated as the guardians of the ancient inheritance of wisdom. The Kings lie in the grave. But above them like a prophecy there wields the Phoenix. We know from the Grail teaching of Trevrizent that this Phoenix contains the Mystery of a continuous rejuvenation.

Processes, presenting riddle after riddle to us, pass by the one invited to the King's wedding. They could appear arbitrary and confusing, if not an unrelenting law which at the same time encourages the seeker to the highest, penetrates all events. But this means, what is still active as forces and gifts in human nature has to be sacrificed so that it can arise again rejuvenated. Mysteries of transformation are presented. Processes of soul and spirit are presented as natural processes; laws of an inner chemistry are revealed. Out of the soul's self-transformation a higher nature is produced, a 'super nature'. In this lies the seed of a future world. But the human being whose spiritual eye is awakened can behold those deep hidden processes, and not only this—he feels continuously called to participate actively with all his forces in generating this higher life.

The Parzival legend has shown us the spiritual seeker who has first to learn to question. For if in beholding the sick king he feels called to be responsible, on this his degree of maturity can be recognized—the strength of his consciousness-soul. This member of the soul is still a young force. It is, as is proved during Parzival's first visit to the Grail Castle, still in need of many experiences before it can ripen towards its high destination.

The Rosicrucian Mystery also describes a guest who enters a castle full of riddles. But how different it is! He does not remain in astonishment; he strives unceasingly to research the mysteries of the Castle. Nothing escapes his wakeful spirit. He seeks to observe even such intimate things which initially should remain veiled for him, in the many situations he feels challenged to act. Although in all modesty bearing witness to it, Christian Rosenkreuz proves to be an individual who with fully awakened forces of the consciousness-soul passes the trials of the spirit. Consequently, he can be called to be the Guardian of the new Phoenix Mysteries (17).

12. Goethe as a Seeker of the Grail

Goethe's Rosicrucian inspiration and the poem 'Die Geheimnisse'

Despite all the decline in Christian traditions, souls continue to be impressed by the Mystery of Good Friday. The picture of the Son of God suffering on the cross, dying for humanity's guilt, always shocks the human mind. On the other hand, the Easter fact disappears from the consciousness of the present day. For life with the Risen One demands the unfolding of most tender soul-forces, a receptivity for the life-processes beyond the threshold of death. And yet for Christianity today, the decisive test lies in finding the realm of life of the Risen One. The Rosicrucian brotherhood seeks to prepare this Easter mood. For them the Rosy Cross appears on the place of the crucifix as the symbol of sacred feelings. Joseph of Arimathea had taken the body of the Tormented One from the cross; a cross of red roses blossomed in the place where He suffered death.

It is known that Goethe harboured an inner shyness concerning showing the Suffering One on the cross. In this he felt a profanity of the highest Mystery. 'We draw a veil over these sufferings because we venerate them so much', he has the wise educators say in *Wilhelm Meister's Apprenticeship*, answering Wilhelm's question why in their Institute of Education the picture of the Crucified is nowhere to be seen. Goethe found the symbol of the highest spiritual striving in that cross which appears surrounded by roses.

Just when an estrangement from Church Christianity, in which as a boy he had lived with great warmth, had reached its climax—it was around his 35th year—Goethe wrote his profound work [*'Die Geheimnisse'*, 'The Mysteries'] that appears to us like a search for the Grail.

On his pilgrimage away from the usual paths of human beings, the young Brother Marcus is led towards a monastic building in a hidden valley, in which a group of twelve wise men who gather around a Thirteenth live in devotion to pursue the future aims of humanity. Over the entrance he sees for the first time the cross surrounded by roses. Later, he finds it once again in that hall in which the venerable group is accustomed to gather. These men have gathered in the sign of the rosy cross, to prepare in a mysterious way the universal religion that will arise out of the harmonization of all religious streams and worldviews. For, according to the intention of the poet, these twelve represent the twelve different worldviews, or religions of humanity. Through the venerable Master who forms the centre of the community, they have learnt the deepest tolerance in which, despite the various creeds, one can live together harmoniously in a mutual complementary manner. The Christianity of the Church did not yet know the ideal of complete acceptance. But whoever can begin to comprehend in its depths the Mystery of *Wandlung* (transformation, metamorphosis), can acknowledge the standpoint of each religion besides his own, because he values them as stages of the human soul on its way to the truth. Through the destinies of time and peoples, limitations are given; they disappear where that sphere begins to shine where death is transformed into higher life. The exalted Master is called 'Humanus'.[47] His name expresses that he has overcome those limitations that hinder our living the comprehensive human spectrum.

Goethe left this magnificent work unfinished. Asked by young people, he indicated in later years how he had intended to lead the reader through 'a kind of ideal Mont-Serrat' [the Grail mountain, Munsalvaesche] and how the whole action was to take place during Holy Week. This should 'reveal comfortingly the eternal duration of heightened human conditions, confirmed by Easterday'. 'Nevertheless,' he emphasizes, 'if this poem had been completed and had appeared thirty years ago when it had been thought out and received, then it would have been vastly ahead of its time.' He consequently concluded that the time was not yet ripe for presenting such 'heightened human conditions' that would lead into openly receiving the world of resurrection.

With the expression mentioning Montserrat in the world of ideas, Goethe, to our knowledge the only time, pointed to Grail symbolism. Through his whole life, however, we find a Parzival striving, especially the wrestling and seeking of his youth. Rudolf Steiner mentions how the impulse to that poem can be traced right back to Goethe's development as a young man. At the end of his student years in Leipzig in his nineteenth year, he entered a difficult crisis in his life. We know from Goethe's autobiography [*Poetry and Truth*], he had reached the exhaustion of his life-forces and due to a kind of stroke had approached the edge of death, hovering for weeks between death and life. In this condition

---

[47] At one level, Herder has been suggested as meant. See: Julius Goebel, https://www.jstor.org/stable/27700746?seq=10.

his soul approached those sublime Rosicrucian inspirations. Rudolf Steiner speaks of a kind of initiation,[48]

> To begin with, he was not actually conscious of it, but it worked in his soul as a kind of poetic inspiration and the process by which it flowed into his various creations was most remarkable. It flashes up in his poem entitled 'The Mysteries', which his closest friends have considered to be one of his most profound creations. And indeed, this fragment is so profound that Goethe was never able to recapture the power to formulate its conclusion. The culture of the day was incapable of giving external form to the depths of life pulsating in this poem ... Then, however, the Initiation took increasing effect in him and finally, as he grew more conscious of it, he was able to produce that remarkable prose-poem known as 'The Fairy Tale of the Green Snake and the Beautiful Lily'—one of the most profound writings in all literature. Those who can interpret it rightly know a great deal of the Rosicrucian wisdom.

The sign of such Rosicrucian inspiration is the call for a change in the whole soul-condition, in the context of the striving human being, a soul-rejuvenation that can penetrate right into the deeper layers of the bodily organization. For the young Goethe this indeed meant a life-saving situation. In the following months in his parents' house in Frankfurt the convalescent develops completely new interests. He begins to study mystical writings, such as Johannes Tauler, but in particular alchemical writings representing the Western occult tradition. Later he relates how right into his student days in Strasburg he carried out such experiments as is common in alchemy, and in this the primal motifs for his poetic drama *Faust* was to be sought. For only in connection with the Rosicrucian spiritual stream can one deeply understand the figure of Faust and everything Goethe poured into it as substantial experience during its long period of its gestation.

The impulses of Goethe's youth

The way the young Goethe lives into his age bears several traits of Parzival. Certainly, unlike the son of Herzeloyde this young lad does not grow up in the peace of the forest separated from the world. From his well-to-do family he received a rich education that early on opened for him the sense for everything noble and beautiful in the world, at least his father protected him from any set form of education by not

[48] Rudolf Steiner, *Theosophy of the Rosicrucians*, lecture 1, Munich, 22 May 1907, GA 99.

sending him to a local school. Deep religious feeling awakening in the lad sought its own expression, away from all ecclesiastical forms. One thinks of the altar the seven-year-old made on his father's music desk, ordering on it representatives of the realms of nature in a pyramidal form, topped by a candle of incense as an image of the sacrificing human soul. The 'young priest', as he calls himself, wants to make a path to 'the great god of nature' through his own ritual. And so, with the help of a magnifying glass with which he gathers the rays of the morning Sun rising over the rooftops of the city, he ignites the sacrificial fire directing his devotion before the smouldering incense candle on the altar. Do we not feel in such a service of light as the soul of the boy himself created it, Ancient Persia re-emerging out of depths of being? Herzeloyde once taught her son when he asked the first question concerning God's nature, that He is brighter than any light. Right into later times, but above all in the way he built up the monumental scientific work of his *Farbenlehre*, the *Theory of Colours*, Goethe fosters a service to the light. It expressed his Persian inheritance, we can also say, his true Manichean attitude, to behold the mystery of the world in the picture of the battle between light and darkness and to venerate its reconciliation, indeed marriage, in the pure phenomena of colour.

The young Goethe approaches the phenomena of the world as out of deep soul-impulses not dulled by the compulsions of a schooling or of professional influences. Does not his natural way of dealing with people, the pure readiness towards impressions and what they can impart, recall Parzival's storming into life, the temperament of that untamed youth, whose appearance nevertheless delighted the world and whose simplicity so quickly transformed into maturity of soul?

The unbroken inquisitiveness—'that I recognize what holds the world together in its inner core'—is deeply inherent in Goethe's nature. It makes him shake the gates of knowledge. A certain stubbornness appears in the youth when he does not immediately meet the goal of his searching and striving. Later in his autobiography, regarding divine guidance Goethe confesses a certain suspicious conceit, for when his path initially led him into a dead end, he was unable to forgive God that he had allowed such a thing. He even said, 'This conceit arose out of my inexhaustible goodwill that, as it seems to me, He would have done better to help me.' At times, this mood increased in his soul, as far as a Promethean rebellion: 'I honour You? For what?'—'Have You not achieved everything Yourself, You Holy glowing Heart? And you burn youthfully and ardently.'

At the court of Arthur, when Parzival receives Cundrie's message and through her is shocked out of his youthful dreams about life, a similar mood comes over him. 'Who is this God now?', the boy calls out. From now on, we know that doubt lays hold of Parzival's soul, since for the first time he must rely completely on himself; he has to experience how one becomes guilty in life before one is conscious of one's actions. And yet, even in doubt, his innermost mood of striving, that unerring faith in what he feels to be his life's task is not broken. In no situation does he avoid life's adventure. His path passes 'right through it'. So, too, is Goethe's life path.

In his *Wilhelm Meister*, in reflection he reviews the path he had taken, believing he recognizes the mysterious law of his own guidance of destiny. When this young man strives away from the firmly grounded forms of family tradition and with his inclination towards the theatre initially seeks a non-bourgeois environment, he becomes unknowingly guilty and seems to lose himself in some illusions. Yet behind his path of destiny a very conscious leadership is apparent that nevertheless does not shy away from allowing him to face biting errors, because without fully experiencing this he would never come to full self-knowledge and with it to autonomy. Wilhelm, when he regains his freedom in the castle of Lothario, gets to know the mysterious group of leaders who attentively accompany the development and searching of this young person and at decisive turning points of his striving, seemingly by chance, repeatedly interfered as soon as it was necessary to help him to find clarity concerning his deeper intentions. This group made up the 'Society of the Tower', a kind of Lodge, founded by some friends out of the selfless interest in human nature and its pure unfolding. From the position of an ancient seat of nobility, in a hidden manner it dedicates itself to the development of certain chosen people. Masonic ideals gain shape in this novel in the sense of the free spirit of the eighteenth century, as they also illuminated Goethe's view. The significance of this seems to be—life itself is raised here to a mysteriously working school; human meetings contain awakening forces. Destiny leads into situations, challenging conscience. They test the human being; they initiate him by degrees.

This, too, is the innermost conviction emanating from Wolfram's *Parzival* poem, that life itself possesses an initiating force for the one who does not avoid it but is prepared to give himself to it with an open heart, accepting challenge. Through this that deep feeling for the sacredness of all earthly existence is awoken. The presence of the divine in all human destiny becomes conceivable.

Wilhelm Meister

It is remarkable how the coming-of-age in *Wilhelm Meister's Apprenticeship* is connected to the readiness to balance out life's outstanding debts. Then in *Wilhelm Meister's Years of Travel*, Wilhelm revisits his life paths accompanied now by young Felix, his own lad, and how through him he finds the gifts of a new beginning—he is once more allowed to behold the world through the eyes of a child. Out of the forces of 'reverence', as they by themselves mature in the soul through the revelations of life, he now learns to lay hold of the Mystery of Christianity in a completely free manner. Human encounters repeatedly become for him 'what the ideals are within, examples not to be imitated but to be striven for'. Thus the journeyman, by understanding and learning to value the nature of many groups of people, can also develop and expand his own being—it undergoes change.

He meets a highest aim of human striving in the wondrous individual, Makarie. Goethe himself describes this figure in an 'ethereal poetic narrative':[49]

> Makarie has an association with our solar system which is of such a kind that one scarcely dares to speak of it. She not only cherishes and observes it in her mind, soul and imagination, but, so to speak, herself forms a part of it; she is aware of being drawn along in those heavenly orbits, but in a quite particular way; from her childhood days she has been moving round the Sun, and in fact, as has now been discovered, in a spiral, moving ever farther from the centre and circling towards the outer regions.
>
> If it may be assumed that beings, in so far as they are corporeal, gravitate towards the centre and, in so far as they are spiritual, towards the periphery, our friend belongs to the spiritual beings; she seems to have been born only so that she may liberate herself from what is earthly and penetrate to the nearest and the farthest spheres of being.

Goethe wants to present a soul that within her earthly existence may already experience a part of that cosmic life destined for our life after death. Although confined to live in an earthly body, she grows into starry widths, which, however, in no way signifies an extinguishing of individual consciousness.

> From childhood she remembers her innermost self, as penetrated by luminous beings, irradiated by a light with which the brightest sunshine

[49] Goethe, *Wilhelm Meister*, trans. H.M. Waidson, 'Years of Travel', Book 3, Chap. 15, Alma Classics. Richmond 2013, p. 820ff.

> has nothing in common. She often saw two Suns, an inward one, and one without in the heavens ...

During the years, she has grown with her inner cosmos from one planetary sphere to another. An astronomical friend of hers thoroughly tests her indications on the observations of the external starry sky. He could observe that she is already in the process of passing the sphere of Jupiter and now strives towards Saturn, the outermost sphere in the sense of early starry wisdom.

> No imagination can follow her there, but we hope that such an entelechy will not disappear completely from our solar system, so that she may again be active in earthly life and well-doing on behalf of our great-grandchildren.

Makarie is an inhabitant of the universe, but she does not live an existence fleeing the Earth but stands with full social responsibilities which she lovingly serves as her good parents reared her to master all earthly faculties. She found the balance between the devotion to the supersensory and her faith to the Earth. Consequently, one can trust that she will not disappear for eternity into heavenly bliss but will return and carry ever new forces of transfiguration into earthly existence. Goethe cannot picture a high moral ideal without the view of repeated earthly lives.

In his old age he must have felt certain, although hidden, possibilities in himself through which a soul-development, as the one of Makarie, did not appear for him too remote. His poem *'Eins und alles'* (*'Im Genzenlosen sich zu finden'*)[50] bears witness when he evokes the World Soul as such, to expand into cosmic life, and he feels the longing that he is here already part of an invisible community of spirits, to be lifted towards the creative life of the universe.

> *Weltseele, komm, uns zu durchdringen!*
> *Dann mit dem Weltgeist selbst zu ringen*
> *Wird unsrer Kräfte Hochberuf.*
> *Teilnehmend führen gute Geister,*
> *Gelinde leitend, höchste Meister,*
> *Zu dem, der alles schafft und schuf.*
>
> O, World-soul, come to fill our lives.
> For he who with thy spirit strives
> Attains the height of his vocation.

---

[50] Goethe, *Gedichte (Ausgabe letzter Hand)*, 1827.

Then, sympathetic spirits, speed us;
Great masters, gently higher lead us
To the Creator of creation.

What else is the Grail kingdom, to which Parzival had been called, than an entrance into the Order of those elevated masters who are unceasingly active in transforming the world? When Cundrie appears for the second time, she recites the name of the seven planets to describe the borders of the wide kingdom for which he has to gain fully conscious mastery. His realm of rulership stretches until Saturn. And only because he can and is allowed to wield the Saturnine power, he is given the power to heal the Saturnine illness of Anfortas.

Wilhelm Meister finally becomes a doctor of miracles, after entering the Order of the Renouncers and having undergone a development as a fully conscious member of social life. For the 'glorious image of God', repeatedly brought forth and at the same time always damaged again from within and without, is endangered on the Earth. But from henceforth he will become its guardian.

In his Makarie, Goethe points towards a human constitution that reminds us of earlier conditions of consciousness, which today through intellectual development seem to be deeply covered over. The 'Vala' approaches it the closest, as venerated by the Celtic and Germanic peoples. Within the Grail Mysteries, besides the courageous knights of the spirit, we can perhaps think of such virginal figures living in quietly protected circles, who were able to unfold the Vala-forces in a Christian manner. Repanse de Schoye, the Grail bearer, is characterized as a soul who, out of that pure consciousness with its seat in the solar plexus, is able to make the cosmic revelations shine. But Herzeloyde, too, it is said, had cared for the Grail before her marriage. Thus, we understand a unique law to which Trevrizent points. He explains to Parzival how the maidens sent by the Grail are openly sent, the men on the other hand must work unrecognized in the world. This wants to say—within a female organization the Grail effect could directly unfold, it shone in a sunlight experience of inspiration. The male constitution was not permeable enough; it rather hid membership to the Grail. Only through the way such a person stood and acted in life, could one glean its connection to the Grail. In this sense, we have spoken of the Order of the Swan and the effect of the great ones who have died, who chose certain earthly personalities as their instruments. Within the will-impulses of such men who stayed faithful to the spirit, the Grail inspiration, although deeply veiled, sought to come to the fore. Yet Parzival appears as an individual who appearing in this earthly life can experience the grace of cosmic consciousness; despite the unfolding of his male 'I', he was able to protect and awaken the virginal nature in himself to the highest illumination. With this he lived a future ideal.

Gawain's nature in Goethe

Initial impressions suggest Goethe has a Gawain nature. He lives his destiny under the compulsion of love. But he does ride on a Grail horse as once did Gawain, 'Gringuljet with the red ears'. Love, although he always has to suffer under its power, nevertheless estranges him from his highest aims. For him it becomes a stage towards the spirit. Although in the *Marienbad Elegy* the old man shockingly confesses that he is still subject to its power, he finds those words of 'being pious' with which he can compare love. In veneration of the 'eternal feminine', which draws us on, the Chorus Mysticus [*Faust*, Part 2, conclusion] helps us divine the ascending path of the highest love, as the Grail teaches us—it leads to the transfiguration of the heart.

We have already compared the Orgeluse experience of Gawain [in Chrétien de Troyes] with the Helena mystery as Goethe fashions it in his *Faust*: the purest reflection of his wrestling in the South for the purified beholding of beauty. The Northern person who 'has become young in misty age' becomes a classical artist when he discovers the Southern landscape and cultural world as the archetypal form of beauty. Lynceus, Warden of the Tower, confesses [*Faust*, Part 2, Act 3]:

> 'Waiting for the morning's gladness.
> Scanning East for dawning light,
> Saw I sunrise, thought it madness,
> In the South, a wondrous sight.'

But Goethe's visit to Italy also brings him to the place where Klingsor's magic arts had been exercised. He dives into the abundance of sense impressions, but they no longer enchant him, although they do not leave him completely unscathed. Yet in the depths of his soul as a directing force the Parzival force remains active. For just there in Southern Italy and Sicily, Goethe is able to purify himself in the steady practice of sensory observation to come to the clear beholding of the archetypal plant. Especially here, this is shown in the letters of the *Italian Journey*; nature reveals to him her 'open secret'. He beholds in the body the 'sensory-supersensory form' as it works in the metamorphosis of plants. This is a Blanchefleur experience—the pure beholding of the etheric form for which he had continuously wooed; it has given itself to the searcher for knowledge. At the same time, it is the wedding of the young king with the beautiful lily, which he had celebrated so beautifully in his revelatory *Fairytale*.

'Do not seek the hidden consecration!' the old Goethe can exclaim. The true Mysteries are no longer guarded within the realm of secret brotherhoods, no longer in the darkness of ancient temple centres. They are to be found everywhere in earthly life as 'open mysteries', 'open secrets'. They are expressed in beholding nature and in going through one's path of destiny. The temple is present everywhere. As in the legend, King Arthur disappeared with the Grail Temple into the mountain, so the Temple with the petrified kings in Goethe's *Fairytale* waits in the rocky clefts of the Earth. But it shall be *revealed*; thus says the prophecy. For this 'the time has come'! It wants to rise into the light—visible from afar and accessible to all who are prepared to set foot on the bridge glistening with precious stones over the dividing stream.

The Anfortas nature in Goethe

Besides these highest revelations of Goethe's genius out of which the light of the Grail reaches us, many other riddles confront us to be accepted as the 'all-too-human' side of his biography. It is the Anfortas nature in Goethe, which governed in such a strong way in him and the existence of which in the depths of his being he never denied as someone practising self-knowledge. In a lecture-cycle *The Mysteries of the East and of Christianity*,[51] Rudolf Steiner mentioned this excruciating riddle, of which we are repeatedly to be aware with important personalities in the modern age. The Klingsor effect to which Anfortas once succumbed, because the mind-soul of the medieval Christian person could not face the onslaughts emanating from the union of the great magician with Iblis, is not overcome to this day. For people today still inherit in the depths of their being old soul-forces and at the same time the dead influences of past stages of development. Consequently, the spiritual researcher says:

> In earlier times the two natures of man were not so widely separate in their development; they could not diverge in this way. A person with a biography comparable with Goethe's could not rise to such heights as are revealed in certain passages of *Faust* Part 2, or in the *Fairy-Story of the Green Snake and the Beautiful Lily*, and at the same time be so divided in his soul. That was not possible in earlier times. It has become possible

[51] GA 144. Lecture 4, Berlin, 7 February 1913.

> only in later days, because there now exists in human nature something we have already spoken of—the part of the soul that has become unconscious, and the part of the organism that has died. The part that has remained alive can be so elevated and purified that the impulse which leads on to the *Fairy-Story of the Green Snake and the Beautiful Lily* can be nurtured there, while the other part may remain exposed to the attacks of the outer world. And because the forces described are able to make their abode there, circumstances may arise in which there is very little agreement with the higher ego of the person ... If we keep this in mind, we can see how a soul who in former incarnations could rule the entire person can be led downwards, and then has to relinquish a part of the total human nature, which then lies open to the influence of evil forces.

Especially in Goethe's inner development, we can pursue how a certain side of his being—that is, the powerful artistic impulse—strives back to an earlier cultural epoch. The longing of Iphigenia, who as the priestess was driven into an unwelcome land of barbarians 'seeking the land of Greece with her soul', and Faust being transported to Arcadia where he can pursue the dream-marriage with Helena—yet not without having to accept the sinister Phorkyas as a companion—expresses such a spiritual striving still wanting to work with earlier Mystery-forces. The other side of this great person, standing awake within the demands of the present day and coming to grips with it, is revealed in the way he appears in the stream of time, acting with clear direction. For his whole life he is concerned practically with material tendencies, assembling building-stones towards a new view on nature that brings about a spirit-illumined worldview. In these attempts, the conscience of the time, the young force of the consciousness-soul, speaks in Goethe. Rudolf Steiner continues:

> And because external circumstances are such that only in the course of time will the lifeless elements of human nature be overcome—the elements which can so greatly disturb the initiate of today—we must say that in our time and on into the far future there will still be many natures similar to Goethe's. With one part of their being, they rise into the heights, while with the other part they relate to the 'all-too-human'. Persons who in earlier incarnations showed no sign of these peculiarities, but on the contrary displayed a certain harmony between the outer and the inner, may enter fresh incarnations in which a deep disharmony can show itself between the external and the inner organization. Those who know the secrets of human incarnations will not feel confused in face of this disharmony. For in proportion as these things increase, the human faculty of judgement also grows, so that the old principle of authority comes to an end ...

The duality of human nature is not in the very least to be defended; on the contrary, we must strictly insist on the rule of the soul over externals, but it must still be said that the indicated facts are absolutely true for modern evolution. For the after-effects of Klingsor and Iblis are still always present, even though in another form. A special feature of our time is that these attacks from Klingsor and Iblis, as they gradually lay hold of people, are insinuating themselves into intellectual life, particularly that bearing on education, with its popularization of modern science.

Goetheanism

Particularly in this realm, however, Goethe developed initial attempts that can lead to the victory over the soul-laming effects of this new science. It is no coincidence that particularly in Sicily he reached a breakthrough to his method of observing nature shone through with ideas, with the 'Archetypal Plant' and its laws of life. The metamorphosis which he begins to pursue everywhere in the law of nature is a *law* of formation. It must become a *decision* of formation for the human 'I' that understands itself, towards a new will of transformation from one form of existence to another. For this reason, Goethe also pursued Osteology; he sought to find a view of bone-formation of the vertebrates and to perceive the artistic grip of nature, from simple elements to ever higher forms that, for example, can transform the vertebrae into the bones of the skull. He pursues the forms of living beings in their gradual advance, arriving at the upright human form for whom the skull becomes the pure dwelling of the spirit.

> *Ein Blick, der mich an jenes Meer entrückte,*
> *Das flutend strömt gesteigerte Gestalten.*

> A look, how did it whirl me towards that ocean
> Whose rolling billows more developed shapes embrace.[52]

---

[52] Goethe, poem 'Im Ernsten Beinhaus', later known as 'On Contemplating Schiller's Skull'. A paraphrase by Michael R. Burch:
And at that ecstatic sight, I am back at sea ...
Swept by that current to where immortals race.
https://www.poetrysoup.com/poem/on_looking_at_schillers_skull_translation_goethe_1289340
The original manuscript of this poem is preserved in Hanover, and over it is written, in Goethe's hand: 'For 17th September 1826.' This date Goethe crossed out, writing in its place: 'September 25, 1826.' It was printed during his

Goethe explains:[53]

> To attain the human being, nature performs a long prelude of beings and forms that still lack many human things; however, a tendency to something else is visible still above them.

This manner of perceiving in which Goethe lets the human being organically arise through the series of natural forms is fundamentally different from Darwin's theory of evolution, for whom the coming about of the human form is ultimately an arbitrary product in the battle for existence. This is carried out according to the laws of selection and the faculty of adaptability. According to Darwinism, as a theory still widely ruling biological thinking,[54] the human being can only be a continuation of the animal stage. On such a view, no attitude to life can be founded placing human beings into a meaningful moral context. Goethe's idea of development, even if initially remaining in seed-form, allows us to experience the human being as the aim of nature's entire becoming. Nature urges on like an artist performing a prelude which from the beginning strives towards the theme, intending to unfold symphonically. But this urge is the World-spirit creating in it through all the paths and detours, striving up towards the human form. For only in this dwelling, at the place of the human skull, can the spirit

---

lifetime, without title, at the end of *Wilhelm Meisters Wanderjahre*, published in 1829, and is followed by the words in parenthesis, '*Ist fortzusetzen.*' Only after Goethe's death, in the Cotta edition of 1833, does the usual title appear, '*Bei Betrachtung von Schillers Schädel,*' doubtless added by Eckermann. Nearly all texts, with the notable exception of the Weimar edition, repeat this title. The Jubilee edition has the heading, 'Schillers Reliquien' (James Taft Hatfield).

[53] Goethe, letter to Riemer, 23 Nov. 1806.

[54] For Steiner, the idea of development, of evolution, is already evidence of the Christ-Impulse, if not always acknowledged. 'To understand Darwin [...] you have to make a synthesis of all the laws discovered in the past. To understand Goethe, you have to rise above this to laws which are ever new in Earth existence. Both are necessary.' The problem is 'that people want to follow one or the other rather than one *and* the other' (R. Steiner, lecture Dornach 26 Oct. 1917. GA 177). Other 'theories' of evolution, including S.T. Coleridge, 'Theory of Life', expounded by Owen Barfield in *What Coleridge Thought*, Barfield Press UK, 2014. See also, Norman Macbeth, *Darwinism Retried*, London/Boston, Garnstone Press, 1974, who shows 'classical Darwinism is no longer considered valid by qualified biologists'—*Tr. note.*

itself dwell. It has come home in the fully awakened human form. Such metamorphosed thinking alone can lead the human knower towards the Mysteries of the resurrection. These are Mysteries of the Phoenix shining forth in Goethe's view of nature and the human being. They could not be laid hold of in the nineteenth century. Through the materialism of natural science, any possibility to conceive man's true being was obscured. It also obscured the source of a true recognition of Christ. Goetheanism was reborn in the transition from the nineteenth century to the twentieth century through Rudolf Steiner's spiritual achievement. The worldview was forged able also to lead the Faustian, searching human being towards the fact of the Resurrection.

Goetheanism wants, as it were, to support the maturing of a new Grail Christianity. In the thoughts and feelings involved in the realm of living forms, experience can bring the revelation of 'the eternal duration of heightened human conditions sealed through Easter Day'.

13. Richard Wagner's Grail Message

The mission of art

In an essay 'Religion and Art', which Richard Wagner[55] wrote after the completion of his *Parsifal* drama (he was still working on the instrumentation of this work), he speaks of the true mission of art:

> One might say that where Religion becomes artificial, it is reserved for Art to save the spirit of religion by recognizing the figurative value of the mythic symbols which the former would have us believe in their literal sense and revealing their deep and hidden truth through an ideal presentation.

It is always the sign for the decline of a religion when it sees the necessity to build a dogmatic system. Then 'it only lives artificially', Wagner claims, and with the Christian religion, which he calls 'the greatest miracle of all', this moment occurred when it became possible 'to turn it into a State-religion for Romish Caesars and Inquisitors'. Here begins the purifying task of art that seeks to free up the experiential aspect of the symbols (but leaving open their actual truth). The artist has been endowed with a representative task.

With this Wagner did not want in any way to dismiss Christianity's essential truth. As someone experiencing and recognizing in the nineteenth century, he rather tried to gain a new access to it. As one who recognizes, this is clearly demonstrated by his philosophical wrestling, frequently expressed rather incoherently. In particular, in his subsequent writing 'Hero-dom and Christendom',[56] he pursues the question of 'regeneration', the 'possibilities of ennobling the human race'. One of the reasons for racial decline he thought he saw in the change of human nutrition from the original vegetarian diet to a carnivorous one; this would have changed the basic substance of our blood and made its effect right into moral qualities. Another cause he saw under the influence of Count Gobineau in the commixture of the races. To him the white race seemed the noblest, because it is the most able to suffer. For in the ability consciously to suffer, he saw:

[55] 'Religion and Art', in Richard Wagner, *Religion and Art*, trans. (1897) William Ashton Ellis, University of Nebraska Press, Lincoln and London 1994, 213–52.

[56] 'Hero-dom and Christendom', in Wagner 1994, 275–84.

> the quintessence of free-willed suffering itself, that godlike Pity which streams through all the human species, its fount and origin.[57]

The declining races no longer produce *heroes*. The hero, nevertheless, has to be found where, against the decline of his race, he rises to find himself in the *sacred realm* as a divine hero through a miraculous reversal of his misleading will. He will overcome that will in his readiness to suffer and sacrifice himself. Yet in his modesty he is greater than the hero can be in his pride.

Wagner's Ring *and the Mystery of the Blood*

Wagner asks: What does blood—the quality of the race—mean for enabling such a sacred heroism? 'Evidently the last,' he answers, 'the Christian proclamation of redemption has arisen out of the lap of the extraordinary extensive commixture of the races.' He points to the mingling of Middle Eastern cultures and the people of the later Roman realm, who as the Latin race presents a melting of most varying elements. It formed the Roman Catholic Church with its canonized saints. He admits, 'After centuries of huge perversion of the Semite-Latin Church we see no longer any genuine Saints, no Hero-martyrs of the Truth, arose therefrom'.[58]

'The blood of the Redeemer's self, which erewhile poured its hallowing stream into the veins of his heroes' has entered a decline. It has consequently become curdled as it streams on within the Church tradition. This is the 'lament of the Saviour', as Parsifal heard it from the Grail.[59]

Parsifal:	*Parsifal:*
die Klage, ach! die Klage —	Oh the lament, ah! The lamentation
um das verrat'ne Heiligtum:	from His profaned sanctuary:
'erlöse, rette mich	'Redeem Me, rescue Me
aus schuldbefleckten Händen!'	from hands defiled by sin!'
So—rief die Gottesklage	Thus rang the divine lament
fürchtbar laut mir in die Seele.	in terrible clarity in my soul.

Christian Morgenstern later radically formulated the same experience. 'To save Christ out of the hands of the Christians.'

---

[57] Wagner 1994, 281.

[58] Wagner 1994, 280.

[59] *Parsifal*, Act 2, 2.

At the end of the mystical rite, Parsifal lifts the Holy Grail out of the shrine that enclosed it and which the sick Amfortas refuses to open. The release of the Christian Mysteries out of the shrine of dogmas and the rigidified forms of the Church is pictured. The Grail again pours its full glory over everybody gathered around it, and this is the 'supreme miracle of salvation' that, hardly audible, is softly announced from the cupola of the Grail Temple.

Erlösung dem Erlöser Redemption to the Redeemer!

How can the Redeemer be redeemed? How can the most sacred sacrifice become fully effective for humanity? For Wagner, this is the true question regarding the Grail.

It is a drop of blood, but this blood that flowed from the cross bore in itself no hint of differentiating humanity according to race. In this blood a Being, related in the same way to all people, was able in divine compassion to take into Itself the suffering of the whole human race and to release it by sacrificing Itself. Wagner writes:[60]

> The blood of the Saviour, the issue from the head, his wounds upon the cross—who impiously would ask its race, whether white or other? Divine we call it, and its source might dimly be approached in what we call the human species' bond of union, its aptitude for Conscious Suffering.

It is not a more highly organized individual; with Him a new species has entered existence. Paul calls it 'the new/last Adam'.[61] Wagner writes:

> The blood in the Redeemer's veins might thus have flowed as divine sublimate of the species itself, from the redemptive Will's supreme endeavour to save mankind at the death-throes in its noblest races.[62]

As a person educated in the concepts of modern philosophy and natural science, Wagner dares to fashion some ideas at 'the extreme limit of a speculation hovering between Physics and Metaphysics'. And he even takes a further step. 'The blood of suffering Mankind, as sublimated in that wondrous birth' of the Redeemer belongs to the whole human race, no longer to one favoured race. The religion of the Brahmins, as well as others, always belonged to a certain race. Christ's sacrifice con-

---

[60] Wagner 1994, 280.

[61] 1 Corinthians 15:45 and Romans 5:12–21. Cf. Hebrews 2:5–9.

[62] Wagner 1994, 283.

cerns a renewal of the blood wanting to benefit all human beings:

> [W]e have seen the blood of noblest races vitiated by admixture, the partaking of the blood of Jesus, as symbolized in the only genuine sacrament of the Christian religion, might raise the very lowest races to the purity of gods.[63]

Wagner says this sacrament 'could have been the antidote to the decline of the races through commingling'. It would be an illusion to want to stop this commingling. We have 'lost the nobility of the blood'. There is but one remedy for the degeneration of the whole human race: the blood of the Redeemer permeating human nature—a mystical process that is to be made visible through the sacramental deed. 'And perhaps our earth-ball brought forth breathing life for no other purpose than that ministrance of healing.' Wagner's confession towards the Christian Mystery culminates in this sentence. It is his Christianity of the Grail.

The drama of **Parsifal** *as a new creation*

Already as a young man Wagner was concerned with this Mystery. During his time in Dresden at thirty-years-old he studied Christian origins. He was known to the world at that time as a free spirit and a revolutionary, who a few days later had to flee Germany to live for some years in exile. He was not attached to any confession as he searched for the inspirational sources of Christ's influence in word and musical sound.

For the great male voice festival in Dresden (1843) Wagner composed *Das Liebesmahl der Apostel*, which was performed by 1,200 voices in the *Frauenkirche*.[64] He called this choral work 'a biblical scene'. One may imagine the days after the first Pentecost, as described in the Acts

---

63 Wagner 1994, 283.

64 *Das Liebesmahl der Apostel* (1843) WWV 69 ('The Feast of Pentecost,' 'The Love-Meal of the Apostles') is a piece for orchestra and male choruses. Many years later, Wagner described it as 'a sort of folk miracle play'. Wagner, who had been elected in January 1843 to the committee of a cultural association in the city of Dresden, received a commission to evoke the theme of Pentecost. He had successfully performed *Rienzi* in Dresden in 1842; however, *Der fliegende Holländer*, produced there in January 1843, was not received as warmly. The premiere of *Das Liebesmahl* took place at the Dresdner Frauenkirche on 6 July 1843, performed by around a hundred musicians and almost 1,200 singers from all over Saxony.

of the Apostles. The original community, hidden from the eyes of the world, frequently gathers for the holy meal. The number of believers grows, but also the pressure from without. When meeting the fearful congregation, the Apostles report the threats they experience when they dared to preach in the temple. Sufferings are foreseen. Yet voices from the heights speak comfortingly to them.

> *'Seid getröst. Ich bin euch nah, und mein Geist ist mit euch.*
> *Machet euch auf! Redet freudig das Wort,*
> *Das nie in Ewigkeit vergeht.'*
>
> 'Be comforted. I am near you, and my Spirit is with you.
> Arise! Speak the message joyfully,
> Which will never pass away for all eternity.'

The choir of disciples recognize the presence of the Paraclete, the Comforter.

> *'Welch Brausen erfüllt die Luft? Welch Tönen, welch Klingen?*
> *Bewegt sich nicht die Stätte, wo wir stehen?*
> *Gegrüst sei uns, du Geist des Herrn, den wir erfleht,*
> *Dich fühlen wir das Herz umwehen, mächtig*
> *Erfüllst due unsre Seele!'*
>
> 'What a roar fills the air, what harmonies, what sounds?
> Does not the ground move on which we stand?
> Hail to Thee, Spirit of the Lord, for Whom we pleaded,
> Thee we feel mightily flowing about our heart.
> Fill our soul!'

Can one not recognize in these motifs a preliminary stage of those mystical voices that later in Wagner's *Parsifal* will resound from the dome of the Grail Temple? It is also understandable how the poet, with his studies on the Grail, felt particularly drawn to Robert de Boron's presentation of the original Christian Grail community, whereas Wolfram's interpretation remained less accessible to him.

For Wagner in his 30th to 33rd year, it was the often-decisive time for a Christian deepening. During this period he also produced the two romantic operas *Tannhäuser* and *Lohengrin*. Both according to the legend are taken from study of Middle-Age epics, which he had pursued with zest during his stay in Paris (1841). Such legendary motifs as he could perceive from the early poems, 'the song-contest on the

Wartburg' or the Tannhäuser saga, initially rested in the depths of his soul, always in motion, penetrated with passionate battles for inner and outer existence. In complete transformation and artistic expression, the motifs suddenly erupted out of the depths into the light. Wagner describes on a magic moonlit night at the Schreckenstein, while wandering from Tiblitz in the Elbsandsteingebirge, how that world of the Minne song became alive before him. It is like a transportation to an earlier age, through dream-forces awoken by the Moon—before his inner eye the Wartburg arises as a place of wonderful spirit-flowering, but also of those battles in whose centre Wolfram, the singer of the Grail, had once stood.

A short while after this, in July 1845, the other work was conceived: 'And again I was on the volcanic soil of Böhnen.' He reports in a lively manner of the birth of Lohengrin, which ambushed him in the bath. For a serious ailment the doctor had prescribed a cure in the Marienbad. Wagner, enthused by his story of Lohengrin, jumped out of the bath to put on paper what he had perceived. He now knows that he is not made for such cures. He terminates them and nevertheless lives on. Different warm springs, as eruptive as the ones in Böhnen, had opened in him. A regeneration from within, renewing him right into the nature of his blood, was to take place.

In Wagner's biography the suffering of Amfortas,[65] of the higher human being, comes especially to the fore. We had to mention this regarding Goethe. However interesting Wagner's autobiography might be with the chain of successes and rejections, of financial straits and exuberant spending sprees, of great friendships and embarrassing rifts—from it one can hardly glean the source of his creativity. A second, supplementary biography has to be imagined for this productive person, a mystical one taking place subterraneously. Only from time to time does the latter secret one work with volcanic power into the light of day, placing marking stones of his inner development visible to the world. The contents of the sagas, which in their Middle Age version he finds 'poor and flat', present to him actions full of symbolic power from which he can draw when he wants to present inner 'events'. How much his inner personality remains behind he knew quite well when he confesses in a letter[66] to Mathilde Wesendonck:

---

[65] Wagner changes the spelling of Anfortas to 'Amfortas', Parzival become 'Parsifal'—*Tr*.

[66] Venice, 19 January 1859.

'With my poetic conceptions, I was always so far ahead of my experiences that I can see my moral training only brought about and developed by these conceptions.'

Wagner understood the language of imagination. He knew that neither everyday psychology, nor philosophical ideas, on which he had intensely studied, are able to express those trials and victories which the mystical human being has to undergo. Only the imaginative element offered him the possibility to express himself. But through the world of music there could be revealed what the inspired consciousness experienced full of grace.

*

From the studies in Paris, the content of *Parsifal* also takes place in him. In spring 1857, the source of inspiration opened, leading him into the depths of the world of the Grail. Wagner himself tells of a Good Friday morning when he stepped out of the house which Otto and Mathilde Wesendonck had lent for his disposal on the 'green hill' in a suburb of Zürich. From this place—he called it his 'asylum'—spread before his gaze was Lake Zurich with its charming shores; they seemed to be transfigured by the sanctity of the Good Friday Mystery. A soft voice spoke: Thou shalt not carry weapons on the day the Lord died on the cross.

At that time illumination sparked off in Wagner's soul how the effect of Christ radiates into nature. The creatures are allowed to participate in the deed of redemption. They too long to be accepted as children. But the redeemed human being shall be their mediator. The Apostle Paul expressed this deep cosmic Mystery in his letter to the Romans [Chap. 8]. For Wagner, this became the starting point for his *Parsifal* creation— on this morning the sounds of the *Karfreitagszauber* (the 'Good Friday magic') permeated his soul. It was still to take more than twenty years before this poetic work could gain its final form. Before this the *Tristan and Isolde* creation took precedence with the power of destiny. The love for Mathilde Wesendonck and the denial to which he had to fight through seek their freedom in this work. At that time Wagner thought to weave the figure of Parsifal into the last act of *Tristan and Isolde*. The hero on his search for the Grail was to pass the castle of the dying Tristan. The motif of the Grail search was to be heard. 'Where do I find you, you Holy Grail; my heart full of longing seeks you', thus Wagner noted at that time of his deep soul conflict.

In *Parsifal* that hero was to appear who frees himself from the compulsion of love, the *Minnesang*—as victor over those powers to which Tristan succumbs.

But soon he becomes aware how this theme would exceed the whole composition. The suffering of Tristan appears again in the figure of Amfortas, whom he wants to make the 'centre and main subject' of *Parsifal*. 'It suddenly became shockingly clear to me,' he writes 30 May 1859 to Mathilde Wesendonck:

> it is my Tristan of Act 3 unimaginably intensified. The wound of the spear and still another one—in his heart, the poor man with his terrible pains experiences no other longing but to die; to gain this highest soothing he repeatedly longs to behold the Grail, if it would at least close the wound, for everything else is not possible, nothing—nothing is able to help—but the Grail always gives him only the one thing, that is, that he is *not* able to die.

Wagner sketches the basic idea of the work, drawing from the tradition of Boron. For him the Grail is the chalice of the Last Supper in which Joseph of Arimathea collected the blood of the Saviour on the cross. Here Wagner finds scathing words against Wolfram von Eschenbach. 'Look, on the other hand, how easy Wolfram makes it!' Wolfram, Wagner thinks, without a deeper understanding of the Mystery, only added one adventure after another.

Certainly, Richard Wagner's music drama, seen as a work of art, is more complete than that medieval epic. But his judgement on Wolfram is wrong. Wagner is not yet able to decode the language of initiation. Here a path of knowledge towards spiritual awakening was pursued. To redraw it with the means of the Grail knowledge of the thirteenth century was a life achievement which included soul battles and victories of the spirit that we can only imagine. Wagner's *Parsifal*, however, pursues a mystical path which only runs on the level of the feelings. He gains 'knowledge through compassion' ('*durch Mitleid wissend*'). It is true, feelings of the deepest kind can make one '*welthellsichtig*', clairvoyant for world-issues. In a certain sense, a Christened Buddhism finds its way to the Grail.

At that stage, Wagner was given to the study of Schopenhauer's philosophy. This was the intellectual clothing of that time, in which the Buddha impulse was brought to Western consciousness. For Wagner, it meant orientation and comfort in the soul-battle he had to go through at this time. He found the moral strength to abstain and knew how to transform the fruit of suffering into creative life. In suffering and the overcoming of self-centred suffering, his soul expands to comprehensive compassion. 'This compassion I recognize in myself as the strongest trait of my moral being, and possibly this is also the source of my art' (Venice, 1 October 1858).

At that time, he drafted the plan of a Buddha drama, *'Die Sieger'* ('The Victors'). Ananda and Savitri, the two lovers, go on the path of renunciation. Yet slowly he transforms this couple, the male and female disciples who had chosen the path of the Buddha, into something quite different: Parsifal and Kundrie, who through renunciation fulfil the law of the Grail. Nevertheless, it still takes approximately twenty years before the Mystery drama becomes fully ripe in Wagner's soul for the one 'made wise through compassionate suffering'.

The most significant new creation, apart from the genial condensing of the plot into three acts, seems to be the figure of Kundrie. She is no longer the Grail messenger, as in Wolfram; Wagner does not know the threshold Mysteries connected to this mysterious being. However, he has given her a unique depth into another direction. Traits of Sigune who pronounces his name to Parsifal and can tell him of his mother, but also traits of Orgeluse who has to live in Klingsor's power and led to Amfortas' downfall, smelt into this Kundrie, who is condemned by the curse on Eve, the clinging of female nature to the instinctive powers, to hasten from existence to existence.

With this figure Wagner seeks to reveal the law of repeated earthly lives. She is the penitent in the realm of the Grail, who attempts to atone old debt into a readiness to serve. But, when the demonic nature gains power over her again, she can also be a devil who plays with her arts of seduction through which she triumphs over the noblest of men.

This Kundrie is a female Ahasver; once she met the Saviour on Earth when she lives as Herodias.[67] She recalls this:

'Ich sah—Ihn—Ihn	'I saw Him—Him
und—lachte...	and laughed ...!
Da traf mich Sein Blick.'	Then I met His gaze!'

[67] Hermann Beckh, *The Parsifal Christ-Experience in Wagner's Music Drama* (tr. A.S. and Anneruth Strauss, Temple Lodge 2022; double volume with *The Essence of Tonality*) confirms Wagner's insight. 'It is the greatest dramatic moment in the whole of *Parsifal*, the inner core of the entire *Parsifal*-drama' (p. 109). Beckh, however, suggests the figure should rather be Herodias' daughter Salome, who carries out the latter's will (Matt. 14:6ff.; Mark 6:21–25) The context is the ongoing antagonism of the adversary Iblis-Klingsor throughout lifetimes—*Trans. note.*

Now wandering from world to world, she seeks to meet Him again. When in highest plight she believes that His gaze meets hers, it is always a sinner who falls into her arms. And yet, basically, she seeks the *spirit* in man, the redeeming Spirit. In Parsifal, she meets the man who does not succumb to her magic, but especially for this reason is able to pull her from enchantment, from Klingsor's demonic spell.

Wolfram's Parzival, too, goes undeterred through the sphere of Schastel Marveile; Orgeluse's charm does not seduce him. But how completely differently Wagner was able to fashion this transition of the pure simpleton through Klingsor's world! It is a soul-battle leading to abysses. In his battle Parsifal gains knowledge—'*welthellsichtig*', 'clear vision of the world', through Kundrie's kiss, for only now does he recognize the suffering of Amfortas, before whom he initially remained silent on his first visit to the Grail Castle. Why did he remain silent? Although he beheld the suffering of Amfortas, why did he not ask? Because he had not yet experienced the wound in his own heart, from which the latter suffered. Wagner's Parsifal, when he goes through Klingsor's realm, is exposed to all the temptations that can arise in the sensory world. He must be shaken right into his blood by those powers wanting to estrange him from his true destiny. But in these depths another Power had entered, since he had been chosen to behold the Grail. This Power speaks through compassion; it permeates the blood with the purest feelings. It frees the heart. This holy presence Parsifal feels streaming in his blood is stronger than any natural power wanting to fetter him. The onslaught of the demons breaks on the Grail which shines forth in the blood. (18)

In a psychologically staged progress, Wagner makes the 'simpleton' awaken to this compassion. The first stage is when Parsifal enters the realm of the Grail. In a blind pleasure in hunting, he shot the swan over the sacred lake. A sacrilege happened; everyone is appalled, for in the realm of the Grail no animal is allowed to be killed. Gurnemanz, the Grail teacher, leads the youth before the dying swan, letting him see the dying gaze. 'I did not know', the shaken one says, who immediately breaks his bow. From now on he will no longer kill. With this, Wagner seeks to express a deepest ethical concern with which he stood in the cultural battles of his time. He was involved passionately in the battle against vivisection, in which he saw the modern form of torture. To become a protector of the defenceless, in this case of tortured animals, he felt was the first law of Grail knighthood. For knighthood is obligated.

Wagner also knew how to fashion another law of the Grail that we know from Wolfram's poetic work. It says that the one who comes to the Grail is to bring another along, who out of their own conditions of destiny would not have reached it. Parsifal had chosen Feirfis, his heathen [half-]brother; the latter received baptism in the Grail Temple, and only through this could he perceive the Grail Mystery. In Wagner's *Parsifal*, Kundrie is the soul the Grail-seeker is allowed to bring to the temple. It shows a deep insight into the laws of destiny, how the poet had connected the two paths of these souls.

When Parsifal denies the passionate advances of Kundrie, he receives her curse. The path he seeks, he shall not find, for she casts a spell on all the paths that lead him away from her. His wanderings of many years (musically presented by Wagner between Acts II and III) are caused by her spell. But Parsifal does not leave Kundrie behind in her plight without a promise. '*Du weisst wo Du mich wiederfinden kanst!*'—'You know where you can find me again!' he says to her whilst banning Klingsor's magic with the sign of the cross and sets off on his way to the Grail.

Kundrie will only be able to meet him again in the realm of the Grail. But he will not be able to arrive there before—until she, too, is prepared for this. Only as renunciants will they find each other again. Consequently, Act III begins in the realm of the Grail with the awakening of Kundrie out a death-like sleep. '*Dienen*'—'Serve' is the first word the awakened one utters. Parsifal, too, approaches the holy source. The wandering has reached its aim.

The Good Friday instructions through Trevrizent (who with Wagner carries the name Gurnemanz, the teacher of the young Parsifal) is also within the drama the most moving scene. Actions that lead to the sphere of the Gospel are carried out here. The spirit of the Washing of the Feet [John 13] reigns between the human souls. Like the great sinner, who weeping, bent down to the feet of Jesus pouring out the precious ointment [Luke 7:36, cf. John 12], Kundrie too anoints the feet of the pilgrim, who after long wanderings found the path to the Grail. Parsifal, now anointed by Gurnemanz as priest-king, out of the power of the Grail performs his first service by baptizing Kundrie, the heathen soul. At that moment the miracle of transformation spreads over the whole spring landscape. Creation wants to take part in the Good Friday Mystery; for them too Christ brought His sacrifice of love.

> *Ihn selbst am Kreuze kann sie nicht erschauen:*
> *da blickt sie zum erlösten Menschen auf ...*

Since it cannot see Him on the Cross;
they look up instead to man redeemed ...

In Kundrie herself a piece of nature has been atoned and lifted towards the spirit. For the human beings has been called upon to be a mediator for nature. In human beings and through them the elements want to return to their divine origin. The effect of the Grail is not only an inner human Mystery; it rays out into the light of the Earth. It is the *'Terra lucida'* ['Earth of light' or 'luminous land'], which in seed-form begins to shine forth, the etheric Earth of the future.

Wagner has the action continuously passing into sacramental reality. In Act I of his mystical plot, he has Parsifal behold the Mystery of nourishment of the immortal human being at the Grail Castle, the continuous sacrifice of the love of Christ in the celebration of the holy meal. But now something similar takes place in the baptism, carried out in the power of the Grail. The transformation becomes world-power; it leads nature to transfiguration.

The Mystery of the Spear

Parsifal accomplished the supreme healing deed of healing on Amfortas. For this it needs the power of the Holy Spear, the one which inflicted the wound. No Grail poet has brought out the significance of the Spear in such clarity as Wagner. With this, he gave his poem a turning point which especially for our time gives it a contemporary note.

For what is this Spear? Chrétien and Wolfram initially only knew the bleeding Lance which was carried in during the meal. It is, as we already saw, the Imagination for the instinctive power of the drives at work in the blood. It poisons the most holy striving; it wounds every night when it permeates to the head the hidden human being in us. Only Chrétien's successors who continued his work bring the lance into a mystical relationship with the Sacred Lance or Spear, with which the Centurion Longinus was to have opened the side of the Redeemer on the cross. It played a great role in the tradition of the Middle Ages.

It was felt that it is the selfishness of humanity that nailed the Saviour to the cross and which still crucifies Him. This also inflicted the wound at His side. But out of this misdeed, nevertheless, the highest salvation has sprung for humanity. The sacrifice of love of the Son of God has transformed evil into a higher good. It also had sanctified the Lance that inflicted the wounds from which the blood of the Redeemer had flowed—the blood which in the Grail chalice now radiates like the

Sun. Consequently, the Lance belongs to the Mystery of the Grail. Like the healing Vessel, it too has to be guarded in the right way.

From the chalice of the Grail humanity is to receive *grace*; with the Grail Spear something is given into the hand of humanity, most inwardly connected with its *freedom*. For the same force, which—released as selfishness—bringing sickness and destruction, laid hold of in freedom can be revealed as the creative power of the higher self.

The human 'I' shall consequently not be extinguished; it must be wrested from the instinctive power of the sensory nature.

As Wagner describes it, Amfortas lost the Holy Spear when he forgot the pure service of the Grail and allowed himself to be seduced into Klingsor's magic realm. With this Spear the opponent of the Grail could inflict the wound on him. Sickness, seemingly unhealable, is the consequence. The plight of the Grail begins.

'O, wunden-wundervoller	'Oh, wondrous-wounding
heiliger Spear!	hallowed Spear!
Ich sah dich schwingen	I saw thee wielded
von unheiligster Hand!'	by unhallowed hand!'

Thus Gurnemanz complains when relating this misfortune. (19)

The Grail is revealed ever less frequently, because beholding it increases the pain to the point of being unbearable for the sick Amfortas. Thus, the Grail knighthood begins to wilt. All the means brought to heal the wound prove to be ineffective. The wound is only closed by the wound which inflicted it.

But who is able to wrest it from the opponent of the Grail? Only the one who is so pure that he can enter Klingsor's realm without succumbing to his enchantment. This is Parsifal's challenge. The weapon cannot touch him when Klingsor seeks to destroy him. Parsifal remained awake during the onslaught; he did not lose himself with Kundrie. Nevertheless, he learned to know the depths of suffering springing from passion; in his soul it transforms into the strength of highest compassion. Consequently, in reviewing his accomplished path, he can bless this suffering. He even blesses Amfortas in his suffering, because only out of beholding this suffering can the highest compassion awaken in the timid simpleton.

When Parsifal catches the Spear that remained hovering over his head, he makes the sign of the cross with it over Klingsor's entire realm.

'Mit diesem Zeichen bann' ich deinen Zauber.
Wie die Wunde er schliesse,

die mit ihm du schlugest,
in Trauer und Trümmer
stürz' er die trügende Pracht!'

'With this sign I banish all your magic;
as the spear closes the wound
which you dealt with it,
in wrack and ruin
it destroys your deceptive display!'

One must see through the illusion of sensory enchantment to be able to break its spell. Parsifal has become the victor over it, consequently he is chosen for the Grail kingdom. On a Good Friday morning, bringing the Holy Spear back to the realm of the Grail, he reports on his wanderings and numerous plights. He had to receive many wounds without defending himself in battle. On his path, he had never used the Spear for self-defence. Unblemished, the hero brings the Spear back to the Grail.

Wolfram points to this Mystery in a different way. During all the years of his wanderings, his Parzival leads the battle of self-assertion. But only when his sword breaks in his last battle and he feels defenceless for the first time, can the calling to the Grail reach him.

The force that hitherto had served self-assertion must turn to the spirit. In the struggle with the earthly world, the personality can be strengthened and matured. Out of an innermost freedom it must open to the realm of grace. Those ever-present forces of grace have poured from Golgotha into humanity; nevertheless, the deed of free human beings is necessary to make them effective—creative human beings who know how to wield the spear. Traditional Christianity has kept the healing forces hidden in the shrine of dogmas and traditional forms. Does it know how to wield the Spear? Indeed, this weapon was taken from it by the enemy of the Grail. But only when the Spear is together with the Grail, can the Grail shine at its highest to reveal its power to overcome the world. The world needs a new uncovering of the Grail. Only a Christianity possessing the Spear will be able to accomplish this.

14. Uncovering the Grail

'The Holy Spear, I bring it back to you.' With these words Parsifal moves towards the redeeming deed. He closes the wound of Amfortas; he fulfils the uncovering of the Grail.

In 1879, Wagner penned the climax of his poetic work with this mystical act of its hero. The breakthrough of an age of new spirit-revelations, the victorious luminosity of the Grail, which the Church had kept locked up in a shrine, stood before his inner vision. Now he could start with the instrumentation of the piano score, which with prophetic power penetrated the morning awakening call of the trombones into the deep soul-sleep of the age. It was a festive opening of that epoch in which the Archangel Michael—according to ancient traditions and expectations, which were to be fulfilled with this—took on again the leadership of the age.

This turning point of the new spiritual development, which, for example, Trithem (Trithemius) of Sponheim[68] had exactly calculated and which Rudolf Steiner out of his spiritual research also dated to the year 1879, one can find throughout mirrored in the soul biographies and crises of destiny of many contemporaries when one pursues intimate studies of those years.[69] Perhaps one discovers in the same

[68] Johannes Trithemius (1462–1516), born Johann Heidenberg, a German Benedictine abbot and a polymath, active in the German Renaissance as a lexicographer, chronicle, cryptographer and occultist. He is considered the founder of modern cryptography (a claim shared with Leon Battista Alberti) and steganography, as well as the founder of bibliography and literary studies as branches of knowledge. He had considerable influence on the development of early modern and modern occultism. His students included Heinrich Cornelius Agrippa and Paracelsus—*from Wikipedia.*

[69] In the nineteenth century, Lewis Carroll (Rev. Charles Dodgson) had to write *Alice's Adventures in Wonderland* (1864) under the code of fictional 'nonsense'. As the protagonist, Alice morally develops by overcoming four trials based on the four days of Easter (John Docherty, *The Literary Products of the Lewis Carroll-George Macdonald Friendship*, Mellen Press 1997). In theology, a new theological emphasis on the Incarnation became dominant (*Lux Mundi* 1889); the search for the 'historical Jesus' inspired several 'lives of Jesus'—to research the subject, the more successful writers employ a 'reverse technology' by asking what each important saying meant for the self-consciousness of Jesus himself

year that Edison constructed the first carbon filament lamp and with it opened the age of the electric light [termed 'artificial daylight']. But such events present more the material counter-picture of that inner transformation. The longing of humanity for 'more light', which arises out of the deepest grounds of the soul, initially finds a satisfaction in the realm of the practical, sensory realm. Schastel Marveile has at hand direct solutions through substitution.

Or, to remain within the technological realm, one could look at the use of dynamite to break through mountains and confirm that the St Gotthard Tunnel, Switzerland, was built; natural borders between countries and nations were broken down to enable traffic flow. Certainly, there were souls who longed for quite different breakthroughs.

Rudolf Steiner's spiritual battle before the turn of the nineteenth century

In the autumn of the same year, the young Rudolf Steiner entered the Technical University in Vienna. There that quiet, yet mighty wrestling began for the breakthrough to the spiritual world, which through the natural-scientific manner of thinking seemed completely blocked. From his autobiography, *The Course of My Life* [GA 28], we glean—in that simple form in which he reports about his own path—how here an individuality entered earthly life whom from earliest times onwards possessed access to the supersensory realms. But through this, he was destined to suffer inner loneliness at this time. He reports [Chap. 3]:

> I had to study mathematics and natural science. I was convinced that I should find no relationship between these and myself unless I could

---

(Maisie Spens, *Concerning Himself*, 1937; see also Friedrich Rittelmeyer, *Jesus and Christ*, 2024). The leading nineteenth-century writer of prose in English, John Henry Newman, was made a Cardinal in 1879 (canonised 2019); he began tracing development in doctrine. In 1879 George Matheson, the blind seer of Scotland, began publishing articles that made the experts sit up—he traced development in Paul's thinking and suggested a positive view on evolution could balance the prevailing materialistic Darwinism. In 1879 Henry Scott Holland gave his acclaimed addresses on the Easter events (*Logic and Life*, 1882); in 1879 Phillips Brooks of Boston gave the Bohlen Lectures on *The Influence of Jesus*; in 1879 Andrew Jukes spoke on *The New Man* (pub. 1882), a sustained biblical study on the 12 'Verily, verily' sayings in John's Gospel as a spiritual path; in 1879 George Bowen, missionary in India, produced his *Verily, verily: The Amens of Christ*—*Tr. note.*

> place under them a solid foundation of philosophy. But I perceived a spiritual world, none the less, *as the reality*. In clear vision the spiritual individuality of everyone revealed itself to me. This found in the physical body and in action in the physical world merely its manifestation. It united itself with that which came down as a physical germ from the parents. Those who had died I followed farther on their way in the spiritual world ...

Rudolf Steiner quite clearly recognized this view of the spiritual world that he carried within himself was impractical in his age, unless he could also justify it 'with the forms of natural scientific thinking'. A comprehensive study of the sciences ensued, but especially of philosophy. He became aware, that which gives us a worldview denying the spirit is not only the observation of nature and experiments, but the way the phenomena are interpreted. Thus, in optics he learnt to understand the battle Goethe pursued against Newton. In biology he took on Goethe's teaching of metamorphosis. The task was 'to read the facts of nature correctly'. These efforts to gain knowledge made him in the best sense suitable to edit and publish Goethe's scientific writings. Amongst the Goethe researchers at that time there was hardly a person who had a true understanding of Goethe's works. Karl Julius Schröer, Professor of Literature in Vienna with some intuition in this realm, could bequeath that important task to his pupil Rudolf Steiner, who was then a 22-year-old student. We have already pointed out how a new Grail path opens in Goethe's spiritual approach—especially where he gave himself to practise beholding the spiritual forces wielding in nature.

In retrospect, Rudolf Steiner describes how difficult it was for him, out of his own nature, to live especially in sensory observation. The world of ideas, the direct beholding in the spirit, was natural for him. However, practising unceasingly, he gradually managed to live into the world of tangible sensory experiences. In his concern with Goethe's work, he found an impulse to devote himself to the pure beholding of phenomena, until they themselves eloquently revealed their meaning. *'Beholding the Idea in reality is the true communion of the human being'*, Rudolf Steiner was finally able to express as a blessed experience in his introductions to Goethe's natural scientific writings.[70] He had found the way, which in a courageous diving into the world of sensory experiences did not lead to their denial but, to the spirit.

---

[70] Published version: Rudolf Steiner, *Goethean Science*, Chap. VI. Mercury Press 1988, GA 1, p. 91, emphases original.

The path that had to be pursued was long and painful, and not without dangers, placing difficult soul-trials before the contemporary spiritual seeker, for which he was nowhere able to find support and comfort, except in his own self, when the source of the pure world of ideas had opened. Being thrown back on oneself, part of the Parsifal destiny, had to be wrestled through in the experience of loneliness. *The Philosophy of Freedom* presents the experience of someone who—starting with pure observation without the help of a religious tradition—learns in full consciousness to lay hold of that which is eternal, based in the pure world of ideas of the individual.[71]

This spiritual knighthood is to find its approval in continuous battling, daily challenged by the contemporary buzz-words. It may often appear mysterious on which side the knight stands and what sharp sword he wields in battle. When Nietzsche with clouded consciousness had collapsed after a heroic spiritual battle, he had to be defended against a world of Philistines, who like Pharisees put him on trial. One finds Rudolf Steiner completely on the side of the tragic man. Again, in Ernst Haeckel's dispute, in which his opponents sought with cheap arguments to demolish the great concept of evolution of the keen natural researcher, Steiner steps completely on the side of the latter, although Haeckel went against anything to do with Christian tradition. At that time the spirit of progress was on the side of those who could courageously deal with the concept of evolution and apply it to all the phenomena of existence, even if initially supporting it in a mathematical guise.

As described by Wolfram, we have also found Parzival at times fighting on the side one did not expect. Like him, the spiritual seeker at the threshold of the twentieth century seems no longer able to know when Good Friday arrives. He too lives completely outside the 'Christian calendar'. Pointing towards this are those radical judgements in which Steiner seems to reject the world of Christian faith the closer the turn of the century approaches. He explains this contradiction people often believe they find in his development. In an autobiographical passage,[72] he writes:

---

[71] The basic 'Parsifal' contention is that the achievement of individual struggle in cognition opens the way for those coming after—*Tr. note.*

[72] The passage (*'in seinem Lebensgange'*) is neither found in *Mein Lebensgang* (GA 28) nor in the autobiographical lecture, Berlin 4 February 1913 (GA 250)—*Tr. note.*

> I wanted to speak of what can be found in 'this world' as the spiritual-natural [element], the essentially divine content. In the traditionally preserved confessions, this divine content had become something 'beyond', because the spirit of 'this world', not recognized, was separated from the perceptible world. It had become something for human consciousness that had been submerged in an ever-increasing darkness. Not the rejection of the divine-spiritual, but its insertion into the world, its invocation in 'this world'—is what strongly concerned him at this time.

The rebirth of Christianity

Those who imagined the divine enthroned above the world and guiding it from without, instead of recognizing Its presence in earthly existence itself, cannot find the Grail. In a letter from that time, Rudolf Steiner defends the concept of Prometheus. He understood the Prometheus concept of incarnated humanity, 'not as an outraged being in ceaseless arrogance against world-creation, but as the concept that becomes aware that it has to create out of its own self the highest of what can exist for it at all in the world'.

> When the human being becomes aware that the highest potency of existence in unending love has given up itself to live again in the human soul and here accomplishes the deed of freedom, in that moment one has to see each god standing outside as a pseudo-deity, against whose tyranny one has to rebel ...[73]

Parzival lived in defiance against the god whom he still perceived as an almighty being whom he consequently thought should have steered destiny differently for him. Only when he experiences Him as the One sacrificed into earthly existence, the One giving Himself in unswerving faithfulness to human destiny, does he begin to feel God in His reality. He finds Him on a Good Friday, as the One Who awaiting the human being's free deed. Of the chained Prometheus, Rudolf Steiner writes in a letter:

> ... that the bondage ceases at that moment where the highest potency of existence slumbering within, that is, wisdom and love, are unbound.

Consequently, the laming of the sick Anfortas is lifted when Parzival is able to ask the question born of the heart. For to ask it requires the whole maturity of life—both wisdom and love.

---

[73] From *Briefe*, Vol. 2, letter to Helena Richter, Weimar 29 August 1891.

In this context, only indications may serve to point towards the inner consistency of a path the spiritual seeker is to follow to that threshold, which was the turn of the nineteenth century. It meant at the same time 'a turning about of the nascent process of human development'. Rudolf Steiner says:

> At the time I imagined how the turn of the century would have to bring a new spiritual light to humanity. It seems to me that the separation of human thinking and will from the spirit had reached a climax.

But not from historical traditions—also initially not from the Gospels—could the Christ Mystery reveal its true form at that threshold of time; for him it had to be brought directly out of the spiritual world. Steiner writes [GA 28]:

> The Christianity which I had to seek I did not find anywhere in the confessions. After the time of testing had subjected me to stern battles of the soul, I had to immerse myself in Christianity, that is, in the world about which the spirit speaks.

The first fruit of this Grail search comes to the light of day in the book *Christianity as Mystical Fact* (1902), [GA 8]. Rudolf Steiner confesses:

> The evolution of my soul rested upon the fact that I stood before the mystery of Golgotha in most inward, earnest joy of knowledge.[74]

At that time, the Good Friday Mystery entered his spirit and his soul. It was as if in ceaseless efforts and patience the pure chalice had been polished to receive the most sacred content. The sum of all the sciences, the extract of all cognitive knowledge formed itself as a vessel of salvation in which from now on the blood of the Redeemer is to be protected and brought to shine brightly. The uncovering of the Grail could begin.

The new Mysteries of the Grail

The aim of the above-mentioned book [GA 8] was to understand the appearance of Christianity out of the context of the Mystery streams of antiquity as their fulfilment and at the same time their succession. This book signified a waymark in the history of Christianity itself. During the following years and decades, matters outlined in this book were extended on all sides. The Gospels were step by step regained for contemporary consciousness, beginning with

[74] Rudolf Steiner, *The Course of My Life*, Dornach 1925 (GA 28), final sentence of Chapter 26.

John's Gospel. They were not only interpreted. Out of their sources of inspiration, as it were arising anew, they could reveal their original sound as heavenly Word, soul-awakening, spirit-illuminating. Instead of historical documents intending to report past events, they prove to be stages of ascent to the spirit, directly leading in all proximity to the One wanting to lead through death to a higher life. The paths are still open today; walking them, they still prove the power of their veracity.

A cosmology was built which from the ground up overcame the natural-scientific, materialist worldview—yet paying attention to each detail of the results of research and the objections. In its centre, the Christ-event rayed forth—the sacrifice on Golgotha as the meaning of the Earth and the whole of the starry cosmos. In his *An Outline of Occult Science* (1909), Rudolf Steiner, besides numerous lectures, fundamentally presented this picture of the world and human development. In this book, he called it the 'science of the Grail' and showed the path into the supersensory worlds that can lead to the first stages of this knowledge. Of the Grail, he writes [Chapter 5]:

> If this symbol, as it is given in legend and myth, is understood in its deeper meaning, we shall find that it is a significant image of the nature of what has been spoken of above as the knowledge of the new initiation, with the Christ-Mystery at its centre. The modern initiates, consequently, may also be called 'initiates of the Grail'.

Each age has to re-find the path towards the spirit by connecting to the corresponding faculties of the soul, and at the same time takes note of the cultural conditions. '*Gardevias*' [*Garde-vias* = 'Guardian of the path!'] is read on the *Brackenseil* [a leash]. The Grail seekers of the early Middle Ages willing to walk the path of the spirit were called to 'watch the path!' We heard of souls, who with engagement of their lives and their happiness, wrestled to gain the mysterious *Brackenseil* and to decipher the path to the spirit from the writing, sparkling with precious stones. Today, this path has been re-found for the consciousness of the twentieth century onwards. For the first time, it is openly revealed in the book *Knowledge of the Higher Worlds, How is it Attained?* (1904) GA 10.

Rudolf Steiner's four Mystery Dramas present in dramatic pictures the paths of destiny of individuals stiving towards the spirit. There can be revealed in a living manner what the contemporary Grail seekers have to undergo with these trials of the soul and probations of the spirit. It proves that they, too, can achieve the path of schooling not in the peace of a monastery or as a world-shunning hermit lifting themselves to divine visions. Initiation is met amid one's destiny in life. It demands that they unerringly remain *in life*, working right through it (*'in mitten durch'* [Wagner's *Parsifal*]).

Rudolf Steiner repeatedly attempted to describe the contemporary path of knowledge, in connection with descriptions of early Mystery schooling. On the one hand, to show and foster the continuity of spiritual striving, as it leads from epoch to epoch, but on the other hand to summon out of the divining, beholding of a noble path that 'magic breath' (*Zauberhauch*) into the present time, which always passed through the Mysteries to take up the soul on its wings so that it may not slacken on the path of probation.

Thus in 1905, he began to speak of those centres of wisdom, from which in dim prehistoric times the spiritual leadership of the primordial European people have arisen. Through Wagner's music dramas he initially developed the view of those early Mysteries, because in these works something can become alive most directly for contemporary feeling of the spiritual sources out of which the myths and legends have arisen. It is as if the Merlin magic of a sunken world is summoned again in these works, but especially in the aural magic of Wagner's musical world. These are the Mysteries of the far North mirrored in *The Ring of the Niebelung*, whereas the Western European (Celtic and Germanic peoples) find their purest expression in *Tristan and Isolde* and in the sacred world of the Grail.

*

In Rudolf Steiner's presentations, besides the Druid Mysteries, the *Trotten*, are repeatedly named; in Northern Mythology, the sacrificing priests were called *Drotten*. The word *Drude* (or *Trutte*), later used of magicians and mysterious spirits when the mythical figures were feared as evil, is a variation of this.

Here, drawing upon ancient Mystery experiences through the power of spirit-vision, Rudolf Steiner describes a certain schooling that initially connected to the most tender Mysteries in nature. The pupils—as we read—were instructed to contemplate pure flower chalices and to feel that it is the power of the Sun's rays, under whose effects the seeds ripen. This process takes place without longing in ceaseless innocence. It is quite different in the animal and human realms, penetrated by desire. Only in a divine sphere above, one sees again a realm of innocence and plant-like modesty. And the pupils of the Mysteries were directed towards the future:

> One day desire and longing will disappear. The chalice will then open from above, in the same way as the chalice of the flower opens; it will regard human beings from above. As the Sun-ray merges into the plant, the human being's own purified power will unite with this divine chalice.

In these Mysteries, the creative power working in the Sun's rays, was called the 'holy lance of love'. But if misused in the sphere of lowest selfishness, it becomes the bleeding lance. This, drawn into superstition, later became the magic wand. Through possession of this lance, Klingsor's magic realm received its terrible power. The Mystery of black magic is connected to the misuse of creative powers. The bleeding lance is to be wrested from the sphere of the lower instincts through Christ-filled human beings. They will learn to hold the 'holy lance of love'. But the chalice, opening like a blossom from above, is the picture for the souls who descend into incarnation. Through the purest Sun-like creative powers, sent to them from below out of human souls, the possibility is given to descend. This chalice is the Holy Grail. But to it there belongs the re-won and sanctified lance—the symbol of White Magic. (19)

This picture points most tenderly to a Mystery of the distant human future. Before the prophetic gaze of those ancient mystics, an age stood picturing the end of the sexual generation of humanity. The human race will then take on completely different forms of existence, condensing in a tender etheric medium. Already today, however, in the human blood can be prepared that which one day will be released from it through the Sun-like creative power. For this, the transformation of all human patterns of life is clearly necessary. The blood shall one day pulse through human veins with plant-like purity. It will then be comparable to the sap of the red rose.

Before this, it must be led through the dying of all lower desires. The sign of the cross stood for this, when the Christian Mystery was included in early initiation symbolism. That which is to blossom from it is indicated in the red roses that can germinate from the wood of the cross. Everything connected with this symbolism was once born out of the Grail Mysteries.

In this light we also learn to understand one of Christ's sayings coming to us from the 'secret gospel', the 'lost Egyptian gospel of

Thomas', perhaps intentionally suppressed.[75] '[71] I shall destroy this house, and no one will be able to build it', we read. To the questions of the disciples, when He will reveal Himself and they may see Him, He answers, '[37] when you disrobe without being ashamed and take up your garments and place them under your feet like little children and tread on them'. Still more clearly, He expresses Himself when asked about this Mystery, '[22] … when you make the two one, … when you make the male and the female one and the same, so that the male not be male nor the female female'.

Grail Mysteries concern humanity. They prepare future stages of development. Wagner, whose ideas range around the regenerated human race, with the redemption of Kundrie wanted to point towards the deepest transformation of human nature.

The path of Parzival and the 'starry script'

It cannot be the purpose of this book to collect all the details of what Rudolf Steiner said about the Grail and the figures surrounding it. His whole life's work is a concern to know the Grail and reveal the Grail. Nevertheless, there are certain marking-stones on the spiritual path which he had to meet and about which he gave witness. 1913 can be seen as such a waymark. The visible expression for it was laying the foundation stone of the first Goetheanum on 20 September 1913 on the Dornach hill, near Basel. In this building such impulses are to be fostered, which Goethe felt mightily pressing in the Imaginations of his prophetic *Fairytale*. The rising of the temple out of the earth's rocky abysses, the awakening of the three kings of their enchantment, the marriage of the youth with the Beautiful Lily—in the same way as Parzifal could unite with Blanchefleur in the light of the Grail.

In that year, Rudolf Steiner gave the most significant revelations concerning Parzival's path. It took place in three steps. Firstly, in the lectures on *The Mysteries of the East and Christianity*,[76] he spoke of the successive ages in which humanity, according to its relevant stage of

[75] 'The Gospel of Thomas' in James M. Robinson (Ed.), *The Nag Hammadi Library in English*, Brill, Leiden 1977, 117–130. These gnostic documents were discovered in December 1945—*Ed.*

[76] 1) *The Mysteries of the East and Christianity*, lecture cycle 3–6 Feb. 1913, Berlin (GA 144); 2) *The Effect of Occult Development*, The Hague, 20–29 March 1913 (GA 145); 3) *Christ and the Spiritual World: The Search for the Holy Grail*, Leipzig, 28 Dec. 1913–2 Jan. 1914 (GA 149).

consciousness, had to be led to the corresponding paths to the spirit. What once the culture of Egypt had ennobled as a unique spiritual dignity, the Mysteries of Osiris and Isis, found its decline during that time, when the pupils of initiation stood before the mourning and silent Isis and as 'sons of the widow' had to experience the pain of the dying Mysteries.

For the spiritual gaze, says Rudolf Steiner, the Mystery stream of humanity appears like a river that for a time appears on the surface, then disappears for a certain epoch to reappear again in quite a different place.

How did what had been submerged in Egypt re-emerge? he asks. 'It emerged in such a way that it became visible with that sacred chalice, which is called the Holy Grail, guarded by the Knight of the Holy Grail. And in the ascent of the Holy Grail, one can feel what in the ancient Egyptian had been submerged.' With these sentences the key to many things had been given which can lead into the Mysteries of the Parzival-path. Let us recall that Chrétien introduces him before he is given the name as 'son of the widow' and that Sigune, through whom Parzival receives his name and the first Grail teaching, seems to harbour a Mystery. For is she not the virginal widow holding the dead bridegroom in her lap?

In this contexts, Rudolf Steiner distinguishes three Mystery groups which appear to have melted together in the Grail legend—Arthur's Round Table, the actual legend of the Holy Grail and the path of Parzival. The civilized peoples had successively to develop three soul-forces—the 'sentient soul', which out of an ancient inheritance could still draw on clairvoyant force; the 'mind-soul', which had to pass through a dying of the earlier beholding of pictures but at the same time had to intensify the feelings into inner religious moods. The 'consciousness-soul', moreover, which is being developed today leads towards individual responsibility but thereby dismisses the individual from traditional Mystery leadership, unable to spare periods of doubt and confusion in life. Arthur's Round Table, as Merlin inaugurated it, presents an after-glow of the first-mentioned Mystery epoch. The European peoples were educated in the pre-Christian millennia out of the wisdom of the Druids. With the heroes of the Round Table (for example, Gawain, whose adventures were discussed in Wolfram's *Parzival*) after-images are alive of those great Mystery messengers of an earlier culture that as singers or bards travel through the countries and through the wonderful pictorial language of myths and legends spread wisdom and moral standards amongst the peoples of the West. The task then was with these means to awaken the sentient soul and bring to it some harmony. 'Arthur's knighthood' of the Middle Ages with secret guilds fostered even further that wisdom tradition. Their last echoes flowed later in the Lodges of the Western countries.

As its content, the Grail Legend itself had the esoteric fostering of the Christ-event. The carrier of this spiritual stream always felt how difficult it is to approach the forces of the ruling mind-soul with the mystical depths of Christianity. Initially they were only able to imbue the divining feeling with the sublime Spirit-light that radiated from Golgotha. They had to wait until new forces of consciousness would awaken, able to lay hold of the new spiritual revelation through a fully self-aware *cognition*. (20)

The approach of such an individual towards the Grail Mysteries, which opens towards the spirit out of an inner freedom, was found within legendary attire in Parzival. Consequently, we find a freedom expressed in the trials—the question that can also be left unsaid regarding mistakes in life, which despite the noblest striving cannot be avoided, but also learning from guilt, the awakening through it towards an inner responsibility. Thus, mysteries of the consciousness soul are arising that belong to the future.

In March 1913 the lectures in The Hague follow, where Steiner speaks of Parzival's first entrance into the Grail Castle as a nocturnal experience—as an inner awakening that is mirrored in Imaginations. We have opened discussion in this book with these significant indications and with it gained an initial key to understand Grail experiences.

The climax, however, of Steiner's expositions concerning Parzival's path are the Leipzig lectures from Christmas 1913/14. Here Steiner connects mainly to Chrétien's work, to honour the depths of the Kyot tradition. Significant above all is how the spiritual researcher speaks of his own soul-paths, which only after years of pursuing and repeatedly losing the trail, finally reached its aim—to decipher the writing that appears on the chalice of the Holy Grail and through which Parzival is called to be the Grail King. It is a 'starry script', in which the name of the new initiate becomes visible.

What does that mean? Earlier, we pointed towards the early Nordic legend of Perceval. In it the Grail is called, '*ganganda greida*' (provisions for the journey). During the evening meal, Perceval perceives how with each course the Grail is carried around and repeatedly offered to the old Titurel. The words '*ganganda greida*', says Rudolf Steiner, came to him as an Inspiration from the Nordic folk-spirit, upon being asked for advice on his search for the Mystery of the Grail. Moreover, in immersing himself into Perceval's soul, riding along through days and nights, who through the hermit had received the Grail teaching on Good Friday, above the rider he beheld in the sky the rising and descending Easter Moon—the golden chalice that dwindles ever more from evening to evening, while the dark only tenderly indicates part of the Moon, like the Host appears to grow in the chalice.

A heavenly sign—the 'stone', which at one time in the cosmic battles was dislodged out of Lucifer's crown, for which he wrestles, shines down as a picture from the firmament! Every Good Friday, accord ing to Kyot-Wolfram, the dove descending from heaven puts the Host on this stone. For when the spring Full Moon is reached during Holy Week, the Easter Mystery can take effect. The Moon becomes a chalice, while during the Easter weeks it wanes again. This leaves us to divine something it contains that is hidden.

Spiritual science teaches the Sun is not only the source of light and warmth of our planetary system. It is at the same time the seat of sublime beings of the cosmos, who allowed the highest spirit of love, the Son of the Sun, through aeons to mature within their lap. When the time was fulfilled, He descended from the ether-rays of the Sun from cosmic heights down to the Earth. Cosmically seen, the appearance of Christ was the highest Sun-sacrifice to the Earth.

For in the Sun's rays there lives not only what we physically observe as light, whose chemical origin we attempt to analyse through spectroscopes. What we call 'light' we also see being reflected from the surface of the Moon. But what on the beams of light attempts to stream into the world as cosmic love, is not mirrored back—it penetrates right through. The Moon takes it up into its hidden depths. To the opened gaze of the seer is revealed how in the chalice of the Moon it glows out of its dark part, how it is enclosed in the chalice and carried through space. This is the 'provisions for the journey', which only become visible to the spiritual vision, the eye of the heart awakened through love.

It is the starry script, in which the name 'Perceval' is to be read on the chalice of the Holy Grail. When the gaze begins to penetrate sense-appearances, when the world becomes transparent for it, for the weaving sacrifice of love hidden in all existence, then the world becomes transfigured for the gaze. It is the Easter gaze. It penetrates 'right through the midst'.

*

The poet Christian Morgenstern (1871–1914), through his whole searching and striving from his youth on pursued this Parzival impulse. In his final years he became a pupil of Rudolf Steiner and could consciously practise the Grail path. He has given inner expression to this experience in his poem:[77]

Gib mir den Anblick deines Seins, o Welt …
Den Sinnenschein laß langsam mich durchdringen …

So wie ein Haus sich nach und nach erhellt,
Bis es des Tages Strahlen ganz durchschwingen —
Und so wie wenn dies Haus dem Himmelsglanz
Noch Dach und Wand zum Opfer könnte bringen —
Daß es zuletzt, von gold'ner Fülle ganz
Durchströmt, als wie in Geisterbauwerk stände,
Gleich einer geistdurchleuchteten Monstranz:
So möchte auch die Starrheit meiner Wände
Sich lösen, daß dein volles Sein in mein,
Mein volles Sein in dein Sein Einlaß finde —
Und so sich rein vereinte Sein mit Sein.

Let me behold thy being, World …
Pierce through me slowly with the senses' gleam …

Just as a house grows gradually brighter
Until day's beam rays through it everywhere
And just as though this house could come and offer
Its roof and walls in sacrifice to heaven —
So that, at length, filled full with golden glory,
It stands, as might a Spirit-building stand
Like to a Monstrance steeped in Spirit-light —

So may my walls their rigid nature lose
And thy whole being entrance find to mine,
While my whole being entrance finds to thine:
Then would our beings perfect union know.[78]

---

[77] Christian Morgenstern, *Wir Fanden einen Pfad* (1914), Munich: Piper, 55. Several reprint editions.

[78] *We Have Found a Path,* Poems by Christian Morgenstern, English rendering by Ruth Hilde Bruce. Mercury Press, Spring Valley NY 1994. 70.

Here are tenderly described the most inner growing processes. At this stage, all cognition has become sacramental. It is a *Mystery of transformation.*

To place the religious life into the centre means to renew Christianity in the light of the Holy Grail. This was the basic impulse that enthused a number of young people in the years 1921 and 1922, when after the collapse of the Middle European culture they looked for the path to rebuild practical Christianity today. They found in Rudolf Steiner the teacher of a new recognition of Christ. Through him they were helped to gain the basis of a contemporary sacramental life. They believed they understood the call of the times to build altars on which human souls in offering could raise themselves to the One prepared to give His life-forces—illuminating, healing, overcoming death—into the needs of the time. Before them stood the ideal, to found places on which the Mystery of transformation can be experienced again. This was not to replace an existing dogma with a new one. They knew it is to stimulate processes of growth within the souls that today open to the first rays of a new spiritual Sun—to create and foster an atmosphere into which the rays of the Grail can enter. Out of such an attitude a new Christian priesthood was founded. This draws its spiritual commission not out of past traditions but out of the presence of the Risen One. For this revelation 'The Christian Community' wants ever to be a vessel.

Out of such a deep insight into the cosmic context of the Christ Mystery, it is again possible to celebrate the annual Christian festivals with new meaning, to express that which occurs year by year between Christ's Being, Who lovingly connected Himself to life on Earth, and human nature opening to it. The first Christian centuries, out of their cosmic insights worked out how to date Easter. We know how seriously the various Church traditions have struggled with this. The events of Good Friday were not to be allowed to become an annual memorial festival to a certain fixed date in the year, but the most inner aim was to organize it ever afresh out of viewing the heavenly events, controlled by the constellation of Sun, Moon and Earth. For Easter, the vision of people seeking Christ is to be directed by the cosmos, beyond the merely earthly events. The forces of Sun and Moon are to work together that the highest divine Being can appear in an earthly attire. Their forces are bestowed ever again in a specific manner, if the Risen One is to appear in the etheric life of the Earth. This belongs to the Grail knowledge.

As long as this was still felt by the bearers of Christian tradition, people did not think of touching the moveable date of Easter. In the present-day struggle to reform the calendar, in wanting to fix the date of the Easter festival, the cosmic Mysteries of Christianity are being denied. It arises from a deep opposition to the Grail, belonging to the intellectual attitudes of our century, even in theological circles. Only a Christianity can answer this materialistic onslaught with more than appeals to a noble tradition, that is, with *insights* arising from a spiritual worldview able to protect the cosmic context of the Christian Easter festival. Something beneficial could happen for the lives of the coming generations if the people with insight could succeed in saving for them the true Easter festival, by helping us look up to the celestial signs of the Sun and Moon, also in times to come.

The Moon chalice, which wanes towards Easter-tide to give the hidden gleaming Sun-host increasing room, is macrocosmically the sign for the Grail. The Grail Mystery, however, has to be found in human beings themselves. Moon-forces are at work in the formation of the cerebrum, to form a pure mirror of thinking activity. The Moon reflects sunlight—but in this reflection its light frequently displays a cold light of almost ghostly effect; the thinking of the brain, too, can transmit to us a virtual world. In this sphere of cold appearance there is no room for such facts that with the Mystery of Golgotha are placed into the earthly world. Only where we allow this brain-bound intellectualizing to subside can the cosmic thought that lies behind it be revealed. A Sun-like quality shines forth. Revelations from the heart flow into this pure thought activity, which then seeks to be only a receptive vessel:

> Spiritual brightness appears to you,
> Killing all intrinsic light—

is how a saying of Rudolf Steiner describes this inner process in which the soul can courageously fight its way free from rigidified thought-forms.

*

Cosmic consciousness

In such pure thinking, which thrives behind the sense-bound life of thought, the impulse of will is at work, striving to break through the world of appearances; in it lies the true human self. Imaginatively speaking, it is the 'holy spear' before which the world of appearances shatters. Before it, every enchantment lying over all existence must give way.

Without the highest activity in the ego, the Grail cannot reach the seeker. And yet, all activity is merely a preparatory act, a making oneself worthy of the revealing life of the spirit. For the Grail and its Sun-like radiance are grace, towards which only the mood of expectation is appropriate.

When one begins to delve into the body of ideas, the spiritual science of Rudolf Steiner, the temptation to summarize it in a world-view system is always there; that is, to intellectualize it. The founder of anthroposophy himself counteracted this contemporary trend by building his work from ever new starting points and with ever-changing conceptual formations, as if from the foundation. He, so to speak, continually opened the world of the spirit in new breakthroughs. The spear-like power of the creative ego can be continually felt at work in this Grail revelation. It protects the work from any dogmatization, from ossification in a reliquary. It always remains a *path*. This, however, means: the fruits of knowledge must never be completely separated from the contemplative re-experiencing of the path of knowledge that led to them. Therein lies the Parzival element of this spiritual struggle.

As testimony to a mighty breakthrough into the cosmic heights and expanses, Rudolf Steiner's lecture-course is there, from the last summer of his life, *True and False Paths in Spiritual Investigation* (Torquay, August 1924. GA 243). This lecture-course demonstrates that behind our sensory-bound consciousness there is more than just *one* deeper layer to which we can penetrate. Human beings are constituted with seven states of consciousness. It is revealed how they are constantly active within us in a hidden way. In the picture of the Apocalypse, the Book of Revelation, the Son of Man walks amongst the seven candlesticks. These states of consciousness correspond to what are called the seven planetary spheres, as enumerated in early star wisdom, and how they can still be valid today for a spiritual perspective viewing humanity as a cosmic being formed from them. Ascending to them again in meditative experience, growing toward them from level to level, is a matter of awakening. Initiation takes place in inner awakening processes.

In this lecture series, Rudolf Steiner describes how the sevenfold states of consciousness are connected to the various metals that mysteriously permeate us with their radiance. For example, it is the hidden effects of silver that awaken the inner 'dreamer' within us, the lunar being; or the effects of copper that can awaken us to the forces radiating from the Venus sphere. We are led through seven metal states and thus simultaneously through seven starry spheres, all the way to the boundary of Saturn.

When Parzival receives the news that his name has appeared on the Grail, the Grail messenger recites the names of the seven planets; for that is how far his domain now extends. Only because he can spiritually penetrate Saturn can he also cure Anfortas of his Saturnian illness. It is the hallmark of one called to the Grail that he has become a citizen of the vast cosmos. He is able to fertilize the earthly world with cosmic wisdom, using its powers to re-order earthly conditions.

When Rudolf Steiner laid aside the instrument of his earthly body on the morning of 30 March 1925, we were allowed to approach his coffin. It was located in the simple studio where he used to work on his statue of Christ. At the feet of this sublime wooden sculpture, his earthly remains were laid out. We found ourselves in the pre-Easter period: in the evenings, one could see the delicate chalice of the spring Moon in its first waxing. Albert Steffen, contemplating the life's work of the great spiritual messenger, was able to conjure before us the image of the Grail. In his eulogy, he called him 'the fulfiller of Parzival'.

Gralsnähe

1.

Aus Sternenweiten senkt ein zweites Leben
Sich sanft herab in deiner Tage Drang.
Wirst du den Lichtgesandten Einlaß geben?

Schon kreisen sie mit strahlende Gesang
Und tragen eine Schale zu dir nieder:
Das Heilsgefäß, darin erglüht der Trank,

Der alle labt, die sich als treue Glieder
Der ew'gen Ritterschaft zum Dienst geweiht,
Vom Gral gerufen und geehrt als Brüder.

Sie heben dich aus Erdenangst und Streit
Und lassen dich der Sendung Glück erfahren –
Den Strahl, der Gegen jedes Dunkel feit:
Dich schützt der Sonnenspeer der weißen Scharen.

2.

Der Sonnenspeer, der alle Weltmacht birgt,
Ist zum geweihten Ort zurückgetragen,
Den heil'ge Bruderliebe streng umzirkt.

Der edle Hort, nach dem die Weisen ragen,
Der Wallfahrt Ziel, das Kleinod, der Legenden,
Schwebt strahlend-unverhüllt in unsern Tagen

Hoch über trübem Dunst in reinen Händen …
Der Erde Heil ist blindem Trieb enthoben:
Nun muß das Reich des Zornes-Engels enden.

Ob Schatten streiten, ob noch Wölker toben,
Die Menschheit wächst zur Einigen Gestalt
Nach jemem Bildnis, das die Sterne loben.

Und dessen Preis durch alle Sphären schallt.
Dämonen weichen vor des Speeres Spitze,
Der Funken sät mit zeugender Gewalt:
Der Menschheit Urbild pflanzt sich fort im Blitze.

Albert Steffen

'The Approaching Grail'

(Prose translation)

1.

From the expanse of stars, a second life gently descends into the struggle of your days.

Will you allow the emissaries of light to enter? Already they circle with radiant singing and carry a vessel down to you. The vessel of salvation, in which glows the drink that refreshes all those who, as faithful members of the eternal knighthood, have dedicated themselves to service, called by the Grail and honoured as brothers. They have overcome the fear of earth and the sorrow and let you experience the happiness of your mission—the ray that banishes all darkness: the Sun's spear of the white hosts protects you.

2.

The Sun-spear, which contains all world-power, has been carried back to the sacred place, strictly surrounded by holy brotherly love. The noble treasure sought by the wise, the destination of pilgrimage, the celestial body of legend, hovers radiantly and unveiled in our days high above the murky mist, in pure hands ... The Earth's salvation is freed from blind impulse: now the realm of the wrathful angel must end. Whether shadows quarrel, whether nations still rage, humanity grows into a unified form, in this image which is praised by the stars and whose praise shall resound throughout all spheres. Demons retreat before the spearhead, which sows sparks with generative power—humanity's archetype propagates in lightning flashes.

Additional Notes

Grail research in recent literature

With his work, *Parzival und der Gral in der Dichtung des Mittelalters und der Neuzeit* (Stuttgart 1925), Wolfgang Golther has given a comprehensive overview of the Grail poems from Chrétien de Troyes to Richard Wagner. He attempts to trace the whole development of the legend out of the seed of Chrétien's *Perceval*. He gets carried away, saying, 'The mysterious spell Chrétien's poem casts on all subsequent writers and commentators of the Middle Ages and of modern times lies less in its content than its incomplete form. There were riddles to be unravelled, the solution of which could be sought in various ways ...'

Certainly, it cannot be denied that often wonderful inspirations can emerge from fragments or works of art left as sketches, because it is carried by a *content* in seed-form that goes beyond what has so far been fashioned. Golther stands for the thesis that the continuations of the legend and the transformation of the motifs can be completely explained from the existing literary material. At times, even out of misunderstandings regarding Wolfram, he seeks to prove that he had his planned structure purely from Chrétien's epic. All this seems quite erudite on a philological level, although one cannot call it profound. But that means, the deep layer from which the pictures have been drawn and from which the legend has been continually fed in its wonderous growth, remains completely closed to this scholar. Thus, in his later work, *Parzival in der deutschen Literatur* (1929) attempting to provide a history of the content and the motifs, he writes, 'We have to become free from the illusory beliefs in unknown great ones, who secretly created all that for which the masters of the medieval poetic art were loudly praised and recognized by their contemporaries.' If Golther means one should not look for prototypes, for example, an *Ur-Perceval*, a primal Perceval, whom Chrétien slavishly uses, or a Kyot poem that Wolfram, as it were, only set into German, but that one may finally fully acknowledge the masters of epic poetry for their own creativity—then one can only agree with him. But it is something else when this creativity is introduced as a mere play of the Imagination, or whether it connects to deeper matters that make the poet greater the more carefully he deals with his world of pictures because he is responsible to a higher reality. The poetic figures and events are but the reflection of this. The aim of a real work of art is to lead the reader to experience this higher reality.

Those who know how to read the inner lawfulness of the Imagination become increasingly reticent in judging such texts. They feel reverence towards them. A groundbreaking achievement for new literary research was initially accomplished by San Marte (A. Schulz). In the middle of the nineteenth century he published his life's work, a translation of Wolfram's *Parzival* from Middle High German, and at the same time he made the other works by Wolfram known, at least in excerpts. He did the same with the Titurel epic—*Leben und Dichten Wolframs von Eschenbach* (2 vols. Magdeburg 1836 and 1841). San Marte also researched the secondary sources of the Grail poem, and because he stood for the Celtic origin with great zeal, he pursued the traditions of the Druids and Bards. His book, *Die Sagen von Merlin* (Halle 1853) elucidates much concerning that Celtic world and the 'prophetic figure' of that early Merlin. This researcher above all persevered in holding fast to the Kyot hypothesis. He believed he found in the French poet Guiot of Provins, who penned a war poem against the Pope and the clergy, *La Bible Guiot*, that 'Provençal' whom Wolfram cites. But then Wolfram must have mistaken the little French town Provins with the region Provence. There are many things that speak for San Marte's hypothesis—but more that they are unlikely. Above all, the fact that from such a Grail poem, from which Wolfram has drawn, indeed, which he even recast out of the French, is not mentioned by any contemporary. This hypothesis today is debunked by scholarship. It is another question whether we cannot find behind that Kyot somebody with knowledge who brough the Cathar traditions of Provence to Wolfram, and to veil his actual person and divert attention from it with good reason. In his exposition of Wolfram's work and once more in his Parzival studies (*Über das Religiöse in den Werken Wolframs,* Halle 1861) San Marte attempted to bring out the Christian core of the great work. He sees in the noble personality of the poet the basic impulses of Protestantism in embryo. Even if one has to see this interpretation as insufficient, one can nevertheless gain much from its presentation. These things have flowed out of the reverence of what is humanly and artistically impressive.

Simrock's version (completed 1862) is certainly artistically more mature, yet his explanations are already affected by the comparative research of literature and legends in the nineteenth century. We partly quoted this scholar, but mostly follow the modern translation of Karl

Pannier (Reclam edition), but always compared to the Urtext, the text and critical apparatus of Paul Piper (in Kürschner, *Deutsche National-Literatur*). For the *Perceval* of Chrétien de Troyes, we could use the translation of Konrad Sandkühler (Stuttgart 1929). They were given in prose but in a special degree through its diction could evoke the magic mood and elevated spirit of the poetic work.

Of the following researchers one may mention Adolf Birch-Hirschfeld, who like most later ones, radically rejects the Kyot source. In his work *Die Saga von Gral, ohre Entwicklung und dichterische Ausbildung in Frankreich und Deutschland* (Leipzig 1877) he gives for the first time a general overview of the Grail poems of the twelfth and thirteenth century. Out of the material, he believed he could explain the transformations and continuations of the subject stage by stage, purely as literature. This academic view misses any view on the essence of context of the Orders and brotherhoods of the Middle Ages, whose secret traditions have given the maternal ground for the making of legends. A Grail researcher who wants to remain with this critical viewpoint is doomed to a completely barren yield. It is akin to that comparative Gospel research which had arisen out of historical criticism of the nineteenth century. That was only able to dissolve the substance of the biblical documents but was unable to reach standards corresponding to texts that have arisen through Inspiration.

In our observations, we shall refer to other academic contributions of more recent years. Here we mention the Parzival studies of Walter Johnnes Schröder in *Der Ritter zwischen Welt und Gott* (Weimar 1952). A new reverential attitude towards the poetic work is apparent. I would like to call it a sensitivity for the sacramental substance of Wolfram's work, although not yet penetrating to the spiritual sources of experience. This has certainly come about in a groundbreaking manner through Ernst Uehli. After a thorough discussion of the works of historic-critical research, in his book *Eine neue Gralsucher* (Stuttgart 1921) he courageously approaches the new spiritual-scientific methods. He was the first to use Rudolf Steiner's Grail researches as a key to penetrate the content of the legend and to open the great medieval poem for a contemporary understanding. The thoughtful methodical viewpoints and its succinct deciphering of the Imaginative content makes this work—within its chosen limitations—an example for future research in literature and legends.

2. *The legend of Veronica*

The legend of the Veil of Veronica is woven in the Grail legend. It says that Vespasian, the son of the Roman emperor, suffered from leprosy and had to live apart from everyone in a tower. A pilgrim comes to Rome and remembers the wonderful healings Christ had accomplished during His time on Earth. The Emperor Titus (here the names are confused: Titus is the son of Vespasian) hearing of this sends messengers to Judea to search through the Governor, Pilate, for any objects that had belonged to Christ. Pilate finds a woman, Verrine (Veronica is meant), who possesses a veil on which the face of the Redeemer was imprinted when He dried off the sweat with it on His way to the place of execution. She does not want to part from it, but travels with the messenger to Rome. Vespasian is healed through merely beholding this picture. After this, he is urged to revenge the death of the Prophet by the Jews. He travels with his father Titus over the sea, punishes the Jews and researches the destiny of Joseph of Arimathea, whom he frees from imprisonment in a tower. Through deep teaching he becomes a Christian.

The legend of the origin of the picture of Christ is told in various ways. In a poem written in Middle Franconian dialect from the second half of the twelfth century, the same time as Robert de Boron's *Joseph* was written, we read the Saviour dried His face with a cloth belonging to Veronica, a woman devoted to Him in love, that she had given him during a meal. In this cloth His face is imprinted for ever. By the same author, who calls himself 'The Wild Man', there follows a poem concerning Vespasian. With such legends, one can say we meet belief in relics but also 'superstition'. But if one looks more closely at the Veronica legend as well as the Grail tradition of Joseph of Arimathea, we meet a thoroughly spiritual teaching. For the cloth is not merely such and the Grail chalice is not an ordinary functional object. For the Risen One looks after this chalice, bringing it Himself to Joseph's prison. Not everyone is able to behold this chalice. What is involved here?

The human body of formative forces excretes very fine, fleeting pictures, which weave on in the etheric surroundings. We are continually surrounded by such pictures, but they can only be perceived clairvoyantly under certain conditions. Christ's body was able in a unique way to detach such etheric pictures, as it were, out of the pure devoted will of His being—out of His 'bestowing virtue',[79] part of His Sun-nature,

[79] A phrase from the inserted prayer for St John's Tide, liturgy of The Christian Community—*Tr.*

the etheric life-forces streamed from Him. This communication of pictures of His form to the surrounding world can be felt like an eternally tender form of propagation. Souls who were fortunate to meet Him on Earth, carried such ether-pictures woven into their experience. Rudolf Steiner once described how Christ's disciples, when they spoke of the Master after His death, seemed as if permeated by His being—it was as if His voice was heard from them and their face transformed into His face. Veronica is a disciple who knows how to protect and cherish such a picture out of communion with the Master. Through her presence something of the Redeemer's Life-substance continues—consequently, healing forces can still be conveyed through such a disciple when received in the right way.

If one begins to understand such processes, one will also grasp the extraordinary effect that proceeded from celebrating the Eucharist in early Christianity. In the act of 'breaking bread', which repeatedly connects to Christ's sacrifice of love during the Last Supper, something of the bestowing of the Redeemer's life-forces passes over to those co-celebrating. This is the deeper reality that was experienced in the sacrament of the altar. For in it the Mystery of transfiguration of Christ's body is repeatedly present—through this Christ's body can be propagated in numerous pictures amongst the believers.

The veil of Veronica, consequently, points in a legendary form towards a mystical experience. The *body* of the Redeemer, by being 'broken', is multiplied in earthly existence; it is the miracle of the multiplying bread.

The chalice of the Holy Grail presents the other side of the sacramental Mystery. It is the *blood* of the Redeemer shed for us—but the flow of which can be collected in the human heart. For the human blood is the carrier of the 'I'. With the out-streaming love on Golgotha, the Christ-I became free and began to invade the life of humanity as holy Love. In the mystical contemplation directed to the Mystery of the cross, this 'I' can be found by the soul and be taken up into one's own inner life. It lays hold, in actual fact, of the blood organization of human beings who give themselves to Christ.

Rudolf Steiner could consequently say of the Grail Mysteries that the 'I' of Christ and the Mystery of its multiplication was preserved for centuries. Out of this Mystery stream there will come a time when the radiance of grace of this Life-body giving itself, when the wonderful manner known to early Christianity had come to an end, the sacramental effect will be generated anew. Only through the 'Grail' will the presence of Christ—the immersion of His 'I' into each individual human soul—be summoned anew in human communities. In the lectures 'Spiritual Bells of Easter', Rudolf Steiner speaks of this.[80]

> Today the time has come, when these Mysteries may be proclaimed, when the heart of human beings becomes mature through a spiritual life, so that they can rise to an understanding of this great Mystery.

3. *The Gospel of Nicodemus*

The Grail tradition, which Robert de Boron represents, links to the Gospel of Nicodemus, much respected in the Middle Ages. The '*Gesta Pilati*', the Acts of Pilate that presents the first part of the Gospel of Nicodemus, reports how Joseph of Arimathea is placed before the High Council and describes to them his experiences in prison. On Good Friday 'around the tenth hour', that means immediately after Christ was taken from the cross, he was locked into prison by his opponents. Throughout the whole sabbath he remained there, yet 'around midnight [so we read], when I stood upright and prayed, the space into which you had locked me was lifted up at its four corners, and a light shone into my eyes, so that I fell to the floor trembling ...' Then somebody lifts him up, speaking comfort. Joseph believes it is Elijah, but the voice says, 'I am Jesus, whose body you have asked from Pilate and wrapped in rich linen, you have put a veil on the face and laid me into your new grave and then you rolled a stone before the entrance.' The One Who appears to him in his prison cell is the One risen from death, appearing to him to show His love. He Himself leads him out of his prison to show him the place of the burial and the linen with which he had wrapped the body.

In his Grail book,[81] Adolf Birch-Hirschfeld can say, with a hint of justification, 'We can consequently exactly show the point where the poet begins to introduce the Grail into the legend of Joseph of Arimathea. We found that the legend itself gave the poet the opportunity for this; quite simply the words of the Latin original "mystice" were taken up and its symbol put in the place of the matter itself.' He means, the poet wanted to characterize two important acts of the holy story, that

---

[80] Rudolf Steiner, lectures Cologne, 10 and 11 April 1909. GA 109. *The Festivals of the Year: Easter*.

[81] *Die Sage vom Gral; ihre Entwicklung und dichterische Ausbildung in Frankreich und Deutschland im 12. und 13. Jahrhundert*, 1877.

is, the Last Supper and the burial with the symbol of the vessel of the Last Supper, that is, the Grail. For the latter symbolizes the Eucharist as well as laying Christ in the grave. Although the author then points towards a change the poet has undertaken, he does not describe the freeing from the prison occurring immediately but taking place many years later under Vespasian. Even the legend of Veronica and the punishment of the Jews through the Roman emperor have been woven into the events, but that means the siege of Jerusalem [70CE].

Birch-Hirschfeld, however, does not draw any conclusions from this change. With the long period in the prison tower, he does not see that something essential is expressed. For in this period, Joseph has received the grace to live with the Grail. He is illuminated and nourished by it. As an initiate of the Christ Mysteries, he steps out after the destruction of Jerusalem and founds that esoteric stream that shall take its course through the centuries away from Church traditions. More is involved here than a spinning further of legendary motifs.

In the substantial work, *Ein Gralbuch* by G. Gietmann S.J. (Freiburg 1889), the same viewpoint is taken as Birch-Hirschfeld, although with a completely different tendency. The Grail legend is simply seen as a symbolic attire for sacramental Christianity, indeed, with allegorical means pointing towards the Roman Church itself, although concerning the latter the Grail tradition is obstinately silent. Here it concerns the method to cover the Grail stream by using it for something completely different.

4. The Hiram tradition

The first researcher of the Grail is called 'Flegetanis', which in all probability is not a personal name. Josef Görres derives the word from the Arabic—'*Felek daneh*'. This would mean, 'the one who knows the stars, the astronomer'. In the later poetic work '*Sängerkreig auf Wartburg*' ('The Song Contest on the Wartburg') this person is also mentioned; there he is named 'the magician Zabuloni'. Again, it is said of him that he 'still venerates a calf, is a Jew on his mother's side and a heathen from his father's side'. We already mentioned the master builder Hiram for whom this origin would fit. For Hiram, according to I Kings 7:14, was the 'son of a widow from the tribe Naphtali and his father was from Tyrus'. The expression 'son of the widow' always points in the spiritual mode of expression.

In the Egyptian Mysteries, Horus himself was the son of the widow; the divine Isis had at one time received him out of the gaze of the rays of Osiris, her dead husband. All Isis-initiates were called 'sons of the widow'. In biblical contexts, too, one often meets this expression. Elijah awakens the son of the widow at Sarepta; here it concerns the magical awakening which Elijah has himself to live through in his own being in a Phoenician centre (Zarepta). In this way, in his lecture-cycle, *Wendepunk des Geisteslebens* ('The prophet Elijah in Spiritual Science', Berlin 14 Dec. 1911) Rudolf Steiner for the first time interpreted the destinies of Elijah. In Luke's Gospel, Christ awakens the 'son of the widow'; the youth of Nain is the other person who besides the awakened Lazarus appears in the Gospels as initiated by Christ.

If one has become aware of the meaning of such a formulation, one will no longer find it meaningless when Chrétien begins his poetic work *Perceval* with: At the time of spring, the son of the widow arose in the lonely forest ... [see Part One, line 69ff.].[82] In certain groups it was immediately understood what was meant that Perceval was introduced with such a phrase.

Regarding the name Zabulini (= Sebulon), the following relationship can be suggested. One could have expected here Naphtali, since Hiram on his mother's side is said to come from this tribe. But in the Book of Isaiah, the land Zebulon and Naphtali are mentioned, lying in darkness—this is 'the people who walked in darkness and see a great light' (Is. 8:23 and 9:1). As we know, Matthew quotes this passage when the first appearance of Christ in Galilee is described. Regarding the prophecy of Christ, which especially applies to these two tribes, in the imagination of the legend, Zebulon could merge into Naphtali. The poet of the Wartburg contest, however, adds that the latter had been the first who knew the wisdom of the stars. One night he read in the stars that after 1,200 years a child would be born who would be above all Jewish honours; this is only explicable by his uniting Bileam, knowledgeable in the stars (Exodus 24), with the figure Hiram-Zabuloni. Bileam, or Balaam,[83] was the first who saw the star of the Messiah approaching. He also plays a great role in the legend of the Three Kings. To him links the non-Jewish expectation of Christ, which was fostered as Mystery tradition.

But how was Solomon's Temple different as preparation for the coming Messiah, which needs the concentration of the highest spiritual

---

[82] https://www.poetryintranslation.com/PITBR/French/DeTroyesPerceval-PartI.php?textLinkTarget=Y2hyZXRpZW4=#anchor_Toc536526871

[83] Numbers 22–24.

forces in one place? Hiram, the Phoenician master gave his contribution to this building. The Temple Legend, as told in the Freemason Lodges and repeatedly presented in ceremonies, now connects with this Master individual. It indeed speaks of the work at the invisible temple. Work was to be continually carried out as the visible temple in Jerusalem had been destroyed. Consequently, it is not arbitrary when the Grail legend chooses the moment of the destruction of Jerusalem as the incentive for creating the Grail table through Joseph of Arimathea.

A Jewish tradition exists of 'Sepher Ha-Yashar' that shows great similarly to it. According to our knowledge, in his work *The Ninth Century and the Holy Grail*[84] (Temple Lodge 2001), Walter Johannes Stein was the first to point to this parallel. In the notes to this work, one finds a translation of the Introduction to that book, printed for the first time in Venice, 1625. There we read how the holy city of Jerusalem had been destroyed through Titus and with the onslaught of the Roman army an officer named Sidrus (or Cedrus) when searching for booty discovered a hidden room behind a wall in a large house. Breaking the wall, he found behind it in a clay vessel many scrolls of the Old Testament, but even more precious books. Amongst these treasures sat an old man who read these books. He brought him out and had pity on him.

He takes him with the scrolls in all honour from Jerusalem. They travel from land to land until they arrive in Spain and settle down in the province of Sevilla. There Sidrus builds a great house to foster the secret wisdom, to which he was introduced by the honourable old man. These teachings are now written down and faithfully protected. But the most precious scrolls was the 'Sepher Ha-Yashar'.[85] It contained the genealogical trees of all times and with it the course

[84] Translation by John M. Wood, revised by Irene Groves, of *Weltgeschichte in Lichte des heiligen Gral*, latest edition Mellinger Verlag, Stuttgart 2010, originally published Orient-Occident Verlag, Stuttgart, The Hague, London, 1928.

[85] Composed: Middle-Age Spain, 1300 CE. Sefer Ha-Yashar (The Book of Righteousness); one of the most popular ethical books in the Middle Ages. It was frequently attributed to R. Tam, the tosafist, who wrote a book by a similar name. Some manuscripts attribute the book to Zerahiah ha-Yevani, but there is no evidence for this. Others have suggested R. Jonah Gerondi as the author but his ideas are contradicted by Sefer Ha-Yashar. It remains an anonymous work probably written in the thirteenth century— https://www.sefaria.org/Sefer_HaYashar?tab=contents

of world-history, not only of the past, but also the future up to the appearance of the Messiah.

We see here a Jewish tradition links to the same magnificent moment in time, according to the Christian reckoning to the year 70CE. From then on what had been taught and practised in the temple of Jerusalem went over to the Mystery traditions. Mystical brotherhoods fostered esoterically a spiritual inheritance that later in the form of Kabbalistic wisdom was in many ways to influence the alchemical strivings of the West. The way, in his description of the freeing of Joseph of Arimathea from confinement, Robert de Boron speaks of that 'great book' in which the Mysteries of the Grail had been written, has undeniably a kinship with that Jewish Mystery tradition. It should not be regarded as a coincidence that Wolfram always expressly mentions Sevilla, where Gamuret went ashore and where Trevrizent was to have met him. The Kyot tradition undoubtedly hangs together with the esoterically kept temple wisdom. In this lies the key to all the riddles the Kyot figure has given to Grail researchers. One researcher showing a sense for such contexts, although he does not penetrate to the esoteric content of the symbolic language, is Ludwig Emil Iselin. In his book, *Der morgenländische Ursprung der Grallegende* (Halle 1909), he pursued the symbols of the Grail chalice and of the miracle-working stone. He shows the rich treasure of the legend that has been carried from the late Jewish and Christian traditions (partly Nestorian, partly Arabic-Abyssinian) from the Orient and from which Wolfram too must have drawn—most likely, through the mediation of the person hidden behind the name 'Kyot'. Thus, Syrian Christianity possessed a favourite book of legends, *The Treasure Cave*; it is regarded as the Christian version of the 'Book of Adam'. Our Additional Note 20 is devoted to this, for it mentions the legendary tradition of the priest-king Melchizedek, who had to guard the 'grave of Adam' throughout the ages, that is, at the place of the hill of Golgotha. With this he presents a kind of archetypal picture of the Guardian of the Grail. The motif of the Grail stone is also pursued through several legends that praise the stone of Paradise and other miracle-working stones. In such a motif and in its transformations, one can well study the language of Imagination that was always used by the guardians inheriting esoteric wisdom.

Into the Temple Legend has been woven the figure of the Queen of the Middle East full of legends. She had heard of Soloman's wisdom and had come from Sheba to him to tempt him with riddles, as it is related in 1 Kings. This Sheba was situated in 'rich Arabia', also known as 'Felix Arabia' in the Ancient world. That ancient cultural land is on the SW rim of the Arabian Peninsula, today called Yemen. It was known and praised for its gold treasures. It became rich from the export of incense and myrrh cultivated there. In his *Marksteine der Kulturgeschichte* (Part 2, Stuttgart 1939), Sigismund von Gleich gives a clear overview of the kingdom of Sheba, reporting on the little-known research that can give us an inkling of the elevated Mystery-culture of this land, of this 'diadem of the Earth'. He shows how here the beginnings of the Phoenician Mysteries are to be sought, the knowledge of the 'philosopher's stone'. According to an old legend, in this country the mountain rises on which the Phoenix bird has its nest. From Sheba, those Sun-Mysteries were later brought to Phoenicia, receiving from them its name. What the legend has to tell us of the visit of Queen Balkis (or 'Bilkis' in the Arabic form) to Hiram, points towards the deep connections of the Phoenician place of wisdom with the original Mysteries of Sheba. In his drama *Hiram und Salamo*, Albert Steffen gave these figures artistic life.

5. *The Cathars*

From 1181–1229 the Roman Church undertook Crusades against the blossoming spiritual culture in Provence until the complete annihilation of the Cathars and Albigenses. In his book *Kreuzzug gegen den Gral* (Freiburg 1933), Otto Rahn attempted to present this as the actual battle to annihilate the Grail stream. The way the author approached the traces of this community of martyrs and presented the heroic resistance of their leaders as well as their followers as a historic, sacrificial deed for the sake of the spirit, shows how deeply he feels connected by destiny with that stream.

Rahn describes the essence of the '*Minnehöfe*', the courts of love, amongst which the court of Adeleide, Vicomtesse of Carcassonne, was famous far and wide. It became the gathering place of Troubadours who mostly belonged to the Cathars. Adeleide is described as a very pious woman, but a 'heretic'. Her husband was called Trencavel (= *Scheidergut*, 'good at cutting'), who had earned a bloodguilt as a swordsman. Her son was Raimon-Roger, also a Trencavel. She brought him up to aim for the highest courtly love. Behind this woman, Rahn seeks to recognize Herzeloyde and in her son Perceval.

The Cathars distinguished between the faithful followers (*Imperfecti*) and the more developed (*Perfecti*). The latter were also called 'good men'. Chrétien describes the hermit, from whom Perceval received his Grail teaching, as such a '*bonhomme*'. They lived withdrawn in the caves of the Pyrenees when the persecutions became intense. These goodmen came out of their hermitages mostly to give 'comfort' to those dying, or to tell old myths in the castle halls. The caves of Sabarthès are as numerous as a Troglodyte town. The most sublime is the cave of Lombrives, which the shepherds today still call 'the cathedral'. This miracle of nature was called the 'cathedral of the heretics'. The reception to the inner circle took place through the *Consolamentum Spiritus Sancti*, the sacrament of 'consolation', a kind of spiritual baptism connected to a festive ceremony demanding very strict oaths. Trevrizent, the hermit, bears all the characteristics of such a wise man of the Cathars.

The noble lady from Tabor and of Montségur, Esclarmonde (meaning, 'the shining one of the world') was famous and is remembered in poetry. She was the aunt of the young Ramon-Roger of Carcassonne; her Cathar parents had already dedicated her in her youth to the Paraclete.[86] Otto Rahn claims to see in her the Guardian of the Grail, Repanse de Schoye. In later poetry she becomes the fairy queen of the Castle Monmur. The Old French poem of Oberon has raised this figure into legend. She and her husband are called by the fairy-king Oberon to rule over the realm of the fairies.

The demoralization of the Roman Church had gone so far that the *Cathari* ('the pure ones') could only have deepest disdain for this situation, although Provence was otherwise the most tolerant land. The attitude of tolerance permeates the Parzival poem in a way that was hardly practised anywhere else in Christian groups. The disputes between the Pope's legates and the Cathar communities, especially with the Duke Raimon of Toulouse, who was their most powerful protector, led to no reconciliation. The duke himself is excommunicated in 1207. Pope Innocent III proceeds with unyielding consistency. Since the final blow was felt coming, a stronghold was built on Montségur, difficult of access, to which Esclarmonde withdrew. In 1209 the great Crusade was undertaken from Lyon against the towns of the heretics. Béziers was stormed and burnt down. Carcassonne was emptied and handed over. All the inhabitants had disappeared, most likely to the caves. But Ramon-Roger dies on 10 November 1209

---

[86] Literally, 'called alongside', i.e. councillor or advocate, names for the Holy Spirit—*Tr.*

within his own castle. The Crusades against the 'Albigenses' (named after the town Albi) continues until 1229. Only Montségur seemed impregnable. In 1243 a siege began against the last refuge of Catharism; in spring 1244 the castle fell through betrayal. The heretics' treasure called 'Mani' was said to have been saved in the caves of Ornolac. The entrances to the caves in which it was assumed Cathars were hidden were bricked up. In one of these caves, the following sacred verse was found in 1850.

What is God?

We who came here,
Let us keep silence.
Let us not say His name.
Let us keep silence.
Let us pray silently.
Whoever wants to say
Who He is,
Has to be
Who He is!

Amen.

Clearly, the Mystery mood of ancient times lived on here; the divine cannot be enclosed in dogma. It withdraws from concepts; it wants to be venerated through silence and be experienced through purification of the soul. To make oneself worthy is everything.

We hear the accounts how the last Cathar groups descend emaciated, in ceremonial procession, from the high stronghold of Monségur. Rejecting any conversion from the side of their torturers, out of their free will they jump into the flaming pyre with the jubilant call, 'God is love'. This heroic community grows into a legend.

No doubt can exist that in those decades those who knew—and Wolfram was one of them—looked with admiration to those Cathar communities. While the Crusades were raging against them, they were full of deepest concern regarding the continuation of spiritual Christianity. That this does not become more evident in the Grail poetry (as the literary historians always naively wish), has to do with the extraordinary pressure of Church life. We are to imagine that those in the know gathered in brotherhoods demanding strict oaths of silence concerning certain Mysteries. It cannot be denied that Wolfram (or his representative Kyot, whom he expressly calls a citizen of Provence) with certain figures in his poetic work wanted to point at the same time to famous Cathar personalities. But that does not hinder him from placing the true Grail community—its archetypal picture—into the eighth and ninth centuries.

Although that cultural blossoming in the south of France has been completely extinguished, in their fairy tales, however, the inhabitants of this realm knew how to preserve the afterglow of the Manichaean wisdom and the courageous knightly spirit. Under the title, *Der Mann in allen Farben* (Stuttgart 1952), Konrad Sandkühler has given a German translation of fairy tales of Gascony.[87] 'The Golden Dragoon', for example, appears like a Michaelic fighter, the duke's son, who quick as lightning charges through the clouds on his flying horse. He saves the damsel in the white garment from her tribulations—as once Parzival did for Blanchefleur. When he finally manages to force the Lord of the Night to the ground, who like a Klingsor-figure robs his bride and holds her in magic bands, the latter says to him, 'You are stronger than me, but you cannot kill me. It is written that I will live to the Last Judgement but will not resurrect.'

Until the end of earthly time, human beings need the power of darkness as the opponent. This is a Cathar belief. For only in confronting this darkness is the highest good challenged to reveal itself.

Such fairy tales are like heroic ballads through the way the moral world-order in them is led towards victory. This takes place in a shocking manner in the fairy tale 'Of the singing sea, the dancing apple and the truth-saying bird'. Here the evil queen, after committing her shameful deeds is brought to judgement by her son, the young king. With a just punishment, she is to receive one hundred whiplashes before all the people and then to be executed by the henchman. But because the people shout, 'A son cannot sentence his mother to death!'—the young king himself takes on this punishment vicariously. When the henchman unbinds the bloody body, it is said, 'He was in such a pitiable condition that everyone felt compassion for him. Yet he did not weep, because a man must not weep, especially if he is a ruler and stands before his people. But when the sword of judgement the henchman swings over the king's neck splinters three times like

---

[87] Cf. Jean-François Bladé, Contes populaires de la Gascogne. Maisonneuve frères et C. Leclerc, 1886 (and reprint editions), 3 vols. Jean Rameau: Gascony 50 tales, illustrated by Gaston Rémy, 1939. Le Campagnoi, Tales Told in Gascony, Merlin Books Ltd. 1996.

glass, it is revealed that a divine judgement is satisfied, demanding no further sacrifice.

The style of this fairy tale from the south of France takes hold of the reader directly through its resolute style. One is carried by the rhythm of the hero's step who knows no resistances; he does not allow these things to sway him from the envisioned aim. The tender lyrical tone that gives Grimms' fairy tales their magic mood is hardly to be found here. In them the tone of ballads rules.

Heart-moving, too, is the fairy tale, 'The veiled one'. He who went through deep error, and when he came to realization took a path of atonement, could become a great helper of people. Unrecognized, he carries out his deeds. As the last healing deed, he manages to save his people from the black pestilence. But for that he first has to find the golden flower on an island in the sea—'the balsamic flower, the flower that sings like a nightingale . . .'. It is the healing power of poesy, which as the world-transfiguring power can heal human beings of that black pestilence to which they have to succumb when they lose connection to the world of the spirit. In another fairy tale it is described as the 'blue flower'—'the flower that sings day and night, the flower that breaks iron'. Who is not reminded of the blue flower of Novalis? In such pictures the power of singing is celebrated, the poetic meaning that frees the world of the enchantment cast by an evil magician. In such fairy tales, the wisdom of the Troubadours proclaims the true knighthood of the spirit and its conquests.

6. Precious stones and the mystery of the pineal gland

In the poetic works on the Grail, the way precious stones are mentioned has become completely estranged from the thought-life of today. If one recalls, however, how the greatest natural researcher of the Middle Ages, Albertus Magnus—a contemporary of the Titurel poet—made a study of precious stones, giving an exact description of the effective forces of each stone, then one will not only regard such indications as beautiful ornamentation of the poetic works. Of course, the traditions dedicated to Aristotle and other writers of the ancient world were already greatly obscured. Rudolf Steiner has indicated new ways to understand the hidden forces of precious stones by showing how in cosmic becoming these purest manifestations of the mineral realm arose at the same time as the first seedlike beginnings of the human sensory organs. As pure crystal formations they are as innocent as the human senses will become only after long development and purification.

For the sense-organs are the more perfected the more selfless they can be. Through our *not* feeling the eye and the ear themselves, we can perceive the world. Thus, there corresponds, for example, *chrysolite* to the sense of seeing, *onyx* to hearing. We can imagine how aeons ago precious stones were once fashioned as sensory organs of the soul of the Earth. This soul required the purest minerals in order through them to reflect the influences of cosmic forces.

We read that the foundation of Montsalvat is revealed as a massive block of *onyx*. Titurel removes the mountain scree and has the plateau polished to gain a mirrorlike surface onto which by invisible hands the ground plan of the temple is drawn. Such details are not meant in a casual manner. From the standpoint of a spiritual teaching of evolution, hearing, according to its original conception, derives from the very earliest cosmic conditions; hearing has been fashioned out of the purest life-ether. Its mineral counter-picture, however, appears in the onyx. These are the true foundations we have first to find in the spirit, to build on them something that survives death. This law is also valid in the realm of the dead. This onyx foundation means—that the spiritual hearing, which can only be formed in the soul as far as all self-will in it has died, is the only true foundation on which to build that temple in which the Grail is able to dwell. The first prerequisite for the revelation of the spiritual world is to be able selflessly to listen.

The windows are made of *beryl*—not of simple glass, it is emphasized—through which the light can radiate into the temple. Beryllus, however, is also the name of the ancestor of the Grail dynasty, from which Titurel stems. It is expressly said by the poet that he is named 'according to the stone'. This stone is supposed to have the quality of turning small virtues into big ones. In the tradition, beryl which does allow light easily to penetrate, only mildly dampening it, always receives high praise. This leads to the claim, where this stone is present the devil has no chance of appearing; the stone drives him away. Consequently, the foundation stone of the Grail dynasty is called Beryllus. A spiritual stream is shown here that attempts to purify the soul-forces so that they become transparent to the light. Seen spiritually-scientifically, beryl appeared in cosmic evolution at the same time as the indications of the forces of understanding came into existence. It is consequently the purified thought-force from which this spiritual schooling took its starting point and in which Titurel was involved; it is a thought-force that does not convey cold light, but can transform it into a soul-light, into a mild warmth.

The stone altars in the Grail Temple were made of many *sapphires*, for it is said that this stone has the noble quality to wipe out the sins of human beings and to bestow that virtue to regret them with tears. The sapphire consequently produces in the soul the pure will for atonement, but this is the basic mood out of which each act on the altar is to arise.

From the standpoint of *cosmic* evolution, as taken up by Rudolf Steiner's spiritual research, we would have to speak quite differently about this stone. For when the evolution had reached to the starry sign of 'the Fishes' and had given human beings the first indications for feet—the 'organs' with which they are to learn to feel the Earth in purity—the sapphire at the same time was formed in the mineral realm. Connected to it are those hidden forces in the soul through which the soul can find again its pure origin; it regains the innocence of becoming, as it became effective in Christ's Incarnation, Who wants to redeem us out of the deepest entanglement of guilt.

According to certain traditions, the Grail chalice is said to be formed out of *emerald*. In the cosmic becoming of the human being, it corresponds to the formation of the solar plexus; it has become the seed of that deeply hidden consciousness with which the vegetative processes, the unconscious movements of life, are perceived. From the sign of 'the Virgin', these forces were once active with the fashioning of the emerald. Consequently, only a virgin is allowed to carry the Grail. At this place in Eschenbach, the emerald-green cloth is mentioned—made of Achmardi silk[88]—on which the Grail is carried by Repanse de Schoye. The poetic work *Titurel* says that the Grail itself has brought about all the building materials to construct the Temple. Where the Grail is effective, there the true Mysteries of transformation take place. On the one hand, substances become etherialized, they dissolve into the spiritual element; on the other hand, spiritual-moral forces become condensed, striving towards a new formation of substance. These precious stones for building the Temple cannot of course be found in nature in such quantities. They should not be imagined as consisting of earthly material. Before the Imaginative gaze the Mystery of a new world-creation appears here. This will occur out of the moral substance of human beings—out of that which, as it were, is active in human beings as a super-nature surpassing death.

[88] 'Achmardi'—probably an Italianized version of the Arabic 'Akhmardi', referring to the colour green—from *Wikipedia*.

Amongst the many stones used for the Grail Temple, the significance of *jasper* may be mentioned in this context. It is said that it appears in seventeen colours, thus bringing variety into the building, but especially because it has black veins, without which the other colours could not be fully expressed. From the Revelation of John, we know how jasper in an exclusive manner serves the building of the heavenly Jerusalem. The foundation is to be built of this stone. Such a fact can be viewed from the aspect of modern chemical analysis. If we think how jasper has been formed out of the condensed substance of quartz (unlike marble made of calcite, but out of the permeable element of silica) and is intensively penetrated by iron oxide that gives it many colours, one can give it a deeper meaning that it should serve as the essential building material for the foundations, that means, for the boundary towards the cosmos. For the selflessness of silica unites with the strength of self-assertion contained in iron. This produces the character of jasper.

But one can also approach such an indication from the aspect of spiritual research. Here it may sound strange when within cosmic becoming jasper is connected to the forming of the sense of smell. Because, for human beings smell is a stunted sense, when compared to that of some animals. How more differentiated is the sense of smell of a tracking dog, who with it can perceive matter's finer radiations! We can ask ourselves, where can one find in the human being these sensory abilities in their organization stunted, that is, impeded? We arrive at the fact they are held back in the root of the nose. This ability must have passed over to the thought-processes. What the dog achieves through the sense of smell, human beings strive for through those forces of intelligence that seek to penetrate the hidden element in matter. The tremendous will to penetrate ever deeper into the structural forces of matter to get hold of their radiations chemically and technically, although today it may still carry a strong materialistic note, is an persistent tendency of the time. It presents the human transformation of the sense of smell. But especially these forces of sensing that unfold in confrontation with matter, in the intensive exploration of their hidden qualities, are able to provide the basic substance as the future form of existence humanity will build up in the cosmic process of evolution after this existence is finished. For only by completely investigating the world of matter does the spirit learn consciously to lay hold of itself in its own being.

Later in the poetic work *Titurel*, the mystical force and significance of precious stones is mentioned. When the ancient Titurel feels his forces are dwindling, which no longer enable him to perform knightly deeds, he gathers his children and instructs them about the Grail and its wonderous forces. He tells them that certain stones upon entering the Grail Temple will serve to increase their virtues and protect them from vices. Aaron, the first high priest of Judaism, is said to have worn twelve precious stones when he entered the temple. The Son of God, too, taught His disciples concerning the mystical force of the twelve stones that will be used to build up the heavenly Jerusalem. And nobody could serve the Grail in the right way who had not gained an understanding of precious stones which adorn this temple. Through the way Albrecht of Scharfenberg gives this description, it becomes clear that he must have been part of a stream that fostered the mystical deepening in the quality of precious stones. In the medieval gold-smithing schools this wisdom was still taught, coming from earlier times of a magical culture. The stream of forces that move hither and thither as an extremely delicate fluid between the stones and the human organization were revealed to meditative experience. One experiences being taken up into a net of forces, which makes the human ether organization receptive for the comprehensive influence of the stars. In this net of forces one could at the same time feel connected to the world of those who had died.

In the Grail Castle, Parzival meets the ailing Anfortas, who wears a cap of sable fur on which a shining ruby was seated like a pommel. According to Rudolf Steiner, the *ruby* corresponds to 'the higher organ of the brain'—the pure force of Intuition. This force belongs to the supersensible human being carried within ourselves, even if initially powerless to become engaged actively. Why do we read in the *Titurel* poem that all the towers of the Grail Temple are crowned with rubies? These towers rise above the quires with altars built of sapphires built for all the people of the Earth. What takes place here when the divine services of offering are held transforms the blood of the peoples; it 'Christ-ens' the forces of the blood. Through this, out of the forces of the blood, the pure possibilities of ideas, of selfless Intuition can be released.

Only the middle tower is adorned with the carbuncle, which shines in the night for the Grail knights. Because of it they can always find their way home, wherever on their journey they may have become lost. Through the inner connection to the 'carbuncle' there awakens in the soul the pictorial Imagination that becomes creatively active. But this means that through this ability the soul can become aware at any time what it loves and what for it is sacred. The ideal can continuously shine in the soul. It arises out of the transformation of the forces of the blood and leads with certainty out of any darkness of soul.

*

A strange passage is mentioned in the Grail teaching Parzival receives through Trevrizent. Here the unicorn is mentioned, that being of fable that only becomes gentle in the presence of a virgin and even falling asleep in her lap. This animal bears a carbuncle in its skull that has grown directly under its horn. Unpoetically expressed, but physiologically exact, one would have to say—it glows where the pineal gland is situated. It is what remains of an extinguished organ, which Atlantean humanity still possessed. The eye of the 'Cyclops' [the giant in Homer's *Odyssey*], or appearing in the fairy tale 'One-eye, Two eyes, Three eyes' [Grimms' collection, No. 130] is the mythical memory of that early sense organ, which at the time when the [fontanel of the] skull was not completely closed could glow like a kind of lamp and light with its rays the realm of the night. This nocturnal sense had first to disappear somewhat, so that human beings could fully awaken to the day-world, to be experienced with two eyes in one's head. With the unicorn, a physical animal was never meant; it is an astral figure like the griffins, centaurs and sphinxes that hold fast a very early condition of evolution. But forces that have aged undergo a hardening; they consequently present themselves to Imaginative vision as 'horn conditions'. Only through the purest soul-forces—in that realm of the vegetative consciousness remaining unclouded—can this lost ability be regained in a new way. The unicorn, the fables consequently say, can only be caught when it falls asleep in the lap of a pure virgin; the carbuncle can then be released.[89]

[89] In a sculptural relief of a richly adorned 'Cismar altar' of a former Benedictine monastery in East Holstein, Germany, an especially impressive representation of the Unicorn motif can be seen [cf. online, 'Flügelalter Cismar']. The pictures and carvings arose in the fourteenth century in honour of the holy blood relic, which was kept there forming an attraction for pilgrims. They must have arisen out of a deep spiritual tradition. The way the horn of the tamed animal in the lap of a virgin grows out of the head, losing its rigidity, beginning to bow in devotion, points towards an inner understanding of this Imagination. Cf. in Addition Note 17, characterizing the unicorn within the Rosicrucian language of symbols. [See also Margaret B. Freeman, *The Unicorn Tapestries*. https://www.metmu-

For modern physiology, the function of the pineal gland is something mysterious. Descartes [1596–1650], the forerunner of modern philosophy, had a certain view on this organ. He called it the seat of the soul itself, where the element of soul and spirit takes hold of the body. He must have drawn such ideas from spiritual traditions, for from an anatomical viewpoint the pineal gland is only regarded as an insignificant organ. The importance it once received during the time of the clairvoyant cultures can scarcely be observed in its present rudimentary condition. This wonderful organ of light is surrounded by the purest life-forces. These usually withdraw from day-consciousness, yet nevertheless can be brought to flourish. This first occurs in that region of sleep that cannot be approached by the nature of desire. It concerns ether-streams that continuously endeavour to arise out of the blood and which, when Christ lives in the heart, ray in a specific way to the pineal gland. There other streams are met which—in the moment of falling asleep—begin to ray from the cosmos into the human organization, that is, penetrating from the head towards the heart. In a lecture on the 'Etherisation of the Blood' (Basel, 1 Oct. 1911), Rudolf Steiner concretely characterized the mystery of these two streams. He says:

> In the moment of waking up and of falling asleep a kind of battle exists in the region of the pineal gland, of what penetrates from above downwards and what streams from below upwards.

In this battle, the conflict is mirrored between the lower attitudes rising from within and that which from cosmic heights wants morally to permeate human nature. But if a person harmonizes these two streams:

> ... then around the pineal gland a gentle glimmering light appears to spread out. This, at the moment of waking up or falling asleep, is, as it were, embedded into a small sea of light ... Thus, a moral attitude is mirrored in the human being. And this gentle raying light often extends to the region of the heart.

But something else can unite with what arises from the heart streaming towards the head.

> Like our blood streaming as ether upwards from the human heart, from the Earth's ether since the Mystery of Golgotha lives the etherized blood of Christ Jesus. The ether-body of the Earth is penetrated by what has become of the blood that flowed on Golgotha.

---

seum.org/met-publications/the-unicorn-tapestries—*Tr.*].

Through this:

> A continuous possibility is available since the Mystery of Golgotha that in these streams from below upwards the effects of the etheric blood of Christ is included ... but a connection of these two streams only occurs when the right understanding is brought to that which the Christ-Impulse contains. No connection can otherwise occur; the two streams otherwise repel each other.

All true Grail knowledge wrestles for this new, contemporary understanding of the Christ-Impulse. It seeks to connect the stream of the heart with that which continuously streams from Golgotha. For only the innermost mutual harmony of these etheric streams can kindle that gentle light, which during the moment of falling asleep or waking up becomes spiritually visible around the pineal gland. In this gleam the presence of Christ can be revealed. With such a description, the future clairvoyant forces are indicated that begin to unfold at this sacred place. Speaking pictorially, the 'carbuncle' resting deeply hidden in human nature, waiting to be able to shine again.

For a study of the occult meaning of the pineal gland, an important essay by Dr Greta Bockholt may be mentioned, 'Eine Gralsburg in Gehirn' (*Natura,* Sept. 1926, journal of the Medical Section at the Goetheanum, Dornach). From the situation of the *inferior colliculus* and *superior colliculus* and the pineal gland within the brain, here is shown in the description of Chrétien's imagination, how the finding of the Grail Castle can be understood in detail as exact physiological facts. The pineal gland is the only place in the brain where the finest mineral salts collect, usually called '*Gehirnsand*', 'brain sand'. Out of the group of sensory nerves around this organ an understanding can be gained of Steiner's description, quoted in Chapter One of this book [p. 14], how at this place the noblest element of sense impressions in us may unite with the noblest mineral element. From the anatomical description of the pineal gland and of the adjacent *colliculi,* one is helped to divine that place 'where the Grail continuously hovers, that is, the vessel for the noblest nourishment of the human hero [*Heros*], killed by everything else that lies in the castle of the brain'.

We are aware that for the contemporary consciousness, the attempt to connect the pictures from legends with the anatomical and physiological facts must appear strange. One is inclined to leave them in the sphere of the feelings or religious intuition. And certainly, here too the danger is great to entertain an inartistic element if one has not already learned to behold the structure of the human organization itself as a revelation of the highest artistic powers of the world. What we can describe as anatomical facts, is indeed only the imprint of a wonderful etheric organization in physical matter. The clairvoyant view does not mean those physical features shown to anatomy from the outside. It spiritually beholds the wonderful etheric structure, the sculptor of all the material organs. This too is only a microcosmical mirroring of mighty world-powers—of precisely that Grail Castle macroscopically shining in the cosmic ether, which those who have died form and build, as we have attempted to show. If one wrestles through to such an exact beholding of the Imaginations, then the reverence towards the pictorial traditions of earlier times grows immeasurably. For one also knows that in future completely different Grail books can be written, not yet understandable for present-day comprehension.

7. The creation of names

The names occurring in Grail poetry present a confluence of various linguistic roots. San Marte, the pioneer in Grail research from the mid-nineteenth century, contributed much to clarify the names; furthermore, Karl Bartsch in his *Germanistik Studien* and Karl Simrock, the greater imitative poet of the medieval epics.

Titurel could be a Germanic root: 'Tiether' (= 'Diether'), recalling the Old Gothic name 'Theoderich', or 'Dietrich'. For two important kings of the Visigothic Empire were called thus, also mentioned in Note 15 below. His son's name 'Frimutel' (= 'Frimunt') is formed similarly with the same Romanized ending 'el'. But the name 'Titurel', as San Marte suggests, could also contain the Romanesque root 'tutor' (carer, protector). Most likely it has to do with names of the Visigothic dynasty. But in passing through the Romanesque world, they were no longer understood as such and consequently connections to Latin words were sought. This one can well understand with the word 'Titurel'; it gave him as the grand 'Guardian of the Grail' an essential, intrinsic meaning.

The name *Anfortas* was traced to 'Enfermas' (the infirm one). *Herzeloyde* could be traced to a German form (Harchehildis), or the Old French form (Herselot). But with Wolfram, the close sound to 'Herzeleide' [suffering heart] is clearly intended. He wants to say: only out of the maternal ground of deepest suffering can the fruit of the highest Grail called mature. A '*Perceval*' is a 'fruit of suffering'. The name itself, nevertheless, is of French origin ('percer' = piercing through, furrow through; 'val' = valley). A spirited interpretation, which Richard Wagner found and accepted by Joseph Görres: *der reine Tor*, 'the pure simpleton' indicates a Persian origin, for the *Parse* is the 'pure one' (*parselh-fal*). Although this interpretation is unsustainable, it is nevertheless not too far-fetched. In the Grail legends, Manichaen Persian traditions can be found throughout, as is recognized today on various sides.

Sigune is clearly of Germanic origin. Facing this *Schionatulander*, the name of her beloved, is an example of how Wolfram formed names out of misunderstood French: *li joenet ù l'alant* (= youth with a hound). *Orilus* is also derived in this way: *li orgueillous* (= the proud one) or *Orgeluse*: *la orgueillouse* (= the proud woman). Thus, Wolfram also fashioned several other names that clearly derive from the French. *Kondwiramur*, the name of Parzival's wife, San Marte derives from *conduire* and *amour* (= she who leads to love); K. Bartsch, on the other hand, believes it says: *coin de voire amors* (= ideals of true love). The latter as a French word-formation would be more conceivable. Then, Wolfram most likely took it from his Kyot tradition and in an amateur fashion transformed it with the sound of 'the one leading to love'.

Schoysiane (= the giver of joy) and *Repanse de Schoye* (= the essence of joy) are clearly French, as well as *Terdelaschoye*: terre de la joie (= land of joy), as Wolfram called Morgan (Morgan le Fay) by exchanging her name for the name of the place where she lived.

The names from the Arthur's Round Table are mainly Celtic, like *Gawan* or Gauvain: Gwalchmai (= falcon of the battle) and *Ginover*, the name of the queen: Gwenhwyvar (= the lady of the far region?). *Gamuret*, too, is sought to be derived from 'camgredwr' (= heretic), which then nevertheless would be adjusted to the French as: 'game' (gemma) 'amorous' (= gem of love). If one still includes how several Arabic and Oriental words have flowed into Grail poetry, one can sense with this fact the international character of the Grail Mysteries.

8. 'The L'estoire del saint Graal' ('The great Holy Grail')

The '*L'estoire del saint Graal*' is the most comprehensive prose story written about the origin and destiny of the Grail. Some decades after the Grail narration by Robert de Boron, and based on it, it nevertheless reveals quite a different genealogical tree of the Grail dynasty than the one in Robert's *Joseph*. Here a son of Joseph of Arimathea takes centre stage, named Josephe (Josephus). With him and a small community, which he converts to Christ after his release from imprisonment by [the Roman Emperor] Vespasian, Joseph travels to the country of Sarras (it is interpreted as the land of the Saracens). Here he finds a Sun Temple. He converts the old King Evalach to Christianity, who was in great difficulties from the Egyptians, and helps him to victory over his enemies. An abundance of adventures and people woven into the events are contained in this Grail narration. One may have no great opinion regarding the artistic value of the story, but it cannot be denied that it consists of legendary traditions which flowed to it in abundance, pointing towards a spiritual tradition as it was fostered in Christian communities with a devout sacramental life. It must have been a Rome-free tradition that decisively ignored any connection to Peter and the known Church hierarchy.

The depiction of the sacrifice of the Mass is here traced back directly to Christ, that is, to a supersensory revelation which Joseph is said to have experienced. We read that Joseph of Arimathea, after his arrival in Sarras prays before a shrine in which there was a precious chalice as that contained the blood of the Redeemer. There his son Josephe saw in it the crucified Christ surrounded by five angels. One of the angels carried a bleeding lance and with it pierced the side of the Crucified, so that blood and water flowed from the wounds into the chalice at the feet of the Redeemer. Then Josephe strives to enter the shrine to help the Crucified, but an angel restrains him. Now, Joseph his father also became attentive and looks into the shrine. He perceives an altar covered with a red cloth; on it lay a piece of bleeding iron from a lance and with it three nails. A golden vessel stood there as well. Angels carry incense vessels and other altar instruments. Finally, somebody carries in the chalice on an emerald-green cloth. (We recognize this green cloth, on which the stone of the Grail is carried, from Wolfram's *Parzival*.) Now Christ Himself appears in priestly garments: angels permeate the whole palace to purify it from demons, but Christ consecrates Josephe as the first Bishop of Christendom. He is clothed by Him with the garments and insignia of the Bishop's office and anointed with sacred oil; he celebrates Holy Mass. Chalice and paten stand on the altar and when he speaks the words of institution the transformation of bread and wine into the body of the Redeemer takes place. In the transformed substance he believes he beholds the body of a child. At the end of the Holy Service, Christ commands him to celebrate this sacrament daily from now on and to ordain priests and bishops in each town.

In this legendary narration an extensive description is given of the Guardians of the Grail and their Apostolic activities. The concern is to show how the true sacramental stream of Christianity was carried from the East to the West—without any Roman mediation, it found its sanctuary in Great Britain.

The meaning of *Sarras* may be pointed out here, which wants to establish the connection to a certain spiritual stream. In the middle of the course of the River Nile in Nubia a town exists with this name. This region once belonged to the great Ethiopian realm, of which today Abyssinia exists as a remnant. The 'devout Ethiopians' were known in antiquity as the guardians of early Sun Mysteries, which they had received from the places of wisdom of Saba (at the adjacent shore of the Red Sea). [The ancient Greek historian] Herodotus reports on the '*Heliotrapezium*', the Table of the Sun of the Ethiopians, which every night was covered afresh with meat and fruit.[90] In Grail research, people liked to point towards this sacred symbol that appeared so akin to the knightly feeding miracle of the Grail. This connection rightly exists, although not in the outer sense of a borrowing of legendary motifs. The Saba Mysteries were still for a long time fostered in Ethiopia and the esoteric stream of early Christianity could consequently connect especially effectively with these traditions. The Grail narration speaks of the 'Sun Temple' Joseph of Arimathea is said to have found. These realms, starting from Egypt, took up Coptic Christianity with its rich treasures of wisdom. Pantaenus, the first known leader of the Christian school of catechism at Alexandria, which had been the spiritual light of the early epoch of Hellenistic Christianity, set out c. 200 on a missionary journey into this region. It is said he went to 'India'; in the use of language at the time this meant Yemen, the coastal realm of S.W. Arabia, in which the ancient culture of Saba was blossoming. The homeland of the wise ones from the Orient is also placed into those ancient Mystery countries. The Oberufer Mystery Plays from the Middle Ages still carried this tradition; before the palace of Herod the Three Kings have to testify of their origin.

> *Aus keniglichem Stamm san ma olli drei geborn,*
> *Zween kumma aus Sabam der Dritte aus Mohrn.*
>
> [Prose tr: 'All three are born of kingly line, two come from Saba, the third from the land of the Moors.']

---

[90] Herodotus, *Persian Wars*, Book III, 23. https://www.loebclassics.com/view/herodotus-persian_wars/1920/pb_LCL118.31.xml?readMode=recto

'Your Kingly love we fain would win
To hear our journey's origin.
In Saba, in our land afar,
Rose in the East, a wondrous star ...'[91]

But this means, from the southern Arabian realm of Yemen and Ethiopia, the adjacent country. In his contributions to *Die Mysterien and Geistesgeschichte der Menschheit* (Dresden 1938), Gunter Wachsmuth, after describing the blossoming of Christian Gnosticism in the Egyptian-Coptic world and its disappearance, writes: 'What had ripened on Egyptian soil of Christian primordial wisdom, was later mostly wiped out. Abyssinian Christianity had preserved in secret the early Christian traditions.'

It is consequently significant when we read in another Grail narration (the *Queste*) that the Holy Grail was expressly brought back later to Saras by its guardians. There Galahad and Perceval are said to have returned to God [died].[92] In this legendary tradition the 'ship of Solomon' is mentioned, on which they undertook the journey into the Orient. This symbolic picture points towards brotherhoods who must have had their place in the temple symbolism as they had traditionally still found their echo in the Lodges. Such groups consciously foster spiritual exchange with the places of initiation of the Middle East.

9. *The Queste del saint Graal*

In the genealogical tree of the Grail guardians and the destinies of the Grail—its journey via Sarras to Great Britain—the '*Queste*'[93] is closely related to the Grail Legend concerning which we have spoken. It aims to show a figure of Christianity still completely based in the experience of beholding the Mystery of transformation for those who set off to the quest to seek the Grail. It always concerns a renewal of the archetypal

[91] Tr. A.C. Harwood, *Christmas Plays from Oberufer*, Rudolf Steiner Press, London 1973, 47. These traditional plays were preserved by sixteenth-seventeenth century German-speaking immigrants from around Lake Constance, living on an island in the River Danube near Pressburg. The plays were collected by Karl Julius Schröer, Rudolf Steiner's teacher and friend, performed in Dornach and subsequently in the first Waldorf School, Stuttgart, and from there a performing tradition arose in many Waldorf Schools in Europe and worldwide—*Tr.*

[92] *The Quest of the Holy Grail*, 15. Tr. Pauline M. Matarasso, Penguin Classics 1969. 283f.

[93] *The Quest of the Holy Grail*, tr. P.M. Matarasso, Penguin Books 1969.

Christian spiritual blessing as it was to be revealed within the Grail community of Joseph of Arimathea. This impulse is characteristic for the carriers of early Celtic Christianity. Lancelot, the famous hero of the Round Table, is able to receive the revelation of the Grail in an ancient chapel in the woodlands, that is through a dream-vision. But when he arrives at the Castle Corbenic and at the midnight hour in fervent prayer perceives a ray of blinding light from an open door, tempting him to behold the Mystery of transformation, he is thrown back from the threshold to the room by a gust of wind. He falls down as if dead and remains lying for fourteen days in a swoon. For because of his forbidden love for the Queen Guinevere he cannot become worthy to receive the grace of the Grail.

Only three from the Round Table are able fully to behold the Grail Mystery—Galahad, Perceval and Bohort. After five years of searching for the Grail they finally reach Corbenic. There they are to succeed in the trial of the sword, but only Galahad is able to put the pieces together in the right manner. Three maidens bring in a bier on which an ailing man bears a crown. He greets Galahad, the longed-for bringer of healing. But here the question is not demanded, as in Wolfram's *Parzival*. Altar Mysteries are revealed to them. Angels glide into the room, carrying burning candles. They bring down the holy vessel and with it the bloody lance and place both on the Grail table so that the blood can drip into the vessel. But before the Holy Grail a man kneels who has descended from the heavens. Joseph, the first Christian bishop, whom the Redeemer himself had consecrated in Sarras (we already know this inauguration ceremony from what is called 'The High History of the Holy Grail'). He had died 300 years ago; now he initiates Galahad and his two companions into the Mystery of transformation. For, the narration wants to say, the true Mysteries of the altar are protected in the realm of the dead while on Earth they have become obscured.

After Josephe had covered the Holy Grail with a cloth, he begins to celebrate the Mass. From the Holy Vessel he takes a Host. But while he carries out the elevation, from heaven a flaming child descends with a radiant countenance; before all eyes the bread transforms into the holy body. For a long time Josephe holds it aloft that they may behold the Mystery, then it is returned into the Vessel. After completing the Mass, he disappears with the words, 'Knights of Christ, you underwent many troubles to sit at this table and behold the history of the Holy Grail. Now you will receive the highest feeding out of the hand of the Redeemer Himself.' Then, emerging from the Vessel they see a human being with pierced hands and feet and a wound in His side. He graciously invites them to participate in His Mystery. He lays hold of the Vessel and Himself distributes the sacrament. On his knees, Galahad is the first to receive the body of the Redeemer and then the two others. After enjoying the ineffable sweet food, they are instructed by Christ Himself concerning the Vessel from which they had eaten. It is the same out of which the disciples received the Passover meal. It nourished all who served it; it is called the 'Holy Grail'.

If one considers how these Grail narrations appeared during an age when the intellectual dispute about the transubstantiation raged through Christendom and the rigidification of the Mysteries of transformation culminated into ecclesiastical dogma, then one understands the concern of those still able to speak in Imaginations; in such pictures they want to indicate the supersensory processes that etherically work through the holy action at the altar. To become aware of these pictures means to receive the grace of the Grail. For in the Grail that strength is active which releases in the soul the new beholding, a strength, which through the sacrifice of Golgotha permeates the Earth in etheric streams and continually wants to unite with human nature, to bring the immortal element in human beings to shine forth. After the discussion on precious stones, we attempted to present this fact in a more concrete manner.

Here it may still be noted that the great English Grail narration written by Thomas Malory around 1470 is mostly an imitation of the French '*Queste*'. England itself did not initially contribute to embellish Grail poetry, although the Grail legend repeatedly connects with Britain and Joseph of Arimathea, especially with the Abbey of Glastonbury. Only with Malory's comprehensive narration, which with the title 'The Death of Arthur' embraces the whole Merlin and Arthur legends, then finds its climax in the search for the Grail. The content suddenly became a classic in English literature. The work's mature art of narration, the style of which can still today be felt as exemplary, essentially contributed to its fame. As in the '*Queste*' here too Galahad is raised to become the main seeker; beside him Perceval appears as a shadowy figure. Thereby the impulse open to the world of the Grail-stream to lead soul development to a free, modern attitude as we admire it in Wolfram's poetic work, unfortunately does not appear in this English version of the Grail legend. Thus, too, the romantic poetry of the nineteenth century, particularly Tennyson's 'The Holy Grail', in the first instance celebrates the spiritualized Grail hero, Sir Galahad. Visionary, as shining from afar, the Grail shines into souls.

10. The Grail sword

Trebuchet, the smith of that mysterious sword, means 'the limping one' (from *trébucher* = 'stumbling, limping'). He is a figure related to the divine smith Vulkan, or Hephaistos. He is active in the fiery forces of human nature. He needs these forces, which he has to master, to refashion within the human organization the life of mental pictures into an instrument of creative thinking, of the free forming power of the Imagination.

Later, we hear through Trevrizent, that the two silver knives belonging to the Grail were also fashioned by that smith. Here it concerns the twofold form of the sickle in which the Moon appears as waxing and waning. Within the human etheric organization, certain effects of the Moon are rhythmically revealed that have their task as regenerative forces. They are mirrored in this Imagination of the two silver knives.

In Trebuchet, consequently, a divine force appears before our gaze. He is active as an artistic smith in the body of formative forces, which initially has to build up the physical organism but then gradually frees its forces for the life of soul and spirit. To be able intimately to describe the processes of the body of formative forces, one has to know how to speak the language of legends. This sword is truly smithed out of an especially good steel. For it is fashioned out of the fine rays of iron active in the human blood. Without them the inner activity of the freely creative possibility of thinking would never arise in human beings. Rudolf Steiner spoke pictorially of a meteoric shower, similar to a rain of shooting stars, in the blood, out of which Michael's sword is to be fashioned, the strength of freedom in human beings, which is a cosmic miracle. With this sword the awakening human spirit fights in the wrestling of thought for beholding the spiritual worlds.

The young person receives this sword initially as in a dream, like a gift of grace. The ability to experience ideals flashes up in the soul. But they are not yet reborn out of the innermost personality. They are still a heritage of spiritual goods that first have to undergo a trial in life. The sword breaks for the youth in the battle of existence. The Grail Imaginations, which are not yet laid hold of by the knowledge born of suffering, fall from consciousness. They have to be freshly created out of the source of the creative life of thought, out of the source of ideas—in the continuation of Chrétien's poetic work through Manessier, this process is described differently. Here Perceval has to return the sword to the smith, who lives near the Lake Cotoatre. But the forge is guarded by two snakes, which Perceval first has to overcome before the smith can weld the pieces together again. But when he rides away, he hears bells pealing. They announce the death of the smith, who after mending the sword has to die. We see those urges that arise out of the lower nature and do not want to set free the power of thinking (the snakes), have first to be overcome. The human being awakening to the spirit grows beyond the wisdom-forming powers as soon as they have forged for him the instrument of creative thinking. Trebuchet can die after completing this task.

In the language of Imagination pictures are valid that are not simply fixed. Experience in the spirit is so rich that it can be expressed in various forms. Where paths towards the Grail are trod, spiritual experience becomes progressively more individual. Accordingly, too, the force of the Imagination becomes increasingly mobile and sovereign towards tradition.

Hereby, it cannot be initially avoided that an element of Imagination is unleashed that frequently cannot completely cope with the abundance of pictures. The forming power of Inspiration has to be involved. It presents a higher level of spirit-experience and masters the pictorial consciousness, indeed, it partially sacrifices it. With Wolfram we see this power reaching a certain maturity. In contrast to this, those who continue the French poetry seem inadequate.

Three poets are acknowledged who attempt to supplement Chrétien. The first is Gautier de Doulens. He leads the narration to the point where Perceval, after many adventures that contain very significant Imaginations, is allowed for the second time to sit at the Grail table. We already heard how at this time he asks about the Grail and the bleeding lance, and about the broken sword carried in by a page. Then it is reported how Perceval succeeds to re-assemble the pieces. After this completed trial, the king embraces him and greets him from now onwards as the Lord of this house.

At this place Gautier ends his narration. Manessier is the next poet who continues from where the broken sword is reassembled. He reports mysterious things that had occurred with the sword, which nevertheless are difficult to harmonize with Chrétien's presentation. However, Gerbert, a third poet continues. He introduces a part of the poem at the place where Manessier began, but this means—also with the reassembling of the broken sword. He says that at the attempt a gap remained in the sword because of Perceval's unatoned guilt. Consequently, the latter finds himself on the next morning amid a field—the Grail Castle has disappeared. He sees a wall before him and with his sword knocks at the gate until it breaks. Then an old man looks out, sees the broken sword and tells him he now has to wander for seven years seeking the Grail. After many trials, Perceval is finally mature to enter the Grail Castle. This time he succeeds to assemble the sword without any cracks. Only after this does Manessier's narration begin and completes the poetic work.

It is evident that the breaking and re-assembling of the Grail Sword is the decisive point with which the Grail poets of that time wrestled. On this the correct completion of the poem depended. The question was—how can one renew and supplement the Imaginations, coming to us as traditional spiritual goods but remaining fragmentary, in such a way that they present a path that in the future can really be pursued; expressed differently—how can the search for the Grail be consciously renewed?

11. Flore and Blanchefleur

The archetypal picture of the unification of the Red Knight with the 'Lily' we find in the old French legend of that youthful couple, their painful separation and glorious reunion, as it was copied already in the twelfth century in Low German minstrel poetry, and around 1220 was fashioned by the German poet Konrad Fleck into the charming heart-rending epic of 'Flore and Blanchefleur'.

The son of a heathen king of Spain and the daughter of a Christian prisoner of war are born on the same day in the same house. Since their birthday falls on the '*paske flôrîe*' (*Pascha floridum* = Palm Sunday), the king's son was called Flore and the daughter of the imprisoned duchess Blanchefleur. This means 'rose and lily'. They are brought up together; already as children they feel a most tender but irresistible mutual attraction. Since the Spanish king will never marry his son with the daughter of a prisoner, he orders an early separation. Flore is sent for a period to a distant city for schooling, while Blanchefleur is sold to a Babylonian merchant. The latter takes her to the Orient; the Amiral buys her and locks her with the other women of his harem into a tower. When Flore returns home asking for his Blanchefleur he is shown a precious gravestone under which she is supposed to lie. But since he is inconsolable about her death, threatening to kill himself, the parents reveal to him that Blanchefleur is still alive and was sold into the Orient. He sets out to seek her.

He rides out on a horse white on one side and red on the other. It is a very special horse—we know such horses from Wolfram's *Parzival*, for example, the Grail horse 'Gringuljet with the red ears'. Those who want to pursue the path to the spirit, have to bear a certain wisdom in the depths of their souls; one could call it an instinct leading the Grail seeker on the right trail. Horses lead a significant role in the world of legends and fairy tales. They always express the power of intelligence by which the human soul is led on its way more or less instinctively. The Apocalyse, too, knows such horsemen. And according to the direction of the will living in the thoughts of human beings, they ride on a white, red, black or pale (or pallid) horse.

Concerning this dual-coloured horse, which Flore rides on his way to the East, it expressly says that this is a work of nature, not of human invention, and only one worthy of a crown is worthy to ride it. We notice with the division of the colours, that in this young knight the forces of the blood express themselves held in balance by the forces of wisdom. Love drives him but it is full of innocence. In his book, *The Ninth Century and the Holy Grail*, W.J. Stein attempted to show how this legend can only be understood out of the symbolic language of Middle-Age alchemy. The significant thing of this work is that for the first time the alchemical bases of Wolfram's poem are shown. Most likely many other things seeking to connect the Grail events to the historical ninth century, one may find insufficiently demonstrated. However, with explanations giving the alchemical key for certain otherwise inexplicable descriptions, Dr Stein's book gives essential contributions for decoding the Grail Imagination. In this sense one begins to understand how the Grail stream could continue into the wisdom of the Rosicrucians.

In a Rosicrucian style, one may also say, it is a 'chymical wedding' to which the young king's son sets out for the East. Here the individual adventures will not be described finally leading him by the sea to Baghdad where he finds the tower in which the beloved is held prisoner. Through bribing the guard, Flore in red clothing (he also appears as 'the Red Knight') hidden in a basket of red roses, manages to have himself carried into Blanchefleur's chamber. They celebrate their reunion, given to each other in most chaste love. Yet one day their hidden happiness is discovered; in his rage the Amiral condemns them both to death. But on the way to the supreme court, how they compete to die for one another softens his heart. An atonement feast is celebrated, and they are released to their homeland. Since his father has just died, Flore takes up rulership of Spain, living with Blanchfleur, spreading happiness, living to his hundredth year. The two lovers die in the same hour. The two bodies are buried in one grave, but their soul enters the divine realm.

The poem says that out of this union, a daughter arose—Bertha, who became the mother of Charles the Great. We may not seek here a physical succession of generations, for Flore and Blanchefleur are not simply the earthly grandparents of the Emperor Charles. In him lived on the noblest maternal inheritance. They live on in him, but this means they are active in his body of formative forces. As the son of Pippin, what he carried as the paternal inheritance connected him to the outer powers. This contributed to his politicising Christianity, not only in a good sense. But what sparked his mind as the son of Bertha as if out of the depths of dreams, opened him to the highest spiritual activities. In him the Grail Inspiration found a significant tool. The wreath of legends surrounding the Emperor Charles points towards this side.

Rudolf Steiner pointed to the deep connection of this legend with the Mystery of the Grail. He describes how the early wisdom that taught the path of complete asceticism appears in the picture of the *lily*; the new path that does not kill off the sensory nature but wants to lift it to the spirit appears as the *rose*. The expression *sub rosa* is still used today to point towards the strict silence of a communication. It arises out of the symbolism of mystical brotherhoods. '*Sub rosa*', truly hidden under roses, Flore enters the realm of Blanchefleur—a picture of a mystical process.

This new path teaches Western esotericism. It does not demand denial of the world, but it starts from recognizing the sensory nature given to human beings. But it leads the forces of the blood through complete purification, until they become like the pure sap of the rose. The 'saints' of the ascetic path appear with the symbol of the lily; this is a bulbous plant and as such does not want to connect completely to the Earth. It is different for the rose. The truly Christian ideal trusts to the transformation of earthly nature. Out of the dying of the lower forces, the higher life is to blossom, the whole human being is to be brought to resurrection. The cross surrounded by roses symbolizes such strivings.

Flore takes this path. The legend calls him the son of King Fenix. It wants to point out that there are Phoenix Mysteries, out of which Flore has come. From Wolfram's poem we already know this symbol of the forces overcoming death. There it relates to the Grail stone. Flore is born as a heathen. But, says the poem, he received his baptism through his love for Blanchefleur that never suffered a doubt. This path initially appears as 'heathen', because it affirms the sensory nature and seeks to open the soul on all sides for the Earth. But on a higher level it leads to a Christianizing of the whole human being, toward a uniting with the Lily, that heavenly part of existence held imprisoned in the tower. Hidden under roses, trusting in the purest forces of his blood, the Red Knight dives into those depths of being out of which he can lead the virginal nature in himself towards disenchantment. With it he can celebrate the chymical wedding. In Eastern wisdom, one would have spoken of the awakening of the 'lotus flowers', where the lily appears. The seeker for the Grail strives to unite with the archetypal wisdom held hidden in the Orient. On this path, however, he brings the power of the human personality, not to be lost. With it the noblest forces of the West penetrate the spiritual striving of Eastern cultures. Flore's journey is characterized as a Grail path, also through the fact that he takes with him a miraculous cup fashioned by the God Vulcan himself, yet the lid is crowned with a carbuncle that shines in the night.

Journeys to the East in this sense were undertaken throughout the Middle Ages. The embassies the Carolingian court exchanged with the Caliph of Bagdad were not only political. They served to balance the cultural impulses that played hither and thither. The legend of Flore and Blanchefleur mirror this spiritual striving. The deepening into its Imagination can prepare us to understand the Parzival path. The localizing of the events in Spain points again to those 'late Gothic Mysteries', of which, following an indication of Rudolf Steiner, we spoke concerning the figure of Titurel.

12. *Grail wisdom in fairy tales*

An educational impulse wanting to draw attention to quite different forces in human nature from the ones fostered in the monasteries and Latin schools of the Middle Ages, tried to be influential through folk tales, which repeatedly trace the simpleton path who emerges as the hero. They sought to express the simplicity of the unspoilt youth as the best prerequisite for the spiritual path, which in the future has to be pursued for humanity's redemption.

We only have to recall the wonderful fairy tale of 'The Water of Life', known from the Grimms' collection. We hear of the sick king, for whom no physician is of any use, as in the Grail Legend with Amfortas.

The three sons of the king are there, who meet the mysterious old man who speaks of the one remedy, difficult to find. After riding out to find the water of life, the two elder sons remain stuck on their way; the conceit of their intellect hinders them from accepting the advice of the dwarf whom they meet. Moreover, as clever calculators, they only went on their way for the reward, not out of compassion as did the third son, the simpleton, who follows the advice of the dwarf and succeeds in the trials. Again, it is the magic castle that can only be entered during the night and which one has to leave before midnight—that means, before being overcome by deep sleep.

Similar situations we find in 'The Griffin's Feather', a fairy tale from Tessin, Switzerland. A hermit at the king's court speaks of a wonder-bird who, shining in marvellous colours, appears once every hundred years to drop a feather from its wings, intended for the noblest. This is the remedy for the king's illness. Again, it is only the third son—who nevertheless on the way undergoes trials regarding the forces of compassion before reaching the longed-for goal. Behind the griffin there clearly stands the mystery of the phoenix. The fairy tale wants to relate, the source of inspiration opens only once each century. Whoever gains the feather from the wings of the colourful bird will become a blessed one amongst the people. It is given to him to heal the ageing, ailing human nature—from it the sovereign power of the spirit has to be set free. For it understands it has to be lifted on the pinions of the imagination, to carry it upwards on the wings of song above all that lames and fetters on the Earth.

There are also fairy tales where the spiritual knighthood in the Parzivalian sense is portrayed. The fairy tales of Graubünden (a canton of Eastern Switzerland) of 'The One in the Bearskin' and of 'The Duke with the Golden Hair' are good examples of this. Such fairy tales mostly concern a threshold crossing, which begins with the coming of puberty of the young person. In the well-known fairy tale of 'Iron John' (Grimms', No. 136) it is nevertheless an eight-year-old lad who is enticed by the wild man to enter the woods and now has to undergo the adventures of his life. Here the forces of iron are impressively indicated, active in the blood; unfettered forces of freedom, which burst the prison of convention, of tradition, now begin to stir in the soul. They announce themselves in the urge for knowledge in the young human being, who wants to explore everything for himself. The lad dips his finger into the mysterious, forbidden well; on pulling it out finds it gilded. The misfortune has happened, the dreamy mood surrounding the child disappears from him. The trial of life begins. The way he is fitted out with the forces of an insurmountable knighthood is clearly a Michaelic trait of the fairy tale. The youth, who three times consecutively appears in red, white and black armour rides to the tournament, reminds one of Parzival. As the Red Knight, he proves to be the conqueror of the nature of the blood, as the White Knight he presents the pure spirit, whereas only the black armour points to the pure emerging of the higher human being into earthly embodiment; at this level he is concerned with the forces of death and overcomes them. In this fairy tale anonymity plays an important role; the hero who appears in the highest plight as a saviour has initially to remain unknown. It is a law of the Grail, the deeper sense of which we shall explore in the Lohengrin legend.

The language of imagination as mirroring the inner development of human nature can be most clearly studied by taking a classical folk tale. Here we may mention the author's two books on fairy tales, *The Wisdom of Fairy Tales* (Floris Books, Edinburgh 1995), and *Die Weisheit der Schweizer Märchen* (Columban Verlag, 1944). As introductions, they seek to develop a method that can lead to decipher the imaginative language. Learning to perceive the lawfulness of this pictorial world through folk tales, opens an important level to understand legends.

Here another fact may be illuminated, which can be irritating particularly in studying certain fairy-tale figures. This applies when studying the Parzival legend. Heroes in fairy tales are usually very young, mostly adolescents at the age of puberty—in some cases, as in 'Iron John,' even younger. But how can they then pass such trials that enable them to achieve the highest deeds of redemption? Initially, it concerns experiences which in the youth, that is, during the time when the 'ideals' in the soul are born, are felt as in a storm of feelings. Nevertheless, only very seldom do young persons in normal life reflect on these feelings as conscious Imaginations. The hidden 'dreamer' in them goes through these experiences; they run under the threshold of their day-consciousness. However, mature persons can, as it were, repeatedly fall back on that protected soul-treasure, in as far as they are not unfaithful to the 'spirit of youth'. They are to learn to draw from it, to become inspired by it.

Whoever is aware of travelling the path of the spirit will now experience that it is good to connect to this 'dreamer' hiding in the depths of the soul. For a conscious unfolding of a higher life, the spirit-seeker can take as a starting point the pure ideals of the heart that shone at a certain moment in life, or the fresh impulses of recognition that experienced an initial breakthrough in a youthful thirst for knowledge. Raised up from the depths of the soul, they appear before the inner gaze as such Imaginations that are found in fairy tales. In his Mystery Dramas, Rudolf Steiner has the 'spirit of youth' appear on stage as an astral figure, in an attempt to portray the soul-development of his character Johannes Thomasius, who at the moment of facing this figure arising from the depths of dream, struggles towards his spiritual awakening.

What Parzival experiences takes place, as Chrétien's presentation shows, between the age of fifteen and twenty. The spiritual deeds and trials, as they are described in Wolfram's poetic work, point towards a high level of initiation. Indeed, at the completion of his Grail's path we are to imagine this individuality in his adult age. No outer biography is traced, taking place in chronological order. Its essential legendary forces are revealed in an Imaginative, poetic manner. The 'human ideal' in the legend is radiantly revealed in such pictures. It is the 'eternal youth' in human beings. When he awakens to the spirit, he begins to lay hold of himself in his unspoilt youthful nature.

13. The leash called 'Brackenseil' ('bracken rope')

A fruitful viewpoint could be to review within Parzival's destiny the stages through the twelve virtues up to true love. Wolfram is also the poet of that tragic adventure with the dog Gardevias. A detailed description of the inscription on the Brackenseil [= bracken leash] cannot be found in his Titurel fragment; it is only given through Albrecht von Scharfenberg. Yet one should not believe that Wolfram did not have a clear vision of it. In any case, in his destiny his Parzival lives these ideals, as drawn from the best Troubadour tradition. He is the true *Minnende*, the true lover.

At Arthur's court, the Brackenseil, for which Sigune so fervently longs after sending Schionatulander for it, is finally deciphered. It contains abundant instructions that find their climax in the description of the wreath of virtues. 'Twelve flowers weave into a wreath when you proceed to the day of honours', says the inscription. That means, 1. Pure cultivation, 2. Chastity, 3. Gentleness, 4. Faithfulness, 5. Temperance, Measure in all things, 6. Care (Attention), 7. Shame (Bashfulness), 8. Modesty, 9. Steadfastness, 10. Devotion, 11. Patience, 12. *Minne* (love).[94]

---

[94] Aristotle's Twelve Virtues (*Nicomachean Ethics*) are sometimes translated as Brave, Temperate, Generous, Munificent, High-minded, Ambitious, Patient, Friendly, Truthful, Witty, Modest, Indignant—*Trans.*

As the wild boy puts on the red armour of the slain Ither, he is already on this path of the soul. '*Pure cultivation*' he receives from Gurnemanz. There he is raised to knighthood; from now on he moves blamelessly in a knightly, courtly fashion. But he immediately internalizes it, when as a knight he takes on a lady in need of help. He enters the land of renunciation, when he comes to Queen Kondwiramur. Her capital city, Belrapeire, is in the grips of hunger, as we hear. Without hesitating, he takes part in their plight. Here his soul shows its virtue as '*chastity*'. To what a high degree this penetrates his whole feeling becomes revealed when the young queen, without protection, entrusts herself to him—but where the heart opens in pure love, everything which is rigid melts away. '*Gentleness*' pours into all his action, even in the heat of the battle it does not leave the hero. This is shown in how he deals with the defeated enemies before Belrapeire and soon afterwards how he shows generosity to the angry Duke Orilus. Now there awakens in him responsibility to what he leaves behind. From now on, Parzival practises '*faithfulness*' in that in his happiness he nevertheless does not close himself to the voice of conscience admonishing him to care for the mother he left behind. Feeling responsible for Jeschute in her misery, of which he is not completely guiltless, shows the same faithfulness. The trial of this virtue, however, is steadfast attitude with which during the years of separation he upholds the marriage bond with Kondwiramur. Nevertheless, the longing of love which becomes overpowering in the deprivation, threatens to throw the lover's soul out of balance. We meet Parzival in the condition of rapture, when beholding the drops of blood in the snow he loses awareness. To find '*measure in all things*' is the challenge, also in the deepest feelings of all. Gawain carefully helps him to direct his gaze to his surroundings; he has to learn to practise '*attention*', to be ready for the dangers of the world and always to meet its challenges. For only through this can he become a member of Arthur's court. Here the middle of the twelvefold path has been reached.

A significant threshold has to be crossed, demanding initially a deep transformation of his being. When the soul begins to practise self-knowledge, it will be overcome by '*shame*'. Here it concerns the deepest shame, far exceeding the life's conventional feeling of shame. From this threshold experience, which is conveyed to him through meeting Kundrie, a decision follows making him renounce all worldly happiness and all momentary success. But in withdrawing from Arthur's court, Parzival chooses the path of '*modesty*'. His striving now proceeds away from outer worldly glory and everything that could satisfy ambition. The knight who has given himself to the Spirit has year by year, unerringly to pursue his aim. *'Steadfastness'* confirms his character. In the German Middle Ages this was called *Stäte*. This anticipates patience, not quite its full development, for we see Parzival pursuing his path with resentment. He bears his destiny without wavering, yet with a sting of bitterness in his deepest feelings. To be able completely to accept his destiny, *'devotion'* is still missing. In naming this virtue, the Brackenseil adds, 'it forgot Lucifer. Now follow the trail and you will not be damned to Hell.' Only on that Good Friday when he receives the Grail teaching through Trevrizent, does true devotion enter the soul of Parzival. The rigidity in defiance is dissolved; he begins to understand the universal meaning of Christ's sacrifice. Trevrizent describes for him the tragedy of Lucifer and how the human being was, as it were, created in his place when he fell into hell. But now those human beings suffer the same temptation who follow Lucifer's path. Consequently, the Incarnation of God has to take place in order to wrest humanity from the abyss, which was threatening them. Only now does Parzival become a Christian.

Now Parzival understands the teaching that one ought not to 'seek' the Grail. Whoever still seeks it will not find it. The attitude of complete submission has to be achieved. The search is a 'non-search'—that is the secret. Only this is true *'patience'* through which the inner human being grows towards the Grail. It concerns a maturing process of hidden organs, which like blossoms open to the highest light when their time has come. Impatience closes the flower of the heart. Parzival pursues the path of the heart's initiation. It is a twelvefold path; in occult wisdom, when development of the heart is described, the maturing of the twelve-petalled lotus flower is mentioned. Parzival appears for a second time before the suffering Anfortas with a fully awakened heart. Out of deepest compassion he can now present the redeeming question. Only now does he become the Lord of the Grail. For the true *'Minne'*, love, begins to enter his heart as love towards God and human beings. From now on he lives to alleviate the suffering of others. Now he may find Kondwiramur again. She is brought to him to live united with him by the Grail. All separations are removed. To become a king in the realm of the Grail means to be allowed to be a fellow of the angelic world, as Titurel learned when he was chosen for the Grail. 'The last flower leads you to the song of the angels', says the Brackenseil, indicating this graded path of trials towards the highest love.

This path should be understood, not in the sense of a rigid scheme, but in a dynamic manner—in the inner wrestling and maturing of the soul the degrees mutually penetrate. It is a key that opens much which otherwise would have to remain mysterious in deciphering Wolfram's *Parzival*. Above all the teacher who has to bring this poem to young people will be able with conviction to bring the sequence of adventures to experience. Only with this key will some of the scenes gain a deeper experience. Ideals can be fashioned, enthusiasm ignited and a meaning for the mysterious guidance of destiny can be awakened. For Waldorf Schools, Rudolf Steiner recommended Wolfram's *Parzival* as a subject for Class/Grade 11. A strong ordering can ray into the youthful soul from the pictures of this poem that can only be seen and completely understood by the one who begins to understand the spiritual lawfulness of such a work. Clearly, it can never be the teacher's task to open the esoteric backgrounds of such a poem before the young people. The colourful pictures of the medieval world may initially become alive for them. In their balance of strong acceptance of the Earth and the fervent love of God, they can foster a healthy feeling for the place of human beings in the wider world. If it were possible that many souls at the right age within Middle Europe could experience this poem within the rhythm of their development, then much would happen to harmonize a puberty that has become stuck or even slept through. One could prevent several neuroses, this ailment of an over-bourgeois society. For the receptive soul, brought in the right way and at the right time, it can indeed become a strong help to kindle the moral experiences of youth, necessary today for an empowered human development.

14. *Manichaean influences*

The insight that the Grail tradition is rooted in Manichaean traditions becomes increasingly evident. Franz Rolf Schröeder (*Die Parzival Frage*, Munich 1928) sought to find Iranian influences, which through the Cathars, or also the Knights Templar, could have been brought to the West in Wolfram's *Parzival*. He points out how in the 'great [Iranian] Bundahishn',[95] a Persian scripture of wisdom, the myth of Gayomard,

---

[95] The Bundahishn is an encyclopedic collection of beliefs about Zoroastrian cosmology written in the Book Pahlavi script. The original name of the work is not known. It is one of the most important extant witnesses to Zoroastrian literature in the Middle Persian language. First pub. 1868—*Wikipedia*. See https://www.avesta.org/mp/bundahis.html

the archetypal human being, is related, of a deep fall and rising again. His body is to be formed of seven metals. Corresponding to these metals, this being stands under the influence of the planets. We read that Saturn returns to the Scales in which he found his exaltation; through this, death is brought to Gayomard after he had been held away for thirty years by the mighty influence of Jupiter. 'Then Gayomard fell on his left side ...' This planetary influence clearly corresponds to the description that Trevrizent gives of the suffering of Anfortas, whose wound with the approach of Saturn always begins again to cause pain.

Or the new silk cloth worked through with gold (called by Wolfram 'Achmardi'), on which the Grail was festively carried in, could remind one of the ceremonies of the Sabians. They fostered planetary cults; the temple dedicated to Jupiter was to have been built of green stones, adorned with green curtains. On Thursday, the day of Jupiter, the Sabians entered this temple in green garments. Consequently, F.R. Schröeder asks whether the Grail was possibly an 'idol of Jupiter'. Yet the discovery of such relationships between the myths and cultic traditions of the Orient on the one hand and Grail symbolism on the other hand will only be fruitful for study when one looks for esoteric sources. That means to recognize the spiritual realities standing behind such motifs.

The Grail is certainly no idol of Jupiter. But in Wolfram's version, which presents it as *Lapis exillis*, as the 'philosopher's stone' gained in a mysterious alchemical process, Jupiter's influence is indeed active. Cosmic wisdom forms the pre-stage for the Grail illumination; Feirifis, the black-and-white brother from the East, possesses the Mystery of the cosmos. He lives in veneration to 'Jupiter'. When he arrives at the Grail Castle, he sees the green silk cloth of Achmardi. But the shining Grail itself, which the maiden carries on this cloth in festive procession, he cannot see while he is still 'unbaptized'. This is intended to express that the old wisdom, despite all illumination, does not yet penetrate to the Mystery of the forces overcoming death in human nature. It is not able to behold how in the dying body the seed of resurrection is being prepared. It is blind to the Grail. The Manichean spirit permeating the Parzival poem is to be sought less in the individual motifs carried over from the East. Much more important is how Wolfram's Manichaeism is expressed in the whole ethos of the work, how the striving human being is placed into the battle of light and darkness.

In recent years surprisingly much new material of the earliest Manichaean texts has come to light. Through the documents of the

Christianized Parsis (Parsees) one will increasingly clearly see this noble religious pioneer. Here we point to the spiritual-scientific study of Albert Steffen, *Mani, his Life and Work* (Dornach 1930). Those who can take up this presentation drawn from intuitive sources will see a figure arise in its glory, whose deepest being seems to shine again in Parzival's being and striving.

15. The impulse of the Visigothic Empire

There are world-historic sacrificial deeds that give the direction to a whole age and like a stream of rejuvenation are able in a subterranean manner to pulse beneath the growth of cultures. Belonging to this is the meteoric appearance of the Goths on the stage of Europe, their short-lived founding of states and their decline. With a few strokes, the vision of the Visigoths may be sketched. It was they, who after Alarich's death moving through the whole of Italy, initially took residence in the south of Gaul and founded the Visigothic kingdom. In the beginning of the fifth century, it quickly blossoms, extending by the Pyrenees into that significant state in Spain, which in 711 through the victory of the Arabs in Xeres de la Frontera was destroyed.

It was Theoderic (419–451) under whose reign the Visigoths proved their ability to found states. They were probably the first Germanic tribe which through agriculture and consequential town building laid the foundation for a Germanic cultural state, whilst at the same time quickly penetrated it with Roman education that was alive in the south of France. Theoderic falls in the great battle with the Huns, but his son took part in the decisive victory over Attila. Under Theoderick II (453–466) the conquest in the north of Spain takes place. They find people who turn to Roman Catholicism, whereas the Goths themselves belong to the Arian confession. This Arian Christianity they once received through their great missionary and educator Ulfilas.

When on their campaigns they had penetrated from the Black Sea to Bulgaria, they were introduced to Christianity through their Cappadocian prisoners. Ulfilas, who gave them the famous Gothic Bible translation and through it, based on its runic script, created the first Gothic alphabet, was himself the son of a Goth and a Christian female prisoner who came from Cappadocia. If we recall the genealogy of the Grail dynasty from the Titurel poem, then a King Senabor from Cappadocia is named; from him stems that Berillus, who was given the realm in Gaul and Spain. He was the ancestor of Titurel himself. It clearly has to do with a spiritual genealogical tree; for an indication towards those Christian streams, which through Ulfilas and the Cappadocian prisoners were carried into the Visigothic realm. These Arians fostered an internalized Christianity. Because of this, they were regarded as heretics by the Roman Church that stood for the teaching of Athanasius.

What was the essential thing in this quarrel concerning dogmatics, which led the Christian Church to the first great split? It concerns Christology. Arius, a noble ascetic figure of Alexandria, sought to understand Christ's being from the human side. Although for him it was also the Logos, created out of God before all times and aeons, but indeed 'created' and consequently not 'equal in substance' with the Father. The Orthodox stream, represented especially through Athanasius, wanted to save the unity of the Persons of the Holy Trinity; it did not concern itself with the true riddle—the Incarnation of the Logos. The victory this stream gained after long battles was an ecclesiastically political one, achieved in an inhuman manner.

Viewed theologically, both standpoints can be either justified or disputed. In those days the understanding for the 'two natures' in Jesus Christ was already obscure. People no longer knew in what way the human and the divine sides permeate His being. If one pays attention to the influences coming to the fore in this Christological battle, one will be able to say, the Athanasian stream leads into dogmatic abstraction, the Arian stream directs its interest most strongly to the human becoming of the divine and consequently corresponded more to the inclinations of the young peoples who took up the Christian impulse into their inner life and with their personal striving wanted to be carriers of the spirit. This contrast came up later once again in the 'Filioque' battle.

The Western Church had taken into their Creed the confession that the Holy Spirit not only proceeds from the Father but also 'from the Son'. In the life of humanity, new sources of the spirit had opened with Christ's appearance. But who instigated this seemingly so insignificant addition to the Creed? It was the Visigoths. The Arian Goths showed they were by nature tolerant towards the original people of Spain, who adhered to the Catholic, Athanasian Creed. The situation became difficult for them only when the Franks, penetrating from North Gallia towards the Pyrenees, became their rivals. They had taken on the Roman Creed under the Merovingian King Clovis, gaining clear sympathy amongst the Catholic of the Visigothic kingdom. When in the sixth century the Franks took over the Toulousian part of the Visigothic realm and the kings of the Goths were forced to move to Spain, the Catholic direction within their realms became increasingly dangerous for them, however pleasantly they behaved towards it. In 589, the Gothic king Reccared I decided to take on the Catholic, Asian belief and in a festive declamation in a church gathering in Toledo, he declared himself free from the Arian confession. But at the same Synod of Toledo, the Athanasian Creed received the addition of the formal 'Filioque' ('and the Son'). Through this, although only indicated through a little word, the innermost concern of the Gothic Christians became once more evident. For a long time, Rome did not recognize this 'Filioque'. Only when Charlemagne recognized it in the year 809 for his Frankish Church, did the whole of the Western world slowly follow.

With the arrival of Tariq on Spanish soil (in 711) and his entry into Toledo (712) the Visigothic realm was conquered. Only in 732, Charles Martel at Tours is able to bring to a standstill the seemingly unstoppable surge of Arabs. But throughout the Middle Ages it remained the destiny of the Goths to have to live on the same ground with the culture of Mohammed. In the legend of Flore and Blanchefleu, the son of the heathen king in Spain and the daughter of an imprisoned Christian, this interpenetration of these two worlds is mirrored; at the same time, however, what can result as the innermost inclination of the soul from two contrasting cultural realms. Here the seeds of the Rosicrucian spiritual stream are laid.

In outer history we see the clash of feuding peoples, the centuries of heroic battles in swaying hither and thither of victories and defeats. But in the depths of spiritual life, a more intimate exchange of forces takes place. Out of the spiritual marriage of Gothic Christianity and Moorish wisdom the impulse is born in which in that 'later Gothic Mysteries' was cultivated in the north of Spain. Rudolf Steiner pointed emphatically to these Mysteries as a still true place of wisdom which existed in the early Middle Ages in Europe. For here, the Mysteries of the Holy Spirit were guarded, whereas the Christian Church after the Council of Constantinople of 869 steered increasingly towards a denial of the spirit, as far as it can manifest in human nature.

What Gothic culture in the north of the Pyrenees—that is, the rest of the Toulousian realm under the Frankish regime—meant for the spiritual life, we have pointed out in the account of the Cathars. Then it was the Gothic nobility, which with the Duke of Toulouse and the high castles of Provence, gave heroic resistance to fight and die for the free spirit.

16. The singer contest and Wagner's Tannhäuser

In the chronicles of the thirteenth century and in the legend of St Elizabeth of Thuringia, the song contest is treated as an historical event, dated to 1206 and 1207. It is told when Heinrich von Ofterdingen at the contest bargained his head and lost the bargain, he received a year's respite to fetch Master Klingsor from Hungary as a protector and judge. He succeeded in finding him and gains his support. Through magic they arrive at the given date in Eisenach and live in an inn near the gate of St George. Klingsor, who can read the stars, announces one evening that in Hungary a daughter is born to King Andreas, that is St Elizabeth who one day will become the wife of the future Landgravine (Duke). Four years later, in 1211, she is brought from the Hungarian court to the Wartburg to be betrothed to the young Ludwig and to be brought up with him.

For modern historical research, all this belongs to legend: the figure of Klingsor, as well as his prophecy from the stars and the taking of the four-year-old Princess to Eisenach. The fact itself cannot be denied, and the appearance of Elizabeth as the carrier of sublime Christ-forces, the radiance of which was of extraordinary significance for that age, will always remain a riddle for academic history caught in prejudice. However, if one begins to see through the mighty spiritual battle, which in the thirteenth century raged around the destiny of the Christian West and in the context of which stood the Wartburg, then one can gain a different relationship to such communications.

A mystery of the stars relates to the appearance of such an individuality, who through her whole existence, throughout her short, devoted life, carried holy forces of love into her time—similar to her somewhat older contemporary Francis of Assisi and the sister of her own mother, St Hedwig of Silesia. A sacrificial stream, glowing through with heroic courage for love, breaks through with this figure. She seems meant to be a heavenly counterforce for the century which, struggling hard with the arising Arabism, finds itself in a tremendous plight of the heart. The soul is set upon by doubts of all revelations, and with the awakening of these strong intellectual forces there goes hand in hand the unleashing of lower love. The sanctifying of the forces of love as it is lived by some great souls brings into balance again that which of necessity had to darken hearts. It is now exceptionally profound that especially from the same country from whence the black magician is brought, there also comes the great saint, indeed, that he himself has to announce with his astrological art her entrance into earthly existence.

Richard Wagner saw the deep connection of the 'song contest' with the appearance of Elizabeth. In a genial way, although completely unhistorical, he wove the saint into the plot, making her the daughter of the Landgravine Hermann. She appears as a maiden who has her say in the contest of the singers. In this drama, a mystical event takes place in which Elizabeth solves Heinrich von Ofterdingen's entanglement of guilt (here he is called Tannhäuser) through her vicarious sacrifice. For it requires the highest exertions of atoning love to break the power of the lower Venus in the erring Minnesinger. But Wolfram, the Grail singer, recognizes the great soul of the saint. With his 'song to the evening star' he glorifies the wonder of Venus Urania, heavenly love, whose carrier on Earth has been Elizabeth. In this mystical event, the deepest wrestling of that time is mirrored in which Wolfram von Eschenbach had to announce and strongly represent the Grail path for a fallen love-culture that had erred into unbridled activity.

17. The Chymical Wedding of Christian Rosenkreuz

Concerning this mysterious writing, one may initially think with scepticism; it is able to accompany the most sacred seriousness with a healthy humour, but consequently is interpreted by historical critics only as a satire on alchemists. Yet if one is open to test it on its innermost attitude, one perceives in it a tremendous courage towards the spirit, which is paired in the soul of the spiritually daring seeker, a deep humility. Through it one can gain the experience of a wonderfully balanced soul. Solely through this the writing has a genuine Christian ring. One values, too, the flavour of the humour accompanying the deepest seriousness, in the sense that the true knower never succumbs to the danger to confuse in himself the everyday human being with the other one who is allowed to experience elevated spiritual grace.

For a deeper experience of this spiritual document, an essay by Rudolf Steiner may be mentioned that appeared in 1917. It gives the key towards the mysterious Imaginations, which want to mirror a mighty breakthrough to the Spirit. This essay is included as an Appendix in a recent edition of the *Chymische Hochzeit* by Dr Walter Weber (Dornach 1942).[96] This beautiful edition gives for the first time a translation of the Rosicrucian text in modern German. It is consequently

---

[96] Rudolf Steiner, *Collected Essays on Philosophy and Anthroposophy 1904–1923* [GA 35], 13. The Chymical Wedding of Christian Rosenkreutz. (https://rsarchive.org/Articles/GA035/English/SOL2024/13_The_Chymical_Wedding_of_Christian_Rosenkreutz.html)

more accessible to study than the archaic style of the original text, which nevertheless gives the spiritual presentations a unique aroma.[97]

The *Chymical Wedding anno 1459* is concerned with new ways to the spirit. How this takes place may be shown with an example. When the wedding guests are precisely weighed on the scales and most are found to be too light, according to the strict judgement only a few remain from those rejected. They are those who do not seek to obtain access to the spiritual world by taking over spiritual forces that are spurious or have become outdated. But in what does a legitimate, that is a contemporary path consist? Rudolf Steiner claims that from now on 'the possibility begins to use the ability to understand in such a way that is appropriate for the spiritual world. The owner of this ability places himself before the soul as the Imagination of the unicorn that bows down before a lion.' The brother of Rosencreuz reports his characteristic experiences on the way to the chymical wedding. He describes how after the strict judgement a short silence ensued; then there came a beautiful snow-white unicorn with a golden neckband. It went to the well in the castle garden, bowing down on both front feet before the lion as if to give honour, who unmoving like a statue remained on the well. Then the lion took his unsheathed sword, held it in its paws, and broke it in two, letting the pieces sink into the well. Then he roared until a white dove appeared bringing a twig from an olive tree in its beak, which he swallowed. Then he was satisfied, and the unicorn, too, returned to its place ...

This capricious being of fable, difficult to lay hold of, we already met in the discussion on precious stones (p. 235f). It is said that the unicorn with its horn can become quite dangerous; it can only be tamed by a pure virgin. But here it changes its behaviour. It bows down before the lion. It this Imagination it is shown how head and heart now harmonize. The forces of the consciousness-soul that in its whole behaviour frequently has something 'pushy', are initially unwilling to listen to what comes from the heart. Consequently, the lion takes a stern, rejecting stance towards the unicorn, until the latter decides to bow down to him in devotion. Only then do quite new possibilities arise for the consciousness-soul. The forces of the heart begin to come into effect; it is the lion who now calls in that spiritual power appearing in the picture

[97] The first English translation by E. Foxcroft (1690), *The Hermetick Romance, or the Chymical Wedding,* Forgotten Books, etc. Online version: https://archive.org/details/ChymicalWeddingOfChristianRosenkreutz

of the dove with the olive branch. The heart now begins to unite with the life of thinking. But with this the consciousness-soul has matured towards awakened recognition of the spiritual world.

In the following scene, the three kings, each with his queen by his side, are presented in a peculiar way. But then, their beheading is described and all those invited are to watch the deeply shocking drama. Before the execution is carried out, the guests have to commit their faith to those who enter death. They are to understand that it depends on them whether out of this death new life will arise. After many preparations, carried out under the leadership of a virgin (her name is 'Alchemia') it is finally achieved to awaken to life the phoenix bird out of its egg. It is described how it unfolds and then is ready to be sacrificed. Its ashes are used to prepare the dough out of which the young royal couple can be formed. Only the sacrificed heart's blood of the phoenix is able to make these beautiful angelic creatures, which initially entered into embryonic existence to grow magnificently, as the blood is administered to them, drop by drop. In the Rosicrucian sense, *knowledge* which recognizes its activity in the spirit—a sacrificial action cannot lead to the goal unless the heart's blood is continually given to it. How deeply this alchemy, in which the life of the higher human being is born, lays hold of the processes of the body, re-fashioning them in an intimate manner from the spirit, Rudolf Steiner has repeatedly presented in describing the seven degrees of the Rosicrucian path. He characterizes the fourth degree as a deep transformation of the breathing process. In the fundamental lecture-cycle, *Theosophy of the Rosicrucians* (GA 99, Munich 1907), which concludes (lect. 14, 6 June 1907) with a presentation of this path of schooling, he describes how the 'Grail pupil' has to develop a special relationship to the world of plants. He shows how the human being initially depends on plants to sustain his existence. Plants continually give back oxygen for human breathing out of their chaste life-processes, whereas to build up their plant-form they assimilate carbon dioxide which human beings exhale. This achievement of the plant for human beings, we read, shall in future by taken over by human beings. This Rosicrucian schooling teaches to produce these transformations of matter within one's own inner being.

> What plants today are doing outside, later on through an organ of the future, human beings will carry out in themselves. Already now they can perform this through [Rosicrucian] schooling. This is being slowly prepared; through the regulated process of breathing, the human being

> becomes instrumental to prepare oxygen in himself. He will then become one with the plant, whereas now he is at the mineral stage. He will retain carbon dioxide within himself, building his own body with it, whereas later his body will be more akin to the plant ... This is called the transformation of human substance into a substance, the basis of which is carbon dioxide. This alchemy will lead to his building up his body as the plant does today. This is called the preparation of the 'philosopher's stone'; carbon is its outer symbol. But it only becomes the philosopher's stone when, through his regulated breathing, the human being can produce it himself.

Trevrizent taught Parzival that the Grail is a 'stone'. During our presentations, we have characterized this 'stone' in very different ways. To the superficial gaze, it could appear with contradictions. But whoever can feel how, in studying the Grail legend, we have gradually penetrated to ever deeper layers of reality will also find the unity which nevertheless links these presentations. In Eastern wisdom, such methods were always known that proceeded from the conscious regulation of breathing. That highest spiritual force accessible to the human being, which from breathing can be brought into the bodily organization until it finally gives mastery over the hidden life-processes, was consequently called 'atman'. In the Rosicrucian schooling, one becomes a 'knight of the golden stone'[98] through the awakening of this atman. For in atman the building mysteries of a future corporeality are enclosed. Atman is the builder of the invisible temple.

Among the Grail Imaginations we know from Chretién's poetry the mysterious figure of the old man whom Perceval only perceives resting in the background, kept alone alive through the power of the Host, corresponds to atman. With this atman is indicated as the deeply hidden builder of corporeality. With Wolfram, it has become the ancestor Titurel, the builder of the Grail Temple.

In his *Occult Science, an Outline,* Rudolf Steiner nevertheless emphasizes that this deep effect, which stretches right into the bodily processes, should no longer be directly produced from the breathing of the meditant today. Western schooling proceeds in a consequential manner only from the awake consciousness; it avoids everything forceful in mastering the bodily nature. But when the meditative life has proceeded to the unfolding of the pure force of Intuition, the spiritual pupil will notice that gradually certain expressions of the physical body, for example, the

[98] A website exists devoted to the Knights of the Golden Stone—*Ed.*

breathing, is mastered almost by itself; it can be brought into harmony with exercises of the soul. 'The ideal of development is that through the physical body itself no exercises would be carried out, including breathing exercises, but that everything that happens to it *only* occurs as consequence of Intuition exercises' [Chap. 5, vii, last sentence].

18. Music as mediator of the work of the Grail

The language of the musician can lead into the depths of Christian experience. To this, pictures can only point as from a distance to something a concept can never completely grasp. Here the deep research of Prof. Hermann Beckh may be mentioned—*The Parsifal-Christ-Experience in Wagner's Music Drama* (1930) [double volume with *The Essence of Tonality*, Temple Lodge 2022]. An example of psychological-artistic analysis is how Beckh develops the 'Gaze motif' from its first sounding through the stages of the drama until, with the admonishing, painful suffering, it finally transforms into the 'redeeming gaze of Christ'.

In addition to this comes the original question of the musical keys, with which Beckh was particularly concerned, *The Language of Tonality in the Music from Bach to Bruckner* (1937). He arranged the twelve major and minor keys [the circle of fifths] to the zodiac circle. Artistic people may initially feel such an arrangement speculative, compromising the immediate experience. But if one takes the abundant musical examples from the musical repertoire and can follow Beckh's tactful, sensitive language then a lawfulness is revealed in a brilliant way, which can no longer be ignored.

This can also intimately awaken the sense for *what wants to be revealed* in music. Here Wagner's mastery to speak through *the musical keys* is concretely worked out. Thus, we learn to recognize A-major as the voice of deepest inner feeling; it sounds in *Parsifal* as the actual Grail-key. 'In the etheric A-major we experience the super-earthly shining of the holy blood', whereas the dominating key of A-major of *Lohengrin* is characterized by Beckh [2015 ed., p. 238ff., towards the end of the section, 'A-major and F#-minor in Wagner']:

> The A-major of the cosmic heights in *Lohengrin* points to the Holy Grail in far-off, unreachable cosmic heights ... In *Parsifal*, however, we are transferred directly into the Grail sanctuary itself; from the very beginning we penetrate to the heart of this sanctuary.

Out of the spiritual-scientific depths, Rudolf Steiner had pointed to that ability in Wagner to announce the Grail Mystery to his age through musical means, which would not have been perceived through other means. He says (Landin, i.e. West Havelland, near Brandenburg. 29 July 1906. GA 97), 'The ether-body is connected to all the ebb and flow of the blood. Richard Wagner understood the Mystery of the purified blood. In his melodies are contained the vibrations which must be in human ether-bodies when people purify themselves in such a way as is necessary to receive the Mystery of the Holy Grail.'

Nevertheless, in concluding his last lecture-cycle in which he gave once more a summary of his spiritual message (*True and False Paths of Spiritual Investigation*, GA 243. Torquay, August 1924), Rudolf Steiner mentions the limits of this art. 'That which for human development is the highest, the approach of the figure of Christ'—to express this would first have to be found in music. Although in Wagner this urge was there, he attempted in his *Parsifal* to conjure up the Christ-Impulse in the sensory world. But just here, where he wanted to be most Christian, he remains stuck in symbolism—the Dove appears, and so on. 'The musical element is capable of placing before the world this Christ-Impulse in music, in formed ensouled and spiritually permeated sounds. If music allows itself to be inspired by anthroposophical spiritual science, it will find the way ...' Then is described in a sequence of specific degrees of the scale, of musical intervals, this Mystery can be expressed, that is, purely musically, *how the soul finds Christ*.

This monumental lecture-cycle of Rudolf Steiner sounds like a testimony, ending with a prophecy. 'And so it can come about (it only depends on people) that the Christ-Impulse in its true form can come to manifestation precisely in the sphere of music.'[99]

In considering how arduously the most light-filled ideas wanting to come to human beings today from cosmic heights can be taken up—not because intelligence for it is missing, but simply because the heart-forces necessary for recognition out of experience are extensively stunted—one will appreciate the spiritual mission of music. Feelings

[99] Rudolf Steiner's concluding words on the mission of music (22 Aug. 1924) are inadequately translated in all the three English versions. The lecturer is trying to find words to express deep feelings. It is reported that he missed a particular musician (Kathleen Schlesinger?) whom he was expecting to be present. An accurate translation appears in Lea van der Pals, *The Human Being as Music*, Anastasi 2014, 120–23. In his pioneer studies, Hermann Beckh finds Wagner's *Parsifal* theme fits Steiner's musical sequence, published in a double volume: Hermann Beckh, *The Essence of Tonality; The Parsifal-Christ-Experience*, Temple Lodge 2022, 153—*Tr. note.*

for the Mysteries can be awakened through music. An extension of the feelings right to the limits of the cosmos and at the same time an intensification opening the soul to receive the sacred element—this double pursuit can take place through the pure musical element.

Mysteries have to be deeply *felt* before one is able to *recognize* them in the full light of day.

19. The sacred spear

In the collection of Irish myths and legends mentioned in Chapter 4, footnote 21, p. 59, the 'Spear of Victory' plays an essential role. Here the Celtic expert Ella Young writes of the gods of light; led by the heavenly Brigit, they descended to Earth and chose the island of Ireland as their dwelling place, from there to transform the whole Earth into beauty. We read:

> Nuada, the wielder of the white light, planted the spear of victory in the middle of Ireland like a great fiery fountain. It was like a singing flame. It burned unceasingly and each fire in Ireland was lit from it.

The spear symbolizes all the creative forces that once were guarded by the Sun-Mysteries and given to the surrounding world. It contains the Mysteries of 'white magic'. For the foundation of the Sun Oracle, which towards the end of Atlantean times was to have its place in the vicinity of Ireland.

Through its creative radiance, the spear forms an extensive circle of light around itself. Misshapen creatures of darkness, the Fomor, approach the rim of this circle of light and bathe in it. Through this, they slowly gain strength and in them the longing grows to possess the spear of light for themselves. Balor with the one-eye, is king of this tribe of Fomor. We already saw how the carriers of a retrograde Atlantean people (Homer characterized the Cyclops in this way) always appeared as people with one eye. Nuada swings the 'Spear of Victory' against the intruding Fomor, the spawn of the underworld. Indeed, Nuada charges destructively through their halls, but Balor is able to catch the weapon, and it remains with him. The spear of light now transforms into a fiery serpent. It is described how from its presence demons of air emerge. It now proves to produce destruction. With this, the Fomor make themselves lords of the island and make the light dynasty of the Dana their slaves. The legend points towards a sublime hero of the Sun who breaks the power of darkness. One day he shall plant the sacred spear in the centre of Ireland, before the end of the world.

The same spear standing for the victory of light can consequently in evil hands transform into demonic power. Then it symbolizes black magic. Through the unlimited misuse of the life-forces the Atlantean world was driven into decline.

Richard Wagner cannot have known this myth, but how he placed the Mystery of the spear into the centre of the poetic libretto on the Grail proves that his genius was able to draw out of the deepest inheritance of the Celtic Mysteries—out of the Hyperborean inheritance, which on their way humanity had lost but which in the Grail Mysteries seeks to arise again. Parsifal, who wrests the weapon of victory from the magician Klingsor, presents the fulfilment of all the prophecies—the rebirth of the Sun-Mysteries, the beginning of a 'age of light' of humanity.

20. References to the work of Rudolf Steiner

Some weeks before he took his leave of this life, Rudolf Steiner once again characterized the special situation in which the guardians of this Mystery stream found themselves at the beginning of our age, the Turning Point of Time. From his sickbed he wrote a series of weekly letters to his pupils (later published under the title *The Michael Mystery*. GA 26). One of these letters contains an assessment of 'Gnosis' from the viewpoint of spiritual science. This spiritual movement belonging to the nascent period of the tremendous growth of Christianity—however, consistently eradicated by the Church—is presented as a heritage of the age of the sentient soul. It is the same age in which the Druids and the bard-culture lived in the West and North of 'heathen' Europe. Such a fruitful manner of acquiring knowledge in Asia Minor and in the whole Greek world was preserved in the Mysteries of antiquity during the culture of the mind-soul age. Here in tremendous pictorial ideas people sought to lay hold of the divine element, but through Greek philosophy forming at the same time the cultural cutting edge of conceptual, strictly logical thinking. Through pictorial thinking an initial understanding of the appearance of Christ on Earth could be achieved. The great Christian Gnostics are a testament for how one could view the sacrifice on Golgotha in a cosmic context. But in permeating exoteric life, Gnosis became increasingly pale and abstract amidst the progressing culture of the understanding.

Rudolf Steiner now describes that in those days there still existed a knowledge of the Mysteries, which developed in strict concealment separated from public life. 'Gods' were involved in it, because out of human forces the sentient soul was no longer able to unfold to such heights of beholding. 'Then,' we read, 'in the highest Mystery places spiritual beings descended out of the spiritual cosmos, who came to assist the efforts of people wrestling for knowledge.' And when human beings in the coming centuries became ever more incapable of raising themselves to such insights, the esoteric wisdom went increasingly to cultivate 'the gods'.

> In these divine Mysteries angelic beings guarded in earthly existence what human beings could no longer guard. Mystery gnosis reigned, while people worked to eradicate exoteric gnosis. Spirit-being protected the cosmic pictures in which the Mystery of Golgotha was living. They inserted, because it was no longer possible, not the content of the pictures but the content of the feeling into human souls when the time had come for it.

The Grail legend points towards this Mystery, by letting the holy vessel for a certain time be kept hidden by angels which only after the building of the Grail Castle is sent down to receptive human, Christian souls. Titurel is called by angels; with him the 'divine Mysteries' slowly begin to become human again. But with his first successors (Frimutel and Anfortas) we see already how difficult it is in the souls of the new, upcoming Western epoch, to unite esoteric striving with the strong personal impulses.

In the lectures Rudolf Steiner held during his last year of life, he repeatedly lifts veils that lie over the Grail Mystery. He points out how important individualities in spiritual life are connected to this Grail stream—incarnated into it. Out of such silently working groups individuals frequently drew those forces they needed in later earthly life to be active in the plans of progressing human culture.

One could not do justice to what is intended with this book to expect a complete presentation of these spiritual-scientific communications; they only arise out of the completeness of the anthroposophical striving for knowledge and can only be fully understood in this context.

It is essential for the method of spiritual research, as practised by Rudolf Steiner, that it repeatedly points back to the spiritual sources whence all spiritual light emanates for the Earth—to the Mystery-centres, as they could still be found in the earlier epochs of humanity in the visible temples and human communities or Orders, and for times were honoured by peoples with sacred awe. In our time they can only be sought in the spirit. Amongst these centres it is above all the 'Sun Temple' from which emanates the highest leadership of mankind from epoch to epoch. It guards, as it were, the blueprints of earthly development. Spiritual science describes how already in Ancient Atlantis the 'Sun oracle' was founded, and it names as its leader 'the great Manu'—the one who understood how to save the spiritual treasures of humanity beyond the decline of Atlantis and entrusted them to a small group of chosen pupils whom he had educated for this task.

In the figure of Noah in the Old Testament, we can recognize a mirroring of this high guide of humanity. The legendary traditions, which were woven around this patriarch during this dim prehistoric time, clearly tell us that he was known to be venerated as that great guardian of the primordial human wisdom. There existed an early Christian tradition of Ephrem Syrus, called the 'Book of Adam and Eve'. Bks. 3 & 4 (also called 'The Cave of Treasures'),[100] but which in its Imaginative style points back to much older traditions of wisdom. This book describes a picture of the 'treasure cave', into which Adam and Eve after the expulsion from Paradise withdraw. Here are the first Mystery Plays of humanity, in which, as it were, the Paradisal memories are stored, in that Adam takes 'from the borders of Paradise' gold, incense and myrrh and with this consecrates the cave. These are the same treasures with which later the holy three kings of Saba were to bring to the child in Bethlehem. It is now told in this Book of Adam, that with the breaking in of the Flood, Noah receives from God the commandment to take out of the treasure cave Adam's body that had been kept there and with it to take those three sacrificial gifts and keep them in the 'Ark'. These sacred treasures were to be saved beyond the great Flood into the future. Noah gives instructions to his son Shem, after his death secretly to carry the corpse of the primal ancestor Adam out of the Ark into a distant land—'to the centre of the Earth'. Under the leadership of the angel of the Lord, Shem sets out and takes the boy Melchizedek. When they arrive at the hill of Golgotha, the angel teaches them that this is the centre of the Earth. The Earth opens and takes the body of Adam into itself. This is the place where now Melchizedek founds his Mystery-centre. We know him from the Old Testament, how from Salem he meets Abraham to administer to him the Mystery feeding under the sign of bread and wine. Abraham bows before him as a Mystery leader. 'To the priest of the highest God'—that means, of a

[100] https://www.academia.edu/36483685/The_book_of_Adam_and_Eve_books_3_and_4

higher God than Yahweh, the God of Abraham. And the New Testament characterizes the being of Melchizedek passing through all ages, by saying, 'He is without father or mother or genealogy, and has neither beginning of days nor end of life but resembling the Son of God he continues a priest for ever' (Heb. 7:3).

In his lectures on Matthew's Gospel (lect. 4, Bern 1910. GA 123), Rudolf Steiner describes Melchizedek as the 'great initiate of the Sun-Mystery', who only in special circumstances—and initially only in the guise of other figures—is able to show himself. The presentation of the Melchizedek's Mysteries in Emil Bock's *Genesis* (*Studies on the Spiritual History of Humanity*, Vol. 1) may be mentioned, in which this figure of an initiate in the great human context is explained.

When Abram, the founding father of the people of Yahweh (who practised a lunar religion) is being prepared for his mission, the leadership of the exalted Sun-Mysteries withdraws, as it were, behind a curtain. For 2,000 years humanity had to pursue a path into earthly depths, until the One appeared Who accomplished the great Sun-sacrifice for this Earth. But under the sign of bread and wine, He gave Himself to humanity. In the Letter to the Hebrews [5:6, 10], Christ is described as 'a priest for ever in the order of Melchizedek'. Those able to behold the Sun-Mystery in this sacrifice on Golgotha were always the Guardians of the Grail, to whom the *glory* was revealed, which pouring into Earth's darkness could be sensed as a shining seed under the forms of bread and wine. For the eyes that are opened, however, it can radiate in the form of the Grail.

Titurel appears like an echo of that exalted Sun-Initiate. Some traits with which the legend had fashioned this spiritual hero remind us of the figure of Melchizedek—he too is a priest-king. He works as out of an unapproachable realm; he protects what is sacred; sends out his knights and waits for those who, penetrating to the spirit, find the strength, for the true 'Percevals'. For he needs them. At the threshold of the twentieth century, for the first time in an unveiled language this great Sun-Mystery was proclaimed. Today the same period has passed since the sacrifice on Golgotha as the period prior to it in which the Abraham-mission of the pre-Christian Age had to be accomplished. Now not individuals are chosen by the Grail but the whole age is called to seek for the Grail. The graded path is free, the 'spoor' is found.

Behind the spiritual activities of Rudolf Steiner, there shines the figure of one of the highest Guardian of the Grail—of Melchizedek.

Appendix: 'A Comparison of Eschenbach's *Parzival* with other Grail Romances'[101]
by Eileen Hutchins

After the spread of Christianity among the Germanic tribes, the Church discouraged interest in the great pre-Christian epics, but from the eleventh century onwards, in France and later in Germany, the Troubadours and Minnesingers developed a new art in their popular romances. The earliest of these were the *Chansons de Gestes*, celebrating the heroic deeds of Charlemagne and Roland, or Dietrich of Bern. Then Celtic legends became popular, probably through the influence of Breton minstrels, and there appeared a whole series of Arthurian romances. Into these in the thirteenth century was woven the Grail theme.

If we accept the suggestion of many scholars that the concept of the Grail was a revival of the Celtic imagination of the Cauldron of Plenty, we are failing to recognize the change of consciousness between the pre-Christian and medieval times. The religious leaders of the Celts were well aware that our physical bodies are nourished and enlivened by spiritual powers, but the tellers of the Grail stories were inspired by a new impulse. They were concerned with the problem of sin and its destructive effect on the human bodily organism, which had been degenerating since the loss of ancient spiritual wisdom. In pre-Christian times it was considered necessary in many tribes to expose children who were born deformed and to condemn to death any whose conduct threatened the tribal law, but through Christianity there had been fostered the impulse to heal and redeem. Owing to the increasing dogmatism of the Church, this could not be openly proclaimed, but these who possessed supersensory knowledge were able to present this teaching in the form of Imaginative pictures. These appeared in the Grail stories.

In medieval romances the Grail is presented in many different forms, but it has always the quality of receiving and bestowing spiritual grace and wisdom. It can be described as a stone, a cup, a chalice, or the vessel used at the Last Supper. The Moon can appear as a Grail, not only because the crescent before Easter can be seen as a chalice,

[101] The final chapter of *Wolfram von Eschenbach: Parzival, an Introduction*, Temple Lodge Press, 1979, 108–119.

but also because it receives light and power from the Sun and passes them on to the Earth to awaken life-processes in plants, animals and human beings. The human body can also be regarded as a vessel the soul and spirit inhabit in order to transform the Earth. In this sense the most noble expression of the Grail is the body of Jesus of Nazareth that became the bearer of the Christ.

When Eschenbach describes the Grail as a stone, he relates it to the most beautiful jewel in Lucifer's crown which was redeemed and guarded by the Templar Knights to become the foundation of a new spiritual wisdom. Christ spoke of Himself as 'the stone which the builders rejected' [Matt. 21:42, quoting Ps. 118:22] which then became 'the head of the corner'. In the Apocalypse the New Jerusalem is likened to 'a stone most precious, even like a jasper stone, clear as crystal'.

When Eschenbach describes the Grail as 'a thing', this word is not used in the trivial sense taken for granted today. We can compare the expression with Gabriel's words to Mary, 'that holy thing which shall be born of thee shall be called the Son of God' (Luke 1:35).

With later Grail romances, such as the Lancelot sequence translated by Malory, the Grail is the chalice of the Last Supper in which Joseph of Arimathea gathered the blood flowing from the Saviour's side as He hung upon the cross.

We need to be able to judge which of the romances offer true Imaginations and which present confused pictures where the teller is not aware of their real meaning. Unlike Homer many of the poets of the Middle Ages did not receive inspiration from a divine Muse but drew their subject matter from any available source that provided a good story. During the long winter evenings, the inmates of the baronial castles had need of entertainment, so they appreciated endless episodes describing the adventuress of favourite knights. Scenes of magic were all the more fascinating when they could not be explained. Then, to avoid the danger of condemnation by the Church, the teller would introduce passages of moral teaching. Some of the later Grail stories are crowded with biblical allusions or references to holy relics that do not add in any way to the development of the story.

Apart from Eschenbach's poem there are four romances connected with Parzival obtainable in English. The story of Peredur, translated from the Welsh of the *Mabinogion* by Lady Charlotte Guest, is thought to be the earliest. The adventures of the young Peredur, from his childhood in the forest until his appearance at Arthur's Court and the slaying of the Red Knight, closely resemble those of Eschenbach's hero. After this, the adventures become confused. Peredur meets with a lame old man, whose attendants are fishing, and from him he learns not to ask questions. He comes to a castle where two youths bear into the hall a mighty spear, dripping with blood. They are followed by two maidens carrying a salver containing the bloodstained head of a man. There is no mention of a Grail. There follow many disconnected adventures during which a beautiful woman, who turns out to be an Empress, gives him a stone of invisibility. An ugly creature resembling Kundrie drives Peredur from Arthur's Court because he failed to ask the question that would have healed the lame man. At the end we learn that the laming of the old man and the slaying of the one whose head was carried in the salver were the deeds of the sorceresses of Gloucester, whom Peredur with Arthur's help finally destroys.

The confusion of this story seems to show that the teller had heard a version of the Grail legend and gathered incidents from it without any understanding of the central theme. Some of the episodes are told with a primitive vigour which gives them a certain appeal, but this work is hardly a Grail romance.

The High History of the Holy Grail, translated from the French by Sebastian Evans, has as its central theme the quest for the Grail by Perceval, Gawain and Lancelot. Despite the many irrelevant adventures, there is some recognition of the characters of the different knights and the reasons for their failure or success.

The first episode shows that the teller no longer understood the relationship of the dream-world with that of everyday life. A squire, who is due to accompany King Arthur on a quest, dreams that he oversleeps and has to gallop in haste after his master. He comes to a lonely chapel where he yields to the temptation to steal a golden candlestick. He is attacked and sorely wounded. He wakes up to find the whole incident was a dream, but the candlestick is by his side and he is mortally wounded.

Early in the story we learn that the Fisher-King is languishing because Perceval, on visiting the Grail Castle, did not ask whom the Grail served. Through his failure the maiden bearing the Grail has become bald and carries her right arm in a sling.

Gawain is eager to take on the quest but is not allowed to enter the Grail Castle unless he brings with him the sword which beheaded John the Baptist. When he has succeeded in this task and returns, he is reminded by everyone he meets to ask the question which will restore the Fisher-King. But when beholding the Grail procession, he is so swept away by his feelings of devotion and bliss that he forgets everything.

The Grail ritual is different from the one described by Eschenbach. One maiden holds a lance which drips blood while a second gathers the drops into the Grail. To Gawain the vessel appears as a chalice, and he beholds two angels carrying candlesticks of gold, while in the midst of the Grail shines the figure of a child. The narrator is bringing his account nearer to the celebration of the communion than does Eschenbach.

After Gawain's failure Lancelot undertakes the task. On his way to the Castle, he meets with a hermit to whom he confesses his sins. The hermit implores him to renounce his unlawful love for the Queen. Lancelot replies, 'This sin will I reveal to you of my lips, but of my heart may I never repent thereof.' He is willing to do penance but not to change. When he comes to the Castle, the Mystery of the Grail is not revealed to him for he loves the Queen more than he loves the Grail.

When at last Perceval returns, he finds that the Lord of the Castle Mortal has conquered the realm of the Fisher-King who is now dead. With the blessing of a company of hermits and the help of two magical beasts, a white mule and a white lion, Perceval is able to win back the kingdom. After most of his men have been slaughtered, the Lord of Castle Mortal kills himself, and, when the last of the enemies has been driven out, the Grail which has temporarily withdrawn, reappears. The importance of asking the question is never made clear, but Perceval's failure and the Fisher-King's languishment are explained by the hermit as the will of God.

The story does not end here. The three chief knights continue to have many aimless adventures, which offer opportunities for moral teaching. At last Perceval is summoned on board a ship bearing a white sail with a red cross which bears him away into the unknown. Although certain of the episodes are told with great charm, the work as a whole is a notable example of the confusion of themes in many of the later medieval romances.

The Romance of Perceval in Prose, translated by Dell Skeels, still more fully illustrates the storyteller's delight in weaving well-known incidents around his chosen hero, without any consideration for a central theme. The beginning and the end of the tale are concerned with King Arthur, and the narrator has no conception of the difference between the Arthurian and the Grail cults. In the opening chapter Merlin tells Arthur the history of how our Lord appeared to Joseph of Arimathea in person and gave him the chalice containing His blood. This was passed down to members of Joseph's family. However, the present King Bron has fallen into a great sickness. He cannot die until a knight of the Round Table finds his way to the Castle and asks whom the Grail serves.

In the next chapter we meet Perceval, who, in obedience to his father's dying wish, rides to the Court of King Arthur, where he is kindly received and in due course becomes a knight. He falls in love with Gawain's sister and, when fighting in her honour, surpasses all other knights including Sir Lancelot. The twelve chief knights occupy the twelves seats at the Round Table, but there is a vacant thirteenth reserved for the best knight in the world. Despite Arthur's refusal, Perceval claims the right to this place. As soon as he sits down, the stone seat with a violent crack splits in two. Then a voice proclaims that never will the stone be reunited or the Fisher-King restored until the best knight in the world finds the Castle and asks whom the Grail serves. Many knights, including Perceval, set out in quest.

Meanwhile, unknown to Perceval, his mother has died of grief. However, he does not go in search of her, as related by Eschenbach. Later, when meeting with his sister who tells him of her death, he visits his hermit-uncle to confess his fault.

Perceval has many adventures and encounters with dark magical forces, but these have little connection with the main theme except to make clear that he is the best knight in the world. When at last he comes to the main Grail Castle, although he has been told about the importance of the question, he does not ask because his mother has taught him that he should not talk too much. There is no mention of his passing a disturbed night or of his being thrown out of the Castle, but after leaving it he meets a weeping maiden who reproaches him for his failure. She does not appear again.

When he cannot find his way back to the Castle, Perceval is seized with a fit of madness—an affliction often attributed to Lancelot. He is brought to his senses when he meets a party of pilgrims who reproach him for wearing armour on a holy day. He finds his way to his hermit-uncle but receives no help beyond receiving his blessing. After further adventures, however, he meets the magician Merlin, who tells him that he has failed to find the Grail Castle because he has not been faithful to a vow he made when setting out on the quest. At that time, he swore that, until he succeeded, he should not sleep more than one night in any place. Perceval replies that he has not lately given thought to this. Merlin comments, 'Then you may be the more easily forgiven.' He assures Perceval that in due course he will arrive at his destination.

When Perceval returns to the Castle and asks whom does the Grail serve, the King is restored. The voice of the Holy Ghost then commands that Bron should appoint Perceval as his successor and teach him the sacred words our Lord taught Joseph in prison when He gave the chalice into his keeping. After three days Bron departs from this life and Perceval has a vision of David and many angels waiting to receive his soul.

The moment the Fisher-King is healed, the stone seat at the Round Table is repaired and the story returns to King Arthur. We hear of the last fight and the end of the Order of the Round Table. However, it is told that Arthur does not die; he withdraws to the Isle of Avalon whence he will return when his country is in need.

There is a mood of unreality in the whole story, and it completely lacks the powerful human appeal of Eschenbach's *Parzival*. Very few places or characters are clearly described, and the incidents seem to take place in a world of phantasy. At the end we hear that Merlin has observed everything and his fellow-magician Blayse has kept the records so that nothing may be forgotten. This adds to the impression that the tale belongs to the realm of magic.

Malory's version of the Grail story is the most widely known in England. *Le Morte d'Arthur* is a translation of several French works, and as most of the episodes are concerned with Arthur and his circle, many people are confused about the relationship of the Arthurian Order and the Grail. However, when several of his knights set out to seek for the Grail, Arthur is deeply grieved and reproaches Gawain and Lancelot for deserting him and destroying the Fellowship of the Round Table. This clearly indicates the difference between the two impulses. In the stories adapted by Malory, Lancelot has become the leading hero. He appears in many different adventures, but one theme is common to all—his unlawful love for Queen Guinevere. On this account he could not be presented as the one to attain the Grail. Nevertheless, storytellers felt the need to link their most popular hero with this ideal, and so he was made to appear as the father of the one who would become the Grail King. In the version followed by Malory, the way in which this is brought about may not seem justified. It is told how in the Grail circle it was known that according to destiny, Lancelot was the one appointed to marry the daughter of its Guardian, King Pelles. However, owing to his love for Guinevere, he would never consider accepting this position. A deception was then practised upon him. He was led to Pelles' daughter Elaine and cast under a spell so that he imagined he was lying with the Queen. From this union was born Galahad of whom it was foretold that he should achieve the Grail. We might well consider such a ruse unworthy of a spiritual leader, but it is possible to view this episode in a different light. Lancelot was 'human, all too human', and therefore unfitted to serve the Grail, but through trials and sufferings, like most of mankind, he was willy-nilly acquiring nobler qualities. Galahad can be regarded as an Imagination of what Lancelot could become in the distant future. He is presented not as a human but as an angelic being, protected from all temptation and untouched by any sin. His deeds appear in the light of miracles. If we accept the view that after many incarnations the human being can free himself from the fetters of the sensory world and become the embodiment of his spiritual ideals, we can think of Galahad as a reflection of Lancelot's higher being.

In *Le Morte d'Arthur*, the Grail was not guarded by a community which through its grace was able to serve the outer whole. It bestowed an individual mystical ecstasy, granted only to those who were free of all human desires, though in certain cases the blessing might be received through the mediation of another, as is later illustrated in the cases of Sir Perceval and Sir Bors. At Lancelot's first meeting with Pelles he was granted this vision, perhaps as a summons to awake to his true destiny and renounce the Queen. It is told that, as he and the Guardian sat together, a dove came in at the window, bearing a little censer of gold, whereupon they were provided with all the nourishment they required. Then a maiden entered carrying a vessel of gold before which King Pelles knelt and said his prayers. Lancelot asked, 'What may this mean?' 'This,' said the King, 'is the holy Sangreal, and when this thing goeth about the Round Table shall be broken.' However, after his union with Elaine, Lancelot was no longer granted such an experience.

When Galahad became its Guardian, the Grail disappeared from the West, which had sunk too far into materialism, so he was guided to the Holy City of Sarras. At this time, it was widely believed that only in the East, where Christ had lived and suffered, could one truly be united with His impulse. Perceval appears only as a minor participant, experiencing the Mystery under Galahad's leadership.

Galahad prayed that he might be permitted to leave this earthly life and, after he had served for a year as King in Sarras, his prayer was granted. He was received into the spiritual world and the spear and the lance were taken with him to be seen no more on Earth.

The healing of the sick King plays little part in the story. Pelles had seized a sword which he was not worthy to wield and had been wounded through both thighs. After attaining the leadership of the Grail, Galahad restored him to health, but neither Pelles nor his son was any longer connected with its service.

In *Le Morte d'Arthur* many of the episodes connected with the Grail are beautifully told and deeply moving, so that readers often find themselves in an enchanted world where they are willing to be led from one adventure to another without feeling the need to understand their meaning. But for those who look for a well-constructed development, the endless series of disconnected incidents, visions and dreams serving to illustrate religious teaching become somewhat wearisome.

In comparing Eschenbach's poem with the three narratives described above, we can marvel at its consistency. He preserves a fine balance between descriptions of the supersensory and of the earthly realms. On the one hand, he reveals the deepest strivings of the human soul, yet on the other he recognizes the demands and duties of everyday life. The story is developed step by step, each incident playing a necessary part and each single detail having its significance. The hero's character unfolds in its steady progress from dullness through doubt to blessedness, and the attainment of the Grail leads, not to an escape from earthly responsibilities, but to their fulfilment. The whole work is remarkably free from any dogmatic teaching. Whatever he wished to impress upon is audience was given through Imaginative pictures or through incidents in the story. As the poem appeared in the form of a romance, Wolfram was able to give free expression to his imagination without danger of being accused of heresy. Although he did not actually contradict the teaching of the Catholic Church, like Dante he was able to indicate through a work of art deeper esoteric truths. The Grail ritual took place in a castle not in a church and was administered by a woman and not by a priest. Trevrizent, who absolved Parzival, had never been ordained, and Parzival's election as Grail King received no sanction from any established religious Order. At the beginning of the thirteenth century, it was still possible for a certain freedom of thought to flourish without being suppressed, and the poem was widely known and appreciated. It was with the advent of Protestantism that the medieval romances fell into disfavour, but in times of need great works of art reappear to give their inspiration to a new age.